DANDY
Guide to Dating

VINTAGE
MENSWEAR

WWI through the 1960s

• SUE NIGHTINGALE •

4880 Lower Valley Road Atglen, Pennsylvania 19310

Other Schiffer Books on Related Subjects:

Clothing & Accessories from the '40s, '50s, & '60s: A Handbook and Price Guide.
   Jan Lindenberger. ISBN: 0764300237. $16.95
The Clothing Label Book: A Century of Design.
   Tina Skinner & Jenna Palecko Schuck. ISBN: 0764317466. $39.95
Fashionable Clothing from the Sears Catalog: Early 1950s.
   Desire Smith. ISBN: 0764305190. $29.95
Fashionable Clothing From the Sears Catalogs: Mid-1960s.
   Joy Shih. ISBN: 0764303406. $29.95
Men's Clothing & Fabrics in the 1890s.
   Roseann Ettinger. ISBN: 0764306162. $24.95
Spalding Aviator's Clothing and Equipment in the 1920s-1930s.
   A Schiffer Military History Book. ISBN: 0764304038. $9.95

Designed by Justin Watkinson Cover by Bruce Waters
Type set in Bernhard Modern Bd BT/Arrus BT

ISBN: 978-0-7643-3890-8
Printed in China

Schiffer Books are available at special discounts for bulk purchases for sales promotions or premiums. Special editions, including personalized covers, corporate imprints, and excerpts can be created in large quantities for special needs. For more information contact the publisher:

Published by Schiffer Publishing Ltd.
4880 Lower Valley Road
Atglen, PA 19310
Phone: (610) 593-1777; Fax: (610) 593-2002
E-mail: Info@schifferbooks.com

For the largest selection of fine reference books on this and related subjects, please visit our website at **www.schifferbooks.com**
We are always looking for people to write books on new and related subjects. If you have an idea for a book, please contact us at proposals@schifferbooks.com

This book may be purchased from the publisher.
Include $5.00 for shipping.
Please try your bookstore first.
You may write for a free catalog.

In Europe, Schiffer books are distributed by
Bushwood Books
6 Marksbury Ave.
Kew Gardens
Surrey TW9 4JF England
Phone: 44 (0) 20 8392 8585; Fax: 44 (0) 20 8392 9876
E-mail: info@bushwoodbooks.co.uk
Website: www.bushwoodbooks.co.uk

{ Contents }

{ Introduction }

ew to you. Hand me down. Used. Pre-loved. Wearing vintage elevates "used clothing" to a different level as a new and interesting way to recycle.

You can pick up a few vintage garments because you like them and easily incorporate them into your wardrobe. Most vintage garments are better made and will last longer, some vintage garments will already be broken in for comfort, and a few vintage items will add a touch of whimsy or quirkiness to your daily garb. In wearing these items, you have quickly become retro-urban with your own unique style and display of self confidence.

A Signal® Overalls ad in a 1905 magazine states: "Say what you will, a man is judged by the clothes he wears. If he is careless, slovenly and indifferent as to what he wears, it is a pretty safe guess that he is careless, slovenly and indifferent about his work." These words are just as true today as they were over a century ago.

In writing this book, I am focusing on my favorite eras of the twentieth century, specifically the WWI and Edwardian period of the teens into the Peacock Revolution of the 1960s, and the clothing that was worn during this time.

I am not an "expert," just someone who happens to love flamboyant ties from the Forties, staid suits from the Twenties, unique accessories, and who wants to help you enjoy buying, selling, collecting, and wearing vintage. I have taken notes and collected some "bits and pieces" of information throughout my years of working with vintage clothing and participating in vintage discussion boards. I've researched them further, checked for accuracy, simplified into my own words, and added to my information treasure trove.

There will always be new information coming to the vintage collector's attention; we will find older garments that help us discover existing style features, or previously undiscovered details can come to light that changes our preconceived perceptions as to dating a vintage garment. Because of the aforementioned, this book is to be used as a guide to help you with the decision of whether a garment is vintage or not.

"Knowledge is Power" and Power is Strength

Advertisement with sage advice no matter the subject. *McClure's Magazine*, c. 1902.

I share this passion for vintage by giving you, the reader, the knowledge to identify and date your own fantastic vintage finds with this simplified and easy to use guide. My hope is that you enjoy discovering the subtle clues to dating vintage menswear, learning about clothing history, and having a little fun along the way.

The illustrative photos in this book are from the authors private collection, or noted if from other sources, and are used for reference or educational purpose only. Please remember that the photos are of labels from used garments or items that are between 60 and 125 years old, and therefore not in pristine condition. Not all illustrative photos are strictly from men's clothing items.

SECTION
1

WHAT'S ON THE LABEL(S)?

You've found a garment that you really like, fits well, and you would like to know its age. Luckily, lots of information about an item can be gleaned from its label(s), so that's one of the best places to start the dating process.

The label information presented here is generic and could be used for any garment: men's, children's or ladies, coats, shirts, or slacks. I have also included label criteria much more current than the 1960s stopping point so that newer garments can be ruled out as true vintage. Always remember to take other dating criteria, such as style, fabric, and construction, into consideration along with what you learn from the label.

It wasn't until the turn of the twentieth century that a few garment makers and retailers decided that a label might be a great form of advertising. If the wearer loved the style of the garment, it was long wearing, or it fit them well, they would be more likely to engage in brand loyalty and purchase either the same item or from the same company again. This was made easier if the store name or the company name was on the label to help the purchaser remember such information. This idea took a while to catch on, and labels didn't come into widespread usage until after WWI and moving into the 1920s.

The main label will have the name of the company the garment is attributed to (a.k.a. maker). This label is usually found in the back neck of shirts, sweaters, tees, and casual jackets, and the inner waist band of slacks or trousers. Or, it can simply tell you what the vintage garment is.

Collage featuring labels from the 1950s and '60s.

Label telling that the garment is a swim suit, c. 1930s.

Certainly it will be one of the first things that you notice. For the most part, the information contained on the main label is regulated by the United States government.

Then we have what I like to call secondary labels, small labels usually attached to, placed beside, or printed on the backside of the main label. Or, they can be a Union or similar label placed elsewhere on the garment. A secondary may have no more information than a size, or may contain fabric content and / or fabric care. The luckiest secondary label that you can find would have a date listed. All this criteria will be covered a little further along in this section.

Hint: When a label is hard to read, it sometimes helps to take a clear, well-focused close-up photograph and then "fiddle" with highlighting or shadows, or even sharpen the focus, to see if it becomes more readable. It also sometimes helps to look at the label carefully with a good magnifying glass. A rubbing of the label with a pencil and paper can yield results.

▓ Secondary label tells about the special collar, c. 1930s.

▓ Secondary label tells about collar care, c. 1930s.

▓ Backside of the main label showing information, c. 1990s.

▓ A suit label showing the tailor's date. June 1929.

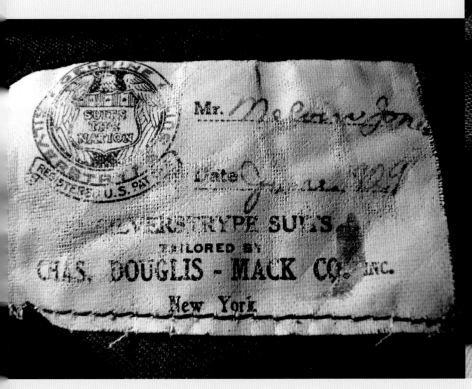

{ Trademarks }

T-shirt showing trademark notation for Caterpillar, c. 1960s.

Label showing trademark notation for Silverstrype, c. 1920s.

Label showing trademark for KODA Phantom Prints, c. 1940s.

Label showing trademark for Manhattan (shirts), c. 1950s.

Label showing "Licensed Trademark" instead of "Trademark", c. 1930s.

Advertisement showing trademark and its wording for Porosknit. *McClure's Magazine*, c. 1902.

A trademark is protection for a name, logo, word or symbol used by an individual or business to identify or distinguish themselves or their products from that individual's / their rivals, or to indicate the source of its origin.

The first known trademark legislation started in 1870 for trade identity during the growth and expansion of America following the Civil War. It was based on the interstate commerce clause of the U.S. Constitution. This was replaced with the Trademark Act of 1881 and amended in 1905.

Although many companies operating in the nineteenth century protected their name and / or the name of their company, there was an influx of trademarks issued about the same time as mass label usage started in the 1920s. Please note that it has never been mandatory to obtain a trademark and many companies, even today, operate successfully without one.

As part of the Trademark Act of 1905, a trademark cannot be acquired through only name usage, but must be registered with the U.S. government. Once a name or mark was registered and granted, the trademark was good for twenty years, then must be renewed. A trademark could be renewed in twenty year increments forever, as long as it remained in use. This remains true today.

Trademarks were applied for through the U.S. Patent Office. Once a trademark was applied for, Section 28 of the Trademark Act of 1905 states: "that it shall be the duty of the registrant to give notice to the public that a trademark is registered either by affixing thereon the words 'Registered in U.S. Patent Office' or abbreviated thus, 'Reg. U.S. Pat. Off.'..." It goes on to say that when this can't be done to the article, then it is to be displayed on the article's packaging.

Once the trademark was granted, many companies did not change the wording on the label to "TM" or "trademark" because of the cost of designing and executing new labels, or they simply chose to keep the existing wording. Below are more examples of various ways that a trademark was written.

There are some circumstances, JCPenney Co.® for example, where others manufactured the goods while a company held and used the trademark under their own name and sold items under that trademark.

Another part of the Trademark Act of 1905 states that the applicant must have done commerce in several states (interstate commerce), or with a foreign nation or Indian Tribe. This provision also applied to Porto (Puerto) Rico, the Philippine Islands, Hawaii, and any other territory under the jurisdiction of the United States.

Label showing that trademark information is for what is previously stated; in this case Sanforized, not Arrow, c. 1940s.

Advertisement showing copyright notation. *The Red Cross Magazine*, c. 1918.

Label showing copyright and date of design. H.D. Lee Mercantile Co., c. 1929-1938.

The Act gave owners the exclusive rights to their mark and set out remedies if the trademark was infringed or violated. Basically, a trademark can only be infringed by a company using exactly the same name and selling the same product, or if someone reproduces, copies or imitates a trademark to mislead the public as to ownership of the goods.

Trademarks can be issued for the same name if the registering companies are selling different products or services. For instance, when I see the word "Arrow®", I think of shirts and ties. However, the name "Arrow®" is also trademarked for percussion instruments, pharmaceuticals, envelopes, travel trailers, cigarettes, and many other kinds of goods.

The "Registered United States Patent Office" or "Trademark" designation only applies to what is mentioned just previous to its notation. The example is the notation "Reg. U.S. Pat. Off." which happens to refer to "Sanforized®" because it is just previous to the notation, not to Arrow (Shirts).

It wasn't until the Lanham Act of 1946, which repealed the Trademark Act of 1905, that owners were allowed to register and be granted ownership of distinctive pictures, words or symbols. Originally, only names and logo's had been considered for trademarks.

An unofficial name change of the U.S. Patent Office to the U.S. Patent and Trademark Office in 1946 would change the wording to "Registered U.S. Patent & Trademark Office" or "Reg. U.S. Pat. & Tm. Off."

The Lanham Act was signed on 7-5-1946 and went into effect on 7-5-1947. If a trademark was granted after the signing of the act, companies / individuals were given a grace period until July 1948 to be able to use the typed words, because in the late 1940s many sewing machines were incapable of producing the trademark logo of ® (R in a circle).

Therefore, any label with an ® will date a trademark registration to after 1946, as this designation was never used prior to the Lanham Act of that year. Under a grandfather clause, companies who had received their trademarks prior to 1946 were allowed to keep their existing wording on their labels, and many chose to do just that.

Before we move on to doing trademark searches, there are a couple other points I want to make referring to terminology or information that causes confusion about trademarks.

Trade Name: An actual business name or assumed name used to identify a product or service. Coca-Cola®, even though it is trademarked, uses its trade name to distinguish itself from other soft drinks. This is opposed to a generic product name such as cola or soda. Common law distinguishes between trademarks and trade names.

Trade Dress: How a product is packaged, labeled, and presented to the public and recognized for its uniqueness. Examples would be the green glass Coca-Cola bottle or the L'eggs' eggs.

Service Mark: Comparable to a trademark, but this mark is only used for services, rather than products or goods, and can be a name, word or symbol. A Service Mark is essentially an ad for what the company does and a way to distinguish that firm from others in the same field. Some examples are the three-tone chime of NBC®, Merry Maids®, and Roto-Rooter®. A Service Mark is shown as the SM symbol in superscript. Many companies will also be trademarked.

Copyright: Grants exclusive rights, usually for written or published works.

One way to do an online search of registered trademarks is to use the Trademark Electronic Search System (TESS), which is part of the United States Patent & Trademark Office (USPTO. gov) website. To search on your own, go to the website; under "Trademarks information" in the middle column click on #2 "Search marks"; click on "New use form (basic)"; type in your label name beside "Search Term"; click on "Submit Query". Then examine the listings that come up for matches to the company name and product you are searching.

Once you find the correct listing, be sure to look at all of the information available. Please note that information from TESS is provided for illustrative purposes and has been abbreviated from its original version. Because we are working with the national trademark site, I will not show the ® beside my illustrations to avoid confusion:

1. "Word mark" tells you the name of the company the information is for.

2. "First use in commerce" will tell when the company starting using the particular name for which you are searching.

This example for first use in commerce is dated Jan. 1, 1937:

WORD MARK SUN VALLEY
Goods and Services (EXPIRED). G & S: Men's and Women's Jackets, Pants, Shirts, Parkas, Ski Suits, and Outer Shorts.
FIRST USE IN COMMERCE: 19370101.

3. The trademark filing date, which may or may not match the first use date, will tell when the trademark registration was actually filed. Note that a trademark can never be older than its filing date, even though the name may have been used for years.

WORD MARK REYN SPOONER
Good and Services. G & S: Men's and boys' swimwear, men's walking shorts, jackets, jumpsuits, trousers, pants, polo shirts, t-shirts, sweatshirts, hats, caps, visors and shoes, etc.
FIRST USE IN COMMERCE: 19640000
Filing Date August 22, 1985
Registration Date September 16, 1986

In reading the above, we see that the company started using their name (First Use In Commerce) in 1964, but that they did not file for a trademark (Filing Date) until August 22, 1985. Therefore, if there is any trademark notation on the label, the garment would have to be newer than 1985.

Label showing "Reg. U.S. PAT. OFF." prompting a TESS search for trademark, first use in commerce, c. 1950s.

Label showing information prompting a TESS search for trademark filing date, c. 1980s.

Label showing information needed to do a TESS search for dating, c. 1960s.

Main label showing information needed to do a TESS search for dating, c. 1950s.

Secondary label showing information needed to do a TESS search for dating, c. 1950s.

4. Check the original ownership vs. the owner's name now. A trademarked name may have been purchased from another company.

WORD MARK THE PANTS KING

Goods and Services (CANCELLED) G & S: Men's, Youths', and Boys' Outer Garments, Trousers. FIRST USE IN COMMERCE: 19010106
Filing Date December 1, 1920
Owner (REGISTRANT) J. Schoeneman,
Incorporated, Baltimore, Maryland
(LAST1 LISTED OWNER) Cluett, Peabody & Co., Inc.
New York, New York
Assignment Recorded ASSIGNMENT RECORDED
Type of Mark TRADEMARK

5. A TESS search of "Levi Strauss®" brought up 333 listings of trademarks, while a search of "Penneys" brought up 923 listings. Some are actual clothing lines, some are trademarked taglines, slogans or advertising campaigns, and some are fabric processes. Unfortunately, sometimes you have to look at many listings to be able to find the one you are specifically trying to find.

6. In a little different scenario, something in or on the garment, like the fabric it is made from, may be trademarked.

A search of "Viyella" on TESS brings up that is was first used in 1894 as a wool and cotton blend fabric and registered in 1907. But, it also shows another listing for "Viyella" as a brand of clothing that was registered in 1951. Both trademarks are owned by William Hollis Co. of England, thus the label notation of woven in Great Britain. Based on the fact that we are dating a shirt and not just the fabric it is made from, plus taking into consideration the style features of the shirt, it dates to the 1950s.

Again, the basic rule of thumb as to trademarks is that the word "trademark" or an ® refers to what immediately precedes it.

7. You can also do a search on TESS to show brands, logos, slogans, or other trademarked information owned by a certain company. When you type in your "search name", you can change the field to "owner's name and address" and this should give you all trademarks owned by a certain company. If nothing shows up, it generally means that the company did not apply or register for a federal trademark, or that the original records are miss from the TESS information. There are probably thousands of companies that manufacture or market garments and have not registered their name for a trademark, or for which that the trademark information is missing.

8. Some words appear on labels that do not state that they are trademarked, but will show up in a trademark search.

Example: We'll say that you have a shirt with the following labels in it. How should it be dated?

Showing shirt style to confirm dating style, c. 1950s. $25-50.

Even though there are no trademark notations, it only takes a couple of seconds to check TESS.

WORD MARK GABANARO
Goods and Services (EXPIRED) G & S: Sport Shirts for men and women.
FIRST USE IN COMMERCE: 19470917
Filing Date September 18, 1947
Registration Date April 18, 1950
Owner (REGISTRANT) Cluett, Peabody & Co., Inc.
Troy, New York
Type of Mark TRADEMARK

and,

WORD MARK SANFORSET
Goods and Services (CANCELLED) G & S: Rayon Piece Goods.
FIRST USE IN COMMERCE: 19400800
Filing Date September 16, 1940
Registration Date January 14, 1941
Owner (REGISTRANT) Cluett, Peabody & Co., Inc., Troy, New York

When we put the TESS information from these two labels together, here's what we get:

* A "Gabanaro" trademark is owned by Cluett, Peabody & Co., which is the legal name for Arrow Shirts. Both names are noted on the label.

* TESS says that the "Gabanaro" name was used as early as 1947, so, the shirt cannot be older than that.

* The "Sanforset" trademark is also owned by Cluett, Peabody & Co.

* "Sanforset" is used on Rayon piece goods; we know our shirt is Rayon because of the label notation.

* "Sanforset" was registered in 1941.

* While not proven, it could be that "Sanforset" does not have a trademark notation on the label because of the push for Sanforizing for cottons from the 1930s through the 1960s.

* "Completely Washable" was a phrase used in the 1950s (see notes about this in the 1971 Fabric Care chapter.)

Double checking the collar points and overall style features of the shirt, I'd date the shirt to the 1950s. As you can surmise, part of dating is by research, part by acquired knowledge, part by style elements, and part by supposition.

9. This final scenario takes into consideration that the trademark wording on the label must match the trademark wording on TESS. We are looking for information on Gantner swim trunks and we see four different entries, all of them filed in 1980 after the company was sold:

WORD MARK GANTNER
Goods and Services G & S: Men's and Women's Swimwear
FIRST USE IN COMMERCE: 19320100
Filing Date January 21, 1980

and,

WORD MARK GANTNER WIKIES
Goods and Services (CANCELLED) G & S: Men's and Boy's Bathing Suits.
FIRST USE IN COMMERCE: 19320132
Filing Date January 21, 1980

and,

WORD MARK GANTNER of CALIFORNIA
Goods and Services G & S: Men's, Boy's, Ladies', and Girl's Tops, Shirts, and Bathing Suits.
FIRST USE IN COMMERCE: 19370100
Filing Date January 21, 1980

and,

WORD MARK GANTNER OF CALIFORNIA WIKIES
Goods and Services (CANCELLED) G & S: Men's, Boy's, Ladies', and Girl's Bathing Suits.
FIRST USE IN COMMERCE: 19580701
Filing Date January 21, 1980

The CANCELLED notation in the above means that the trademark has been cancelled and is no longer active. An EXPIRED notation means that the original trademark time has expired and the trademark was not renewed. An ASSIGNMENT notation means that whatever the trademark is for has been sold or transferred to another company or the original company changed its name.

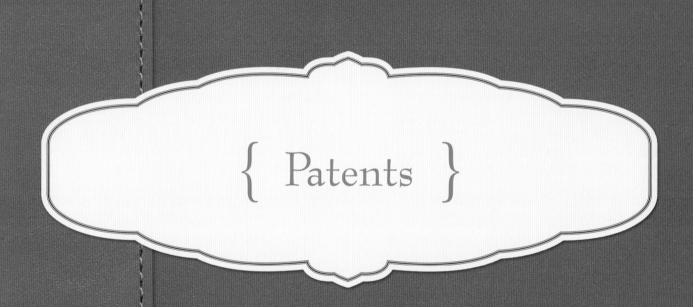

{ Patents }

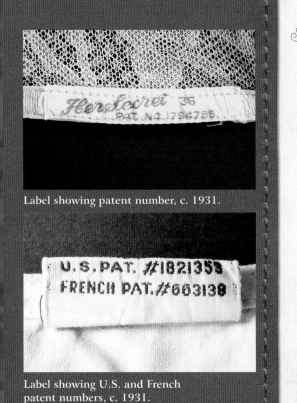

Label showing patent number, c. 1931.

Label showing U.S. and French patent numbers, c. 1931.

A patent is property right protection granted to an inventor for an invention or idea. Each patent has a unique number assigned to it when granted, and is legally binding for only a certain amount of time. A patent notation always refers to the wording just prior to it.

Patents were granted by the individual states until a new Act created the United States Patent Office in 1790. An examination board comprised of the Secretary of State, Secretary of War, and the Attorney General determined which patents were to be granted as useful and important.

Within 3 years, the original Act was repealed and replaced with a new Patent Act which said that a patent would be routinely granted to any U.S. citizen who swore to its originality and paid the fees involved.

The Patent Office was again reorganized in 1836 and began requiring an intricate examination of the inventions and the start of the number system. Any patent records predating 1836 had no numbers assigned.

It could conceivably take years for a patent to be investigated and granted, so sometimes you will see the term "patent pending" or "pat pend" to denote the interim time and warn others of possible infringement.

If you happen to find a vintage garment or accessory that shows a label with a patent number, it is quite easy to determine when the patent was issued by going to the following website:

www.uspto.gov/patents/process/search/issueyear.jsp

At a glance, you can find your patent number in a year by year range and know the year of that patent. Example: Patent number 699 would be dated 1838 because 699 is after 546 (the first patent number issued 1-1-1838) and before number 1061 (the first patent number issued 1-1-1839).

Of course, you will run into higher patent numbers for the items you find, so use the same method of location.

The following table information has been simplified from the USPTO website and shows the calendar year with a starting document number for that year. I have skipped many years to conserve space, but the entire document is on the website.

ISSUE YEAR	FIRST PATENT # FOR THAT YEAR	FIRST REISSUE
1836	1	
1837	110	
1838	546	RE00001
1839	1061	
1840		
1920	1326899	
1921	1364083	
1922	1401948	
1923	1440363	
1934	1941449	
1935	1985878	
1936	2026516	RE19804
	2066309	RE20226

...and so on.

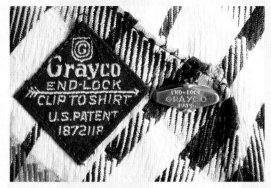

Label showing patent number
and instructions, c. 1932.

Back side of buckle showing
patent number c. 1889.

Showing patent buckle use as
side waist adjustment c. 1889.

To use this table to find patent number 1384706, find the closest corresponding numbers just higher and just lower than your patent number. We quickly see that the patent number fits between 1921 and 1922. The patent number is lower than the starting number for 1922, so the issue year is 1921.

In checking the Patent Number site, we find that the patent number in the picture of a back of the necktie dates to 1932. We are even given an explanation as to what the patent is for: it is a small clip that attaches to the front opening of a shirt to keep the tie in place and avoid unsightly holes from tie tacks.

When a patent is granted, a time limit for the patent is fixed at the time of issue. To correct any problems or mistakes concerning the patent, the original holder must file for a reissue, and if granted the original patent is surrendered. To broaden the scope of a patent, the original holder must file for a reissue within the first two years of the original granting. These are the two instances for the RE #'s and the reissue numbers also appear on the website.

If you have a patent number and want to see what the patent drawings or what the patent is for, sometimes the information is available at:

www.uspto.gov/patft/index.html
or
www.jitterbuzz.com/patget.html

As part of the Lanham Act of 1946, the U.S. Patent Office name was changed to the U.S. Patent and Trademark Office as to reference and labeling, but the name didn't become official until 1975.

I'll close this section with one of the strangest labels I found in a 1940s Botany necktie. At first glance, the patent number on this label would date to 1877, but I found a patent reference to this number for an improvement to mechanical musical instruments in 1897. Since neither of these references sounded correct, I then considered that this might be a reissue number and they just neglected to list as RE19,653.

According to Google Patents, it was a reissue for an original patent filed 08-16-1932 and revised 07-23-1935 as a modification of a machine for sewing together four-in-hand neckties and their linings.

alter vest size, turn this flap inside out, which completely exposes seam. One line of stitching placed either side of present seam will decrease or increase size. Remove original seam, reverse flap to former position and press. This method and structure of SUPER HARMONY TRIM FULLY PROTECTED BY U. S. LETTERS PATENT No. 1,994,956 ISSUED TO ALBERT LITTLE, MARCH 19, 1935.

Label with complete patent information and usage c. 1935.

THIS SHEET CONTAINS THE
SIMPLIFIED DIRECTIONS
for putting in this

TALON
REG. U. S. PAT. OFF. TALON, INC.

SLIDE FASTENER
for
DRESS PLACKET

Package showing trademark, not patent, information because "Reg. U. S. Pat. Off." refers to what is immediately preceding, c. 1939.

Botany
tie
REG. U. S. PAT. OFF.
100% WOOL
BOTANY
WORSTED MILLS
RESILIENT
CONSTRUCTION
PAT. NO.
19,653

Label example for patent reissue, c. 1940.

{ WPL & RN Numbers }

Catalog example of sweaters with Ram's Head logo. Sears, c. 1929.

Catalog example of Ram's Head Fabric logo. Montgomery Ward, c. 1939.

Label showing 100% wool notation, c. 1930s.

Catalog example showing amount of wool in garment. Montgomery Ward, c. 1934.

Label backside showing WPL number, c. 1950s.

Catalog example of the All Wool or Ram's Head logo. Sears, c. 1929.

The Fair Labor Standards Act (FSLA) of 1938, mainly concerning work hours and wages, gave new legislation to protect the consumer. Along the same line and certainly one of the most sweeping acts of the time was the Federal Trade Commission's Wool Products Labeling Act of 1939 (WPL).

This Act required that any person, association or corporation in any form of business, manufacturing, or selling, products containing wool be registered with the United States government. Wool was the basis for the law, but many times it was used for all goods a company produced.

It is interesting to note that many companies had already been marking their goods with Pure Wool, 100% Wool, or the logo below, because of the incredulous popularity of wool knit garments post WWI and into the 1920s.

The All Wool logo was used in many catalogs of the 1920s and 1930s.

Years before the Wool Products Act, many companies had labeled, or at least stated, the amount of Wool that was in the garment.

WPL numbers were issued to registrants starting in 1941 with #00101 and continued until 1959 and ending with #13669. The starting zeros were dropped and numbers were only put on clothing labels as 3 or 4 digits until number 10000 was reached in the 1950s, then all 5 digits were used.

A single WPL or RN number was / is issued to a business that sells, manufactures, imports or distributes products under the Wool Products Labeling Act, Fur Products Labeling Act and is good indefinitely or until the company ceases business. Once a number is issued to a particular person or company, that number cannot be reassigned or transferred. Some of the original numbers are still in use. For example, Levi Strauss & Co. still holds and uses WPL 423. This registration process is still in effect today.

The Fur Products Labeling Act of 1952 came as a result of needed changes to the Tariff Act of 1930 and required information be stamped on the back side of hides or pelts with the original fur still attached. Faux furs and fur blend fabrics like mink & wool blends or seal & wool blends were exempt from this regulation. New registration numbers starting with 00100 and ending with 04086 in 1958 were assigned as requested, but existing WPL numbers could also be used.

The biggest change to the WPL and FPL numbering system came in 1959 with the formation of one set of registration numbers to cover the Wool Products Labeling Act and the Fur Products Labeling Act. These were simply known as Registration Numbers (RN) and commenced with #13670 (following in sequence from the WPL numbers).

WPL or RN numbers *cannot* date a garment, but can be useful in telling the absolute oldest a garment can be, meaning that a garment bearing a WPL number on the label *cannot* be older than when the number was approximately issued.

Unfortunately, there are no records showing an exact date that a number was issued. Therefore, a formula was worked out to achieve this that has been shown to be as accurate as can be expected. It is based on the start year and average amount of numbers issued each year.

For WPL number dating:

Divide the WPL number by 759 (average issue amount per year), round up or down and add to 1941 (start year).

> *Example:* WPL number 9327 divided by 759 equals 12.28, round to 12 and add to 1941 equals 1953.

So, using the above formula, the approximate date that WPL number 9327 was issued is 1953. We now know that the garment cannot be older than about 1953, but is more than likely newer than that date. Other label and dating clues, along with overall style criteria, must be used to date this item.

For RN number dating:

RN number minus 13670 (starting number for RN's), divide by 2189 (average issue amount per year), round up or down and add to 1959 (start year).

> *Example:* RN # 59770 minus 13670 equals 46100, divided by 2189 equals 21.05, round to 21 and add to 1959, which equals 1980.

The approximate date that RN # 59770 was issued is 1980. We know that the garment cannot be older than about 1980, but it is surely newer. Again, other label clues and overall style must be used to date this item.

A database of RN information, with a default of 1998 when it was set up, is available at:

https://rn.ftc.gov/pls/TextileRN/wrnquery$.startup

This database can also tell which company was issued the specific WPL or RN number. The company name can be Googled for start up information, or TESS can be used to see if the company was issued a Trademark for its name. If possible it is always good to cross reference your findings with another source.

This WPL number belongs to Wigwam Mills. Using the formula for dating WPL numbers, it was issued in about 1943, so this garment can not be older than 1943.

Label showing WPL number for checking ownership and when number was issued; belongs to Wigwam Mills and dates to 1943 or after.

Textile Fiber
{ Products Identification }
Act of 1960

Label showing generic fiber name of Nylon Tricot, c. 1950s.

Label showing generic fiber name, c. 1960s.

Label showing fiber / fabric identification, c. 1960s.

Label showing fiber content, c. 1960s.

Label showing fiber content percentages, c. 1960s.

Hang tag showing that information did not have to be on the manufacturers label or permanently attached, from 1960-1962.

In 1960, the Textile Fiber Products Identification Act required that a garment sold in the United States be identified as to its fiber content. The ID was to list the fiber by its generic name. An example would be polyester or Dacron, not Dacron polyester.

When first enacted, many found the generic terms to be quite confusing. The wording of Nylon Tricot, which had been used in the 1950s, is thought to have changed to Tricot All Nylon with this Act; however, the term Nylon Tricot continued to be used until the 1970s.

In 1960, the fiber ID did not have to be on the manufacturers label or permanently attached, and many garments were only identified on a hang tag or on packaging, which upon purchase were removed and promptly thrown away.

A revision of this Act in 1962 required manufacturers or importers to show percentages of different fabrics by weight for each kind of fiber in the garment. Either All or 100% could be used to identify a pure fiber.

The Act also required that the manufacturer be stated, either by name or registered number (see previous WPL & RN information) on an attached label rather than a removable hang tag.

It is interesting to note that many men's suits and Hawaiian tourist garments were not identified as to fabric content on an affixed label when this act first started. There were also certain exclusions to this Act for company stores who made garments for their employees.

{ Fabric Care Label
Rule of 1971 }

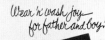

Label showing Dry Clean Only notation
before it was mandatory, c. 1950s.

Label showing Dry Clean notation, c. 1950s.

Label showing Wash and
Wear notation, c. 1950s.

Label showing Washable notation, c. 1950s.

Label showing 1960 care tag. well
before 1971 legislation, c. 1960s.

CARE OF YOUR WOOLENS

WASH automatically on short cycle or
3 minutes in mild liquid detergent and
lukewarm-cold water, rinse and spin.
DRY automatically on low heat for 15
minutes or on hanger at room temperature.
PRESS on wrong side with steam
iron and press cloth.
WEAR with pleasure.

Label showing fabric care as per
1971 Fabric Care Label Rule, c. 1970s.

Advertisement showing a National Dry Cleaning
Machine. The Dry Cleaner, c. 1935.

Before we get into the actual legislation of 1971 regulating fabric care, I think that a clarification needs to be made about garment care in previous decades.

Some companies made voluntary notations on their labels or a secondary label as to care of the garment. "Dry Clean Only" was used on labels in the 1940s to correspond with the WPL Act. The dry cleaning process has been around since the mid to late 1800s, but really didn't catch on until the late 1920s into the 1930s with the use of less flammable solvents.

Companies were known to put Dry Clean labels in their garments as early as the 1930s. You must continue dating the garment with other clues.

"Washable" and "Wash 'N Wear" were marketing at its best in the 1950s by convincing women that they would no longer have to iron their husbands shirts, or send them to the cleaners.

The Fabric Care Label Rule of 1971 was enacted by the Federal Trade Commission (FTC) in December 1971. It mandated that manufacturers provide consumers with the knowledge to clean a particular garment, providing easily readable written information for regular care.

All textile clothing sold in the U.S. was required to have a permanently attached label stating a care method / regular care instructions which had to apply to all parts of the garment, including trims. Two piece garments, such as a man's suit, were only required to have one prominent label in the jacket. If suits were sold as separates, then each piece required its own care label.

Only one method of cleaning was required to be listed, either wash or dry clean, and the rule did not require directions for either. Many manufacturers did, however, include basic instructions for home laundering, such as Machine Wash, Tumble Dry. As time passed, these simple instructions changed to include washing machine water temperatures and drying temperatures, such as Machine Wash Warm, Tumble Dry Low.

Exemptions for fabric care were issued for footwear, hats, gloves, neckties, belts, leather & suede garments, and any items not used to cover or protect the body.

Just remember that to fall under the 1971 Fabric Care Label Rule, a garment must also comply with the 1960 Fabric ID Act.

1984
{ Revision to Fabric }
ID and Care

Japan label predating the 1984 fabric content and care regulations, clearly missing the information the act would eventually require, c. 1960s.

In 1984, the Textile Fabric Identification Act of 1960, the Tariff Act of 1930, and the Wool Products Act of 1939 were modified under a single revision to require garment labels to show the country of origin and to be stated as "Made in ...". The garment had to be entirely manufactured of materials made in that country to have a single country listed. If more than one country was involved, then both or all countries had to be listed. This information could be added to a Maker's Label, or applied to a label of its own and located in the neck area or another easy to find place.

Some labels noted an exporting country long before the 1984 Act. "Made in" countries on labels have been seen on 1930s garments.

Here is some extra information on other countries exporting / importing to the US:

The United States has had the longest standing import status with the British Crown Colony of Hong Kong (full name will appear on label), which began in the 1950s. In 1983, Hong Kong was reclassified to a dependent territory (still under Britain's rule), but known only as Hong Kong or British Hong Kong. In 1997, Hong Kong's sovereignty was transferred to China, but the governments remain independent and they operate as independent countries.

Bangladesh	began exporting to the U.S. in the late 1970s
Cambodia	began exporting to the U.S. in the early 1990s
China	limited trade with the U.S. from 1972-79, then began exporting in the mid-1980s
Egypt	began exporting to the U.S. in the 1980s
India	began exporting to the U.S. in the late 1960s
Indonesia	began exporting to the U.S. in the late 1990s
Korea	known to began exporting to Penney's in the late 1960s
Malaysia	began exporting to the U.S. in the late 1980s
Pakistan	began exporting to the U.S. in the 1980s
Romania	began exporting to the U.S. in the early 1990s
Singapore	began exporting to the U.S. in the 1980s
South Korea	began exporting to the U.S. in the 1980s
Sri Lanka	began exporting to the U.S. in the 1990s
Taiwan ROC (Republic of China)	exported to the U.S. from the 1970s until the early 1980s when it then became known as (just) Taiwan. Not to be confused with the People's Republic of China (China).
Thailand	began exporting to the U.S. in the mid-1980s
Turkey	began exporting to the U.S. in the 1980s
Uruguay	began exporting to the U.S. in the late 1990s
Viet Nam	began exporting to the U.S. in the 1980s

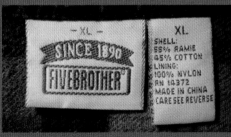

Label showing "Made In ..." notation to comply with 1984 fabric content and care regulations, c. 1990s.

Label showing an example of the 1984 regulation for fabric content and care, c. 1980s.

There are probably other manufacturing countries not listed, but these are the major nations that I have found.

The Fabric Care Label Rule of 1971 was also amended in 1984 by the Permanent Care Labeling Rule. It took the care rules one step further with the clarification of cleaning requirements and standardization of the care instructions.

This amendment required the label to state if the garment must be washed by hand or machine, a water temperature, hang or machine dry, ironed—if necessary, the use of bleach, and warnings such as Do Not Dry Clean, Do Not Have Commercially Laundered, Wash With Like Colors, Wash on Delicate Cycle, or Do Not Wring. In other words, very specific instructions for fabric care.

Exempt from these new regulations were fur and leather goods, reversible garments, items costing less than $3, and special exemptions were granted for items like sheer lingerie.

{ Other Things You
Might Find on a Label }

We signed Pres. Roosevelt's Code

W. B. Saunders Company were happy to co-operate with President Roosevelt in his efforts, through the "National Recovery Act," to increase employment and buying power and to restore the entire Nation to normal prosperity.

Let every citizen do his bit toward Recovery, and it will not be long before the wheels of industry of this great Nation will again be humming.

Example of NRA participation. Journal American Medical Association, c. 1933.

{ NRA Blue Eagle }

In 1933, President Roosevelt enacted the National Recovery Act (NRA), a voluntary program to encourage recovery and combat unemployment. The Act was to declare and regulate fair competition for the protection of consumers, competitors, and employers by dealing with work hours, pay rates, and price fixing. It also gave workers the right to join, or not join, a labor organization or union.

Almost any item with a label, such as razor blades, cigars, magazines & comics, neckties, suits or other clothing could display the NRA "Blue Eagle" to show their participation and agreement with its stated 500 codes of fair practice. Over twenty million people worked under this code, and anyone who did not join was considered unpatriotic.

Contested as authoritarian, the U.S. Supreme Court invalidated the NRA as unconstitutional and the waning program was ended on 1-1-1936. Therefore, the NRA Blue Eagle label will only appear on garments or accessories (or any item for that fact) made between 1933 and 1935.

It is interesting to note that most NRA labels will state something like "under the Merchant & Custom Tailoring Code Authority", "under the Men's Clothing Code Authority", or "under the Cotton Garment Code Authority". Code Authorities for each segment of the garment industry were set up as a form of fair competition and self regulation covering everything from production, quantity, and quality, to prices and distribution. There were hundreds of Code Authorities associated with the NRA and all were dissolved with the end of the program.

Label example of NRA Code Authority notation, c. 1930s.

Catalog example of NRA participation. Montgomery Ward, c. 1933.

Washing

Bleach

Iron

Dry Clean

Dry

Basic International Care Symbols,
c. 1997. *Courtesy of Laurie Moffitt.*

Label showing International Care Symbols, c. 2000s.

Label showing city zones, c. 1950s

Label showing pre-1963 state abbreviation, c. 1950s.

Label showing written city and state, c. 1950s.

International Garment Care Symbols

With the influx of non-English speaking peoples into the United States through the decades, International Garment Care Symbols were introduced to garment labels in 1997. Incidentally, many European countries had introduced these same symbols as early as the late 1970s.

Again, only one safe and reliable method of laundering or dry cleaning was required. In addition was a procedure that might harm the garment, like ironing or bleach, and was shown with an "X" through the symbol, making it a negative, or "do not do this particular thing."

The first two years of the use of International Symbols required written instructions to accompany the symbols. In 1999, just symbols could be used. The five basic symbols are Washing, Bleaching, Drying, Ironing, and Dry Cleaning.

Again, exemptions were granted for fur goods, leather goods, reversible garments, items costing less than $3, and sheer lingerie.

US Postal Zip Codes and State Abbreviations

In 1943, the Post Office implemented postal zones for larger cities. It essentially divided a city into sections or zones to be able to speed up mail service and delivery. An address might have been listed as: Wichita, Zone 13, Kansas or simply as Wichita 13, Kansas.

This system was revised in 1963 with the introduction of ZIP Codes. ZIP is an acronym for Zone Improvement Plan. The U.S. Postal Service divided each state into many three digit areas and added the existing zone to the end. The same address would now be: Wichita, Kansas 67213.

Previously accepted state abbreviations were changed at the same time with each state being designated by two letters, all caps, no periods. Forty nine of the states had previously been known by two letters, but also used other designations. Pennsylvania had used Penn, Penna or P.A. and with the new designation became simply PA.

Not all manufacturing companies choose to redesign their labels to use the new state designations and continued using their existing stock.

Label showing written city and state, c. 1950s.

{ Telephone Numbers }

Telephone numbers on a label can also provide a dating clue. There were as many as seven million telephones in use in the U.S. by 1910 with the majority in big cities like New York and Chicago. Operators handled the calls.

Note the telephone number differences between New York City and Washington D.C. in the two ads from the same year.

By 1925, the semi-centennial year of the Bell System, Americans were still using operator assisted calls as well as dialing for themselves at the rate of over twenty-five billion local and long distance calls a year.

Exchanges for a town or areas within a city started in the 1920s and were normally used with a three digit telephone number in most parts of the country. However, there were already so many telephones in New York City by the 1920s that four digits were used. Exchanges were based on names like Klondike, Amherst, or Murray, but phone numbers only used the first two letters.

For example, a phone number would have been spoken as Klondike-345, but only KL-345 would have been dialed. As towns and cities grew, more digits were added until a maximum of five (5) was reached.

In larger cities, this meant the addition of new exchanges to handle all the telephone numbers needed. The seven dialing digit system that we still use today was implemented in the 1940s—using two letters and five numbers.

Area codes started in the 1950s in the largest of cities. By 1966, all telephone numbers in the United States had been assigned area codes. Party lines, a single phone line serving two or more homes in rural areas by giving each home a different ring, would all but disappear in the 1970s.

If you are looking for an old telephone number printed on a label, usually city libraries have back issues of phone books or city directories on file.

Advertisement showing hierarchy for making a phone call. *Red Cross Magazine*, c. 1918.

Advertisement showing telephone number digits for New York. *Washington Standard Guide*, c. 1922.

Advertisement showing telephone number digits for Washington. D.C. to compare to New York. *Washington Standard Guide*, c. 1922.

Advertisement showing telephone area code for Arizona. *McCalls*, c. 1967.

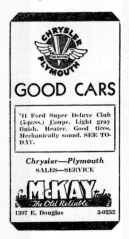

Advertisement showing telephone number digits for Wichita, Kansas. *Wichita Beacon Newspaper*, c. 1943.

Label showing lack of International Woolmark, c. 1950s.

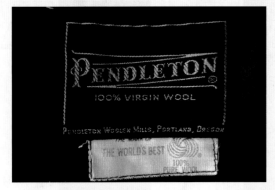

Label showing sewn in International Woolmark, c. mid-1960s.

Label showing International Woolmark, c. late 1960s.

Label showing the Seal of Cotton logo, c. 2000s.

Stamp showing the Crafted with Pride logo, c. 1980s.

{ International Woolmark® }

The International Symbol for Wool, known as the "Woolmark", was introduced worldwide in 1964 and was quickly adopted to be used on all wool garments, whether they were pure wool or a blend. Any clothing label showing this immediately recognizable icon will date to after 1964.

By the 1990s and 2000s, the Woolmark Blend Label, the Wool Blend Label, and the Sportwool Label were added to identify the kind and amount of pure wool in the fabric.

{ Cotton Seal }

In 1973, the Seal of Cotton logo was introduced as a branded ID to allow consumers to quickly identify that the item they were buying was indeed made of cotton. So, any garment with this logo on the label will postdate 1973.

{ Crafted with Pride in USA® }

To combat the influx of imported garments and textiles, the Crafted with Pride in the U.S.A. Council was formed in April 1984. Their mission was to inform the American public of the importance of American manufacturing jobs in the apparel industry and purchasing those domestically made goods. Many companies proudly displayed the logo on the label of their American made goods. There is also the same logo with the word "America" replacing "U.S.A.". Any garment with this logo will date to after 1984.

{ Logo Changes and the Way the Company Name is Written }

Sometimes, the way that a company name is written on the label can give a clue as to dating. Just remember that most companies did not keep exact records of label changes, so sometimes you have to take a little lee-way on the timeline and dating.

To use Munsingwear® as an example, I found that George D. Munsing founded Northwestern Knitting Co. in 1887 and issued his first garment label in 1895 under the name "Munsing". The company name was trademarked in 1918, was renamed in 1919, and early 1920s ads show their products as "Munsing Wear®" with labels that match. This label name was used until 1939 when the labels are shown as "Munsingwear" and written as one word.

As a second example, Champion®, known for t-shirts, used the "running man" logo on their label almost from their start in 1919. The Champion "blue bar" logo was introduced in the 1970s to replace the "running man" and was used just over a decade.

Garments, other than tee shirts, produced by Champion used different logos than shown above or just wording.

The vintagefashionguild.org website has archives for many clothing manufacturers and shows a timeline for some labels. Although this site is mainly for women's clothing makers, there are some listings and examples for menswear.

Label showing how Munsing Wear was
written in the early years until 1939, c. 1930s.

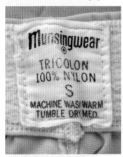

Label showing how
Munsingwear was written
from 1939 on, c. 1970s.

Label showing Champion logo from its early years of
1919 into the late '40s-early '50s, c. 1930s.

Label showing Champion logo
in the 1950s and '60s, c. 1950s.

Label showing Champion Blue Bar logo introduced in
the 1970s to replace the Running Man. The Blue Bar
was used for just over a decade, c. 1970s.

Dry cleaning label showing spikes for attachment used into the 1950s, c. 1940s.

Small hand written price tag showing fold down spikes to attach to garment, c. 1920s.

Dry cleaning label showing unique twisted metal fastener to secure, c. 1940s.

{ Price Tags & Hang Tags }

Label with original glue on sticker, which appeared in the 1930s, c. 1930s.

Hand written hang tag, c. 1960s.

Hand written hang tag, which is still available for purchase today, c. 1960s.

Pin in price tag used into the 1960s, c. 1950s.

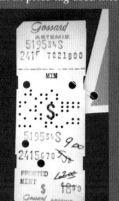

Data processing information "dot" price tag introduced in the last half of the 1960s, c. 1960s.

Inventory number coded price tag, which started in the 1970s, c. 1970s.

Pin in price tag used into the 1960s, c. 1950s.

Price tag with UPC scan code started in 1987, c. 2000s.

This is the "NATIONAL" GUARANTEE TAG

You will find this Tag tied on every article we sell

Advertisement showing hang tag attached with string for pricing or information, which were used from the turn of the twentieth century. *National Cloak & Suit Catalog,* c. 1913.

If you are lucky enough to find some NOS (New Old Stock) garments, the price tag can also offer a clue as to dating. NOS is a common term for any garment that is of vintage age of over twenty-five years old, is unworn, and still retains its original price tag or other proof like original folds and pins that it has not been worn or used. This term is also used for collectibles.

In the earliest decades, a small hand written price tag was attached to a garment with spikes that went through the garment and folded down.

In the 1930s, a similar type of tag was used, but the spikes were thinner and went sideways.

Dry cleaning labels had a similar small tag, but the spikes were much bigger or dry cleaners fashioned their own fasteners. These were used through the 1950s.

Hang tags attached with strings for pricing and notations appeared after the turn of the twentieth century.

Stick on / glue on labels appeared in the 1930s.

Hang tags were an acceptable form of Fabric Identification under the 1960 Act. Of course, the hang tag was one of the first things to go on a garment before it was worn. This Act was revised in 1962 to state that the Fabric ID must be on an attached label. Hang tags were a holdover from the 1950s before the law, and will only come into play when dating a garment if it is NOS.

In the 1950s and '60s, some stores were still using regular hang tags or pin in tags with information either hand written or printed.

Tags with data processing information "dots" were introduced in the 1960s.

Inventory number coded tags (pre-scan codes) came into use in the 1970s.

Scan codes were invented as binary codes for tracking retail inventory and sales. They were first used by grocery stores in 1974. In 1981, the military initialized the system codes for tracking purchases, and in 1982 the United States Postal Service started using the system to track packages.

Clothing retailers and manufacturers introduced scan codes for clothing in the mid-1980s, and it was generally used for clothing industry wide by 1987.

{ Putting It All Together }

Garment that goes with Arotex label for dating exercise, c. 1940s. $50-75.

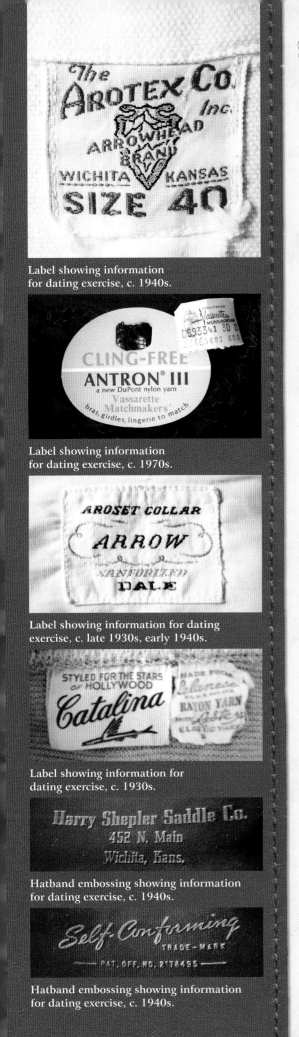

Label showing information for dating exercise, c. 1940s.

Label showing information for dating exercise, c. 1970s.

Label showing information for dating exercise, c. late 1930s, early 1940s.

Label showing information for dating exercise, c. 1930s.

Hatband embossing showing information for dating exercise, c. 1940s.

Hatband embossing showing information for dating exercise, c. 1940s.

By searching the web, I found that Arotex Co. was started in 1924 in Wichita, Kansas, by a husband and wife team as a uniform manufacturing company. The company closed in the very early 1960s a few years following the death of the husband. The style elements and heavy woven duck fabric make me think that this jacket was for a waiter or elevator operator in the 1940s.

Dupont® Antron® III was being used as early as 1970 and was patented in 1973, but was not registered for a trademark until 1985. Upon close examination of the label, we see that Antron is trademarked, not Antron III. Remember that the ® refers to what immediately precedes the symbol. We therefore must conclude that the garment attached to the label is older than 1971 because of the trademark and the fact that a fabric care label is attached.

The only thing known about this shirt from its label is that Sanforized dates it after 1930 (see info in Section III of this book), and no fabric content label makes it before 1962. To narrow this down further, a web search of Aroset® came up with an ad in *Life* (magazine) dated January 23, 1939, for an Arrow® (brand) Hitt® (style name) shirt; a search of USPTO says that Arrow first used Aroset in 1935 and Dale® (style name) in 1922. With this information we have to assume that the absolute oldest this shirt can be is 1935—the newest criteria for dating found.

In a web search, I found that the Catalina® brand was founded in 1928 by Pacific Knitting Mills, Lastex® was introduced in 1925, and Celanese® was introduced in the late 1920s. So, I now know that this swimsuit can't be older than 1928. The overall style of the garment must be taken into consideration when dating—which came out to be 1930s.

Dating the store information on this sweatband took some searching on the web. Harry Shepler bought an existing saddlery shop in 1946 at the location on the sweatband and expanded to a new building at another location in 1961. This hat should therefore date between 1946 and 1961.

Using style dating criteria, the hat that belongs to this label is from the late 1940s. I will mention that I knew Harry Shepler back in the late 1960s after he sold his store and retired; I also have lived in the same town all my life and know some of its history, so this information helped in my search. As an interesting side note, Harry Shepler's store would become Sheplers®—The World's Largest Western Store.

If you find a store label that is from your city, you might want to check with the local library for back copies of old phone books or city directories, or the local newspaper office for advertising archives to narrow a time frame for when the store was in business.

Hat that goes with Harry Shepler Saddle Co. hatband for dating exercise, c. 1940s.

{ Union Labels }

We have covered the basics found on labels and hopefully shown that it is also necessary to look at the label and the garment as a whole, rather than just dating an individual item within the whole.

Since Union Labels and the dating information that they provide are distinct from the Makers / Company labels, their information is being listed and treated separately. I'll present a timeline of the decades and then get into the specifics of a couple of the biggest and most well known unions for making menswear.

This chapter was designed to help date men's clothing items from the best known and acknowledged unions using each one's specific union labels. Just remember that a garment can never be older than its attached union label.

As will quickly be evident, there was much struggle in the clothing industry through the decades, and many influences and pressures on the regulations governing the various unions. But, the struggles of these unions have also played a large part in our country's history and helped to make the garment industry what it is today.

{ Background }

Back in 1888, The *New York Working Women's Society* was formed by two women concerned with working conditions, hours, and child labor in factories. Within three years, the *White List of 1891* was circulated around the city as a compilation of department stores that met certain ladies labor standards—thus making the stores a good place to shop. This was one of the first efforts at consumer education.

At the same time, a *Black List* was put out by various trade unions, informing trade union workers of unsuitable places to work. This was the same objective, but taking a slightly different path to get there. Draw your own conclusion about the use of black lists after that.

The year 1891 is also when the *United Garment Workers of America® (UGWA)* formed under the American Federation of Labor. The UGWA mainly focused on ready made menswear. UGWA and its labels will be covered in depth later in this chapter.

By 1898, leagues from six states had joined New York Society in their work and the *National Consumers League* was formed. The following year, the White List was replaced with their *White Label Campaign of 1899*.

This step added an actual label to the garment, which was virtually unheard of up to this time. The White Label was in a bow tie shape with "Official Label National Consumers League Registered Nov 17, 1899" in the center, "Made Under Clean and Healthful Conditions" on the left, and "Use of Label Authorized After Investigation" on the right. When attached to a garment, a White Label showed the garment was made under fair working conditions.

Since the National Consumers League was formed by and for women and considered to mainly affect women factory workers, the *International Ladies Garment Workers Union (ILGWU),* started in 1900, was thought of as "all the same". This created a competition causing ILGWU to fashion their own label to be added to a garment to show it was produced under union standards.

It also helps to remember that during the early years of the 1900s, men were tailors and factory workers who made menswear, while women were seamstresses and worked in factories making garments for women and children.

The *Amalgamated Clothing Workers of America® (ACWA)* was formed of union workers that wanted to split from UGWA in 1913. This union and its labels will be covered in depth later in this chapter.

The *Federal Trade Commission (FTC)* was created by the Federal Government in 1914 to define and stop unfair trade practices.

The United States Census of 1914 showed that New York state had 2357 factories just for making men's clothing, with Illinois and the Chicago area having 578 factories. With thousands of other similar menswear factories scattered among the remaining states, 983 men's hat factories, 35 shirt collar companies, and so on, there was a big Union influence nationwide as to clothing.

In 1919, the *National Industrial Federation of Clothing Manufacturers* was formed in the four major menswear manufacturing cities to regulate and stabilize the entire men's clothing industry. It became a sort of Union vs. Non-union struggle and was dissolved within a few years.

It was in the 1920s that companies and unions made a real effort by putting labels in their garments as a form of advertising for a particular company or union and acknowledgement of its standards.

The labeling feuds continued and in 1924 ILGWU issued its *Prosanis label,* which was to be a guarantee against disease breeding garments by targeting the health factors of garment workers. The Prosanis label was a bubble-shaped emblem around the words, "Produced under conditions approved by Joint Board Sanitary Control." This label was to acknowledge certain companies in a similar fashion to the White List by their participation in the program. This label is rare and is found only in women's garments.

It is known that many companies contracted with individual states for the production of work garments by incarcerated convict labor at pennies on the dollar. The finished goods were mainly sold in chain stores and dry goods at lower pricing. Union made garments were sometimes as much as twice the cost to purchase.

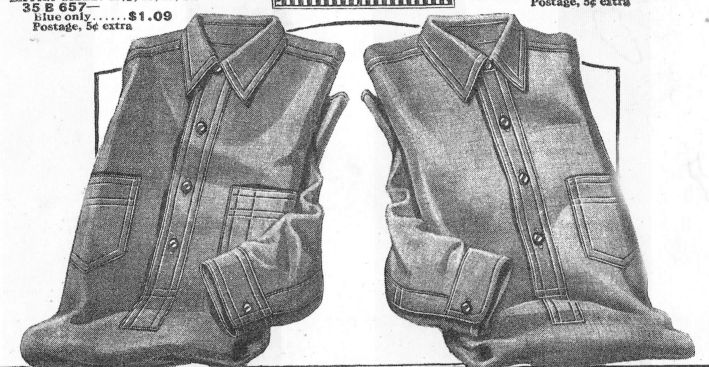

98¢ Heavy Chambray Triple Stitched

Regular and extra sizes in these full cut, roomy Work Shirts made of heavy weight, durable chambray. Six-button coat front. All seams are triple stitched to safeguard you against rips. Flat collar interlined for longer wear. Two pockets, one for pencil, the other specially made to hold a watch. Faced sleeves. One-button cuffs. State size wanted.

HALF SIZES: 14½ to 17.

35 B 656—Blue only.................98¢

EXTRA SIZES: 17½, 18, 19, 20.
  35 B 657—
    Blue only......$1.09
    Postage, 5¢ extra

Ward's Shirts Are Not Prison Made Garments

Khaki Sateen Very Serviceable $1.39

These medium weight Work Shirts are of soft finished sateen in the serviceable khaki color. Attached flat collar and cuffs interlined for longer wear. Two large pockets with buttoned down flaps. Sleeves neatly faced. Ivory buttons. You'll find these shirts extra full cut and roomy and a quality which wears well. They are a bargain at $1.39.

HALF SIZES: 14½ to 17.
State size wanted.
35 B 623—Khaki color only.$1.39
Postage, 5¢ extra

We Never Sacrifice Quality to Make a Low Price

Catalog example stating no use of prison labor. Montgomery Ward, c. 1925.

The White Label proponents and the National Consumers League both endorsed the Prosanis label because of similar objectives. It seems as if the labels for both ceased at the same time while the ILGWU continued to use the Prosanis label until 1929. ILGWU stopped the use of their Prosanis label in 1929.

When the Depression hit later that year, people worried more about their jobs than if the job was safe. Men lined up outside the factories and offered to work for lower wages than their Union counterparts.

The effects of the Depression were also felt in Europe, especially when the U.S. government added new import duties on clothing. These high costs virtually stopped clothing imports, but helped American manufacturers and retailers with their less costly brands.

The **National Recovery Board**, established in 1934, was given new life after the demise of the NRA to be the watchdog of certain sectors of the garment industry to ensure that garments were made following the **Fair Labor Standards Act (FLSA)** regulations. It was most active from 1936 to 1942.

The end of the NRA in 1935 coincided with much unrest among the clothing unions—which all essentially represented the same code authorities. The NRA law had helped everyone, union or non-union, while the unions were only interested in helping their members. Non-union workers, especially women workers, thought they needed a law for protection.

In the background, the **National Consumers League** was impatiently lobbying for all workers and finally got the FLSA passed in 1938. This act was also called the Wages & Hours Bill, and established a national minimum wage, guaranteed time and a half for overtime in certain jobs, and prohibited child labor.

The FLSA was made ineffective and unenforceable during WWII because wartime inflation lowered wages to below the original minimum wage stated in 1938 of 40 cents an hour. Just to give you an idea about wages in past decades:

FLSA Amendment in 1949
  set minimum wage at 75 cents an hour;

FLSA Amendment in 1955
  set minimum wage at $1.00 an hour;

FLSA Amendment in 1961
  set minimum wage at $1.25 an hour;

an Equal Pay Amendment in 1963
  was enacted to prevent sex bias;

FLSA Amendment in 1966
  set minimum wage at $1.60 hour;

an Age Discrimination in Employment Amendment in 1967
  for people over 40;

and it continues through the decades.

On the women's clothing side, the **National Coat & Suit Industry Recovery Board** was formed of 2100 firms that represented ninety percent of the women's and children's coat and suit makers. This label will reverse to **Consumers Protection Label** and states Manufactured Under Fair Labor Standards which was used from June 1938 into the late 1960s.

I only mention the above labels because they have also been found in men's tuxedos, as well as children's & youth's clothing—which would include boy's garments.

The **National Consumer Retailers Council** was formed in 1938 to establish an informative label to be placed on garments. A decade and some advertising later, the council still had done nothing to further its objective.

{ UGWA – United Garment Workers of America }

The invention of the sewing machine brought forth a boom in ready made, ready-to-wear clothing. Even in the last decade or so of the 1800s, custom tailors were forced to machine stitch part of their garments to shorten labor hours and cheapen production costs to keep themselves in business.

New systems implemented for production allowed ready-made clothing to be "custom tailored" to specific sizes—known as "special orders."

Some thought this as a way to deceive consumers into thinking they were getting a custom garment at a cheaper ready-made price. Workers in ready-made factories came to be known as shop tailors rather than being acknowledged for the fine tailoring they had always produced.

The *Tailors Progressive Union of America* consisted of both custom tailors and shop tailors when it was formed. But, for the most part, these workers did not want to amalgamate (join together as one group).

The *United Garment Workers of America (UGWA or UGW)* was formed in 1891 under the *American Federation of Labor (AFL)* as a union of workers for ready-made clothing made in factories. Not only did the UGWA champion for wages and hours, they also tried to restrict output to keep prices up in a down economy before the 1900s.

UGWA recognized its work with a line label sewn in a readily found, but inconspicuous place on each garment: in the hip pocket of overalls, in the inside pocket of coats and vests, and in the hip pocket of pants.

UGWA also made ready-to-wear shirts in their early years, but a disagreement with the *Shirt, Waist & Laundry Workers International Union* in the early teens stopped their production. It was decided that there was to be no overlapping of unions, and no double labels. This was finally resolved with union mergers and / or combining different unions under one label.

More strife followed the UGWA and about 2/3 of its membership left in 1913 to form the *Amalgamated Clothing Workers of America (ACWA)*.

As everyone in manufacturing paid the same price for fabrics, the only way to be competitive on union made garments was through the labor costs. Communists also tried to infiltrate the different unions in the Twenties, and did actually get a foothold in the ILGWU. Strikes seemed to be ongoing and costly to the unions and their workers. All this had to be considered in the wholesale pricing of garments.

Unfortunately, there is no "clear cut" timeline or copyrights to closely date the UGWA labels. This is compounded by the fact that they used two notable and different labels throughout the years: Duck Goods for men's and boy's overalls, and a nondescript label for any other garments they may have produced. I have also seen a few odd labels, which appear very rarely.

There are a few subtle changes that can be noted for both label styles, so here's some of what I have been able to surmise.

The Duck Goods label was introduced in 1913 for work garments made of duck cloth, canvas cloth, denim or other similar fabrics.

Research leads me to believe that A.F. of L. was added to UGWA labels post 1935 with the creation of the rival *Congress of Industrial Organizations (CIO)*. Supposedly, UGWA split from the AFL in 1948, but rejoined within two years—thus the 1950 registration on the label. AFL would also date the label to pre-1955 when AFL and CIO merged.

I want to mention that many work garments only said Union Made on the company label. Be sure to check inside pockets for an actual union label to help date the garment.

Early UGWA advertisement from an unknown magazine, c. 1905.

Early UGWA Duck Goods label, c. 1910s.
Photo courtesy of Dale Vest.

UGWA Duck Goods label used from 1935 to 1955, c. 1930s. Photo courtesy of Dale Vest.

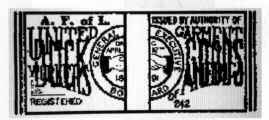

UGWA Duck Goods label from TESS showing 1950 registration, c. 1950s.

Early UGWA shirt label, c. 1910s.

Early UGWA clothing label, c. 1900s.

1977 to 1989 UGWA label, c. 1980s.

1915 ACWA label used until 1934, c. 1910s.

1934 ACWA label used until 1935, c. 1934.
Photo courtesy of Mara Perry.

UGWA (non-Duck Goods) labels were introduced in 1905 (and possibly a few years earlier) for clothing other than work wear. The particular label below states shirts down the right side, dating it before WWI (see previous note as to Shirt Union).

UGWA labels were then changed to have red numbering down the side.

The wording A.F. of L. on the upper left was probably added after 1935 with the creation of the rival CIO. Reads AFL CIO in the upper left of the labels with the merger of these two powerhouses in 1955. Label says AFL CIO CLC in the upper left sometime after 1977 until 1989 with the addition of the Central Labor Councils (CLC) .

I found that UGWA issued "Special Order" labels for military officers' uniforms during WWII that they made. The Special Order was stamped across the regular label like Duck Goods.

And, an unusual all red printed label with an ® was found in a late 1960s garment.

In the 1970s, companies who still contracted with the union usually combined UGWA info with a fabric care label on the garment.

The United Garment Workers of America union was active on its own until 1994. In 2000 it merged with the United Textile Workers of America (UTWA) to form the UFCW Textile & Garment Council.

{ ACWA—Amalgamated Clothing Workers of America }

Amalgamated Clothing Workers of America (ACWA) was formed in 1913 as a revolt against the ***United Garment Workers of America (UGWA)***. It was to be an industrial union representing factories, not just specific craft unions for contract shops, and to represent every worker, not just skilled craftsmen.

Its member manufacturing firms produced men's and boy's clothing other than work wear, which was mainly handled by UGWA, and included: buttonhole makers; vest makers, pressers and basters; pants makers, operators and pressers; coat cutters, basters, operators, pressers and tailors; lapel makers; knee pants makers; clothing burners; palm beach workers; shirt makers; clothing cutters; custom tailors; overall workers; wholesale clothing clerks; and the washable sailor suit union.

From the moment of its formation, the ***American Federation of Labor (AFL)*** refused to acknowledge the new union. ACWA issued its own label in 1915 to be used in each garment they made.

With the pro-union stance of the Federal Government during World War I, ACWA quickly gained a foothold and was able to expand well beyond the menswear clothing manufacturing areas of New York City and Chicago.

As an extremely progressive union, ACWA offered its members unemployment insurance and opened its own banks to serve its members.

The Great Depression took its toll on all walks of life, and menswear factories were not immune. ACWA lost well over half of its membership to unemployment.

ACWA was allowed to join the AFL in 1933 and agreed to use UGWA labels in the clothing they made. Conflicts ensued, and ACWA copyrighted and issued their own labels once again in 1934, and even went as far as crossing over into denim work clothing. This label also added the "80" beside the "Union Bug."

ACWA ended up quitting the AFL in 1935 and again copyrighted and issued a new label for its use.

The Union then joined forces with the *International Ladies Garment Workers Union (ILGWU)* and six other unions to form the *Congress of Industrial Organizations (CIO)* in November 1935.

In 1936, the *Journeyman Tailors Union* became part of ACWA and new labels were copyrighted and issued for that year. This was the first issued label to state "Made in the USA".

The AFL retaliated in 1936 by suspending all union memberships, plus a couple of other unions involved.

By 1937, garments bearing the ACWA label included coats, suits, topcoats, overcoats, trousers, shirts, boy's blouses, pajamas, underwear, neckwear, custom-tailored garments, sheep-lined and leather clothing, dress shirts and even work shirts.

The first CIO convention was held in 1938. The creation of the *Textile Workers Union of America (TWUA)* and the *Retail, Wholesale & Department Store Workers Union of America* necessitated a new ACWA label in 1939. For some reason we find ACWA '39 labels printed both ways with either "Made in USA" or a series.

Labels of 1939 were also issued in sepia tone for use in military clothing during WWII and did not state "Made in the U.S.A.". Instead they stated Series S&G for suit & garment.

During the above five major issues, the labels would designate what the garment was: Union Made Suit, Union Made Vest, Union Made Garment, Union Made Clothing, Union Made Work Clothes, or Union Made Special Order.

Leadership changes, the end of WWII, and the CIO expulsion of eleven affiliated unions for supposedly having communist ties necessitated a total label redesign in 1949. The new label did not state "Made in the U.S.A." and it reverted back to the previous series letter dating system. The numbering system, always printed in red, was moved to the left side of the label, the sewing machine replaced the bobbin and shuttle for the logo, and the copyright date was moved to the end with the series lettering system information.

The 1949 series label became a registered trademark in 1962 and the ® was added to designate this. The numbering system changed from red to black a few years later.

This 1949 (post 62 registration) label remained in use until 1976 when the ACWA merged with the *Textile Workers Union of America (TWUA)* to form the *Amalgamated Clothing & Textile Workers Union of America (ACTWU)*.

I have found ACWA labels in clothing dating as late as 1981, which makes me think that some companies used up their stock of existing labels before starting to use the ACTWU labels.

And, I have noted ACWA labels in women's Shaheen clothing from Hawaii in the 1970s and women's blouses from the same era.

The ILGWU merged with ACTWU in 1995 to form the *Union of Needletrades, Industrial & Textile Employees (UNITE)*.

1935 ACWA label used until 1936, c. 1935.

1936 ACWA label used until 1939, c. 1936.

1939 ACWA label used until 1949, c. 1940s.

1949 ACWA label used until 1962, c. 1950s.

1949 ACWA with 1962 registration (®), c. 1960s.

1949® ACWA label showing date mark of 1978, c. 1970s.

The most important thing to remember is that all ACWA labels, with the exceptions of the special shirt stamp & necktie label, have a copyright date which is found on the label, albeit usually in tiny print which sometimes can only be read with a magnifying glass. New label issues were usually sent out to manufacturers in December, and garment dating will span the life of each particular copyright label plus sometimes a couple of years to use up the excess labels before starting on the newly issued ones. A garment with an ACWA label can not be older than the copyright date on the affixed label.

More about Dating the 1949 ACWA Label

As stated previously, the 1949 label was used from about December 1949 until the formation of ACTWU in 1976. In actuality, I have noted this label in dated garments as late as 1981 which leads me to believe that some factories were proud to have been part of the ACWA and used up their supplies of old labels rather than throw them away.

The 1949 label can be used for more closely dating a garment than sometime between 1949 and 1976 (which I will use as a default). The "Series" on the label is an alphabetical coding system for the date of issue which was put into place on the labels—much like many states today do on their car tags. For example AAA, AAB, AAC, … ABA, ABB, ABC … I don't know how many of each letter set was printed or how often the codes changed, but it has something to do with the (red) numbering system.

This alphabetical coding system started with the letter "S", which was the code for Suit. Like the example, it also used three characters. Note that some of the 1949 labels also used a "G" for Garment designation, which we'll cover a little later.

You have to remember that these labels were issued to hundreds of different manufacturers who more than likely used them at a different rate. The dating method I have figured out is not foolproof, but can be used to get you much closer to an actual date for your suit or sports coat when used in tandem with style features.

Basically, in 1949 with the new ACWA issue, the right edge of the label would vertically state: "Copyright 1949" in tiny print and under it in larger letters "Series SAA". This is our starting point. The last letter ran completely through the alphabet and then the middle letter would change to the next in the alphabet while running the last letter completely through the alphabet again.

With the checking of hundreds of suits and sports coats styling against their ACWA Series set, I have concluded the following:

The first label started with Series SAA in about December 1949 or January 1950.

Series up to SDA or SEA were used in the early fifties, until about '53 or '54

Series up to SHA were used until about '56 or '57

Series up to SJA were used until about '60 or '61

Series up to SKA were used until about '63

Series up to SNA or SOA were used until about the mid-1960s

Series up to SRA were used until about the late 1960s

Series up to SZA were used to the early to mid-1970s

Some leftover labels kept on being used.

My studies have concluded that the "G" series lettering started with the 1939 label using "Series GAA". The majority of these "G" for garment labels were used for military clothing. The 1949 label started over using "Series GAA", but without military contracts weren't used nearly as much.

It was interesting to note that a label from a 1971 garment was designated "Series GLA". This means that the Union didn't produce nearly as many garments with the "G" label as they did under the "S" for Suit label. Almost all the "G" label garments during the late 1960s and early '70s were being manufactured for Hart, Schaffner & Marx.

ACWA Shirt Labels:

The **Shirtmakers Union** became part of ACWA in 1933, so a special stamp was created to show that the shirt was made under the ACWA Union. These stamps were not dated like a usual label, so you have to rely on accompanying specific wording and other dating clues from the shirt.

With the example, note the wording about fabric shrinkage: not more than 1%, and the placement of "union" on the stamp. See the chapter on Fabric Processes in Section three for more information.

Note that the Union Bug is missing on all shirt stamps. The Union Bug signified that the label had been printed by someone in the printer's union, while the shirt stamp was actually stamped on the shirt tail at the time of construction.

By the late 1960s, the stamp was still used on dress shirts with the addition of "Made in U.S.A." added just below.

In the 1970s, ACWA added casual shirts and used sewn in label that also included fabric content and fabric care instructions. The label also lacked the Union Bug.

Another smaller label appeared at the same time and simply stated ACWA or Made by ACWA.

ACWA Necktie Labels:

In 1937, an ACWA special label was issued for men's neckties.

A redesigned label started showing up in neckties after 1949, corresponding with the new clothing label copyright and design starting that same year. This label adopted the sewing machine logo like its big brother suit & jacket label of the same year.

And, another redesign showed up around the 1960s.

ACWA shirt stamp used from 1933 through the 1960s. The patent number on this shirt stamp dates to 1955. so shirt is newer than that date, c. 1950s.

ACWA shirt label used starting in the 1970s, c. 1970s.

1937 ACWA necktie label used until 1949, c. 1940s.

1949 ACWA necktie label used until the early 1960s, c. 1950s.

1960s ACWA necktie label used from 1962 until the late '70s, c. 1960s.

{ Custom Tailors Union }

Journeymen Tailors Union of U.S. & Canada

The *Journeymen Tailors Union* was established in 1883 and is one of the oldest of the clothing unions. It became affiliated with the Union Label Trades Department in 1922 and issued a label under the name Custom Tailors Union Label.

This label sewn into a garment guaranteed that custom tailored and made to measure men's suits were union made. It also drew a distinctive line with United Garment Workers of America (UGWA) and recognized their part in manufacturing something other than custom-made clothing. As time passed, the lines blurred as actual custom-made clothing became standardized sizes made-to-measure and actually produced in factories rather than tailoring shops.

The Journeymen Tailors Union required that their label could only be sewn into a completed garment by a member, and were to be placed inside the breast pocket of coats; or in the middle of the back strap, on the inside of the waistband, or inside the watch pocket of a vest. The idea was to make them concealed, but readily found. The labels were never to be given to the merchant to be applied with a store label.

Unfortunately, I don't know when these labels were implemented, but they stopped being used in about 1936 when the Journeymen Tailors Union joined ACWA.

Closing out the union section is a nondescript Union Label.

If you see that a work wear garment such as overalls, jeans, coveralls, or shirts only says Union Made on the label, it usually refers to UGWA. This was a common practice as far back as the 1930s and as late as the '70s. But, remember that it never hurts to look inside pockets for an actual union label.

Early Custom Tailors Union Label, c. 1920s.

Custom Tailors Union Label, c. pre-1936.

Generic "Union Made" label, c. 1960s.

The Big Three
of America's Best
Known Labels

{   }

ust after the Civil War, one sheet pamphlets called catalogs were circulated in an effort to lure customers to the stores. In 1875, the U.S. Postal Service (USPS) started offering a low cost, bulk rate mailing fee for "educational" literature, which would later come to include catalogs. So, rural Americans found it quite easy to shop from a catalog and then trek to town to pick up their purchase at their local Dry Goods or Mercantile Store. Starting in about 1896, (USPS) Rural Free Delivery got mail order catalogs directly to families outside cities or towns and eventually expanded to nationwide service by 1902.

A combination of mail order and credit terms in 1905 made Spiegel one of the most popular catalog sellers in the U.S. at the time. Many other companies followed suit to keep in tune with the competition.

The addition of Parcel Post Service in 1913 brought the goods to the buyers' home, rather than making a trip to town. Catalog offerings ranged from a cook stove or kitchen table, to clothing for the entire family, medicine, jewelry, guns, toys, tools, horse supplies, and even cigarettes and tobacco, with most of the purchases being delivered by contract haulers.

Montgomery Ward became the first company to accept telephone orders from their catalog in 1934. Again, other catalog retailers followed this example of marketing.

Although this chapter deals with clothing from America's three largest retailers, **Montgomery Ward**®, **Sears, Roebuck and Co.**®, **and J.C. Penney**®, other well known catalog clothing companies have been major players in the mail order and department store business.

L.L.Bean® started his mail order business in 1912 with hunting boots and **Eddie Bauer**® started selling quilted down jackets by mail order in 1920.

Chicago, with its major garment manufacturing facilities and unions, was the home of numerous clothing mail order companies. Many catered primarily to female clientele and only sold very limited amounts of menswear:

National Cloak & Suit, which started in 1888 and was reorganized as **National Bellas Hess** in 1910, then merged with **The Charles Williams Stores** in 1929, and finally went bankrupt in 1974. As National Bellas Hess, the company sold their own line of Gladiator work wear for men starting in 1899.

Montgomery Ward label used in the 1920s and early 1930s, c. 1920s.

Montgomery Ward label used from the late 1920s until 1934, c. 1930s.

Montgomery Ward label used from 1935 into the 1940s, c. 1930s.

Montgomery Ward label used in the 1940s and 1950s, c. 1940s. *Photo courtesy of dvgvintage.*

Montgomery Ward label thought to be used in the 1940s, c. 1940s. *Photo courtesy of Dale Vest.*

Montgomery Ward label used in the 1960s and 1970s, c. 1960s.

Spiegel, May & Stern started its catalog business in 1888 and sold Melville Shirts and Penwood Suits for men. They changed their name to **Spiegel of Chicago** in 1929. I also found that the company carried Oakbrook Coats, which was a brand they purchased from Sears in 1980.

Chicago Mail Order started selling Alden's brand of men's suits in 1899, and added their Glenshire line of menswear in 1940. Their name was changed to **Alden's®**, probably sometime after WWII, and they expanded their own lines of menswear under the Alden's and Aldencrest labels.

Phillipsborn Department Stores started selling coats and cloaks for all family members in 1890 and expanded into the catalog business, finally going bankrupt in 1924. It had no named brands that I could find.

The information offered below is for specific brands of menswear and their labels available through the "Big Three" catalogs or as in store merchandise. Please note that if you have a menswear garment with one of these particular labels, the garment cannot be older than when the label was first used in commerce.

The generic company brand labels have been used for any garment, whether men's, women's or children's. Specific men's brands within a company are listed separately.

{ Montgomery Ward }

Aaron Montgomery Ward issued his first catalog in 1872 under the name **Montgomery Ward**. The company was totally mail order sales until the first Montgomery Ward store opened in 1926. The company closed its last store in 2000. Montgomery Ward was purchased by Midwest Catalog Brands, a division of Swiss Colony, and has been given new life as an online retailer. A Montgomery Ward catalog is currently produced and also has its merchandise available from their website at: www.wards.com.

In their early years, Montgomery Ward bought their merchandise directly from leading manufacturers and mills, then offered the items in their catalogs and stores. This method supported many companies like Talon, Cravenette®, Pacific Mills, Galey & Lord, Bur-Mi® and Arnold Knit Goods.

Many clothing items after the turn of the twentieth century were known to have only carried the name of Montgomery Ward, or just Wards in later years. These are applicable for men's and women's clothing.

Here are some examples of the garment labels and their approximate dating:

Montgomery Ward catalog and clothing logo introduced in 1935. Montgomery Ward, c. 1935.

The 1925 catalog shows Montgomery Ward trademark names of Invincible® for dress and work slacks, and WardWear® raincoats.

In 1927 Montgomery Ward introduced their Brent® line of clothing for men, which included robes, pajamas, shirts, coats, underwear, sportswear, trousers, sports coats, and leatherwear like belts and billfolds. That same year, they also added the first catalog store—a store with displays to show the products available through mail order, to take orders for catalog merchandise, and as a location for buyers to pick up their orders.

Powr House® was the Wards line of work wear introduced in 1929. This line started with overalls and safety shoes, and expanded through the years to include shoes, gloves, shirts, saddle pants, dungarees, jackets, coveralls, raincoats, parkas, caps, and vests.

Commander® (underwear) was trademarked pre-1930 with 101® (denim) following closely behind.

Pleetway® (pajamas) and Homesteaders™ (work clothes) appear as new brands in the mid-1930s.

Did you know that according to snopes.com, the character of Rudolph the Red Nosed Reindeer was created for a Ward's Christmas catalog in 1939?

Healthgard™ (unknown start date, possibly earlier than the 1940s) was their line of union suits and underwear.

Pioneer™, introduced in the late 1930s, was Ward's second line of overalls and jackets.

Jack Frost™ and Windward™ were coat labels started in the 1940s. Windward would expand into service industry uniforms.

Pinehurst Suits™ (unknown start date) was their line of men's ready-to-wear suits, which expanded into shoes by 1939 and shirts in 1941. Note that the labels only say "Wards Pinehurst" and not "Montgomery Ward".

New brands showing up in 1941 were Ashley™ (shirts) and Barclay™ (shirts).

Wards initiated quite a few in-house labels starting in the mid-1970s and include:

Power Denims™ in 1974	Jean St.™ in 1975
Wards Action Pants® in 1980	Hill & Archer® in 1982
Outdoor Exchange® in 1982	Sweater Emporium® in 1982
Highland Park® in 1983	Wentworth® in 1986

{ Sears, Roebuck and Co. }

Sears, Roebuck and Co. got its beginning in 1880 by Richard W. Sears and Alvah C. Roebuck as a single page "catalog" selling watches. By the 1890s, the catalog had expanded to book size and made available many items which Sears purchased direct or wholesale from manufacturers and other companies.

Their first general catalog appeared in 1896, and in the early years the majority of menswear, like suits, were ordered through the catalog and custom made to fit the customer.

Catalog example talking about paper shortages during WWII, c. 1940s. Sears, c. 1944-45.

Sears was also known to use their catalogs to supply information for general use to the public. They explained rationing and how to use stamps for rationed items during WWII. (Please see more about this in the Shoes chapter of the Style section.)

The following partial page tells about the paper shortage during WWII:

The paper shortage continues critical this year. At least 13,000,000 cords of domestic pulpwood will be needed again for Army, Navy, Allied and essential civilian needs. The supply may be maintained and even increased if enough material and manpower to cut it can be found by the country's pulp manufacturers. The War Production Board asks the immediate help of every man with a stand of trees.

Important to farmers with woodlands

PAPER

PACKS A WAR PUNCH

Your trees may go to make the waterproof paper wrappers in which all Army Clothing and Equipment is shipped. Or they may be needed for camouflage strips and netting and parachutes. Or they may become part of the huge amounts of paper board used by the Red Cross for blood-plasma containers.

Every log may be necessary. Harvest your woodland now. Not only will you help the war effort but add to your farm income and your bond-buying power.

Here are Sears menswear labels and their starting dates that I have found:

DATE	BRAND NAME	DATE	BRAND NAME
?	"3 Label"™ (suits)	1905	Pilgrim™—brand ceased in 1964
1935	Armored Crotch® (men's underwear)	By 1940	The Pilgrim line of clothing also had sub-labels, including Positive Wear (socks), Nobility (sweaters, dress shirts), Kingfield (sweaters), Royal Ascot (shirts), Royalton (shirts), Fashion Tower (shirts), and Tru-Point.
1940	Barrington™		
1928-29	Big Ideal™ (denim wear)		
1930s	Chieftain™ (overalls & denim)		
1938	Circle S™ (jeans & jackets)		
1928-29	Double Duty™ as part of the Hercules line		
1940s	Drum Major™ (denim)	1951	Putter® (pants for the leisure activity of golf, but were so comfy they were worn to just putter around the house or yard.)
1959	Fashion Mates® —eventually replaced Pilgrim brand		
?	Fashion Tailored™ (slacks)	1941	Rain-O-Shine™ (coats)
1939?	Fashion Tower™ (shirts)	pre-1916	Rip Proof Brand™ (work wear). Not sure if owned or just sold this brand.
1980	Fieldmaster®		
1914	Footease™ (shoes)	1949	Roebucks® (denim)
1940	Fuzzy Wuzzy® (house slippers)	1974	Rock Bottoms™ (jeans)
1921	Gale® (posture supports)	1975	Rough Housers™ (jeans)
1972	Genuine Roebucks™ (jeans)	1963	Sani-gard™ (bacteria inhibitant for fabrics)
1928	Gold Bond™ (shoes)		
1970	Golden Comfort®	pre-1916	Service Brand™ (waterproof raincoats)
1930s	Good Lucks™ (shoes)	1939	Sta-Cool™ (suits)
1930s	Guardsman™ (overcoats)	1939?	Staunton™ (work wear and suits)
1967	Hasco Moc™ (shoes)	?	Staunton DeLuxe™ (suits)
1908	Hercules™	?	Stoningham™ (suits)
1959	Hoaloha® (Hawaiian clothing)	Early '40s	Sturdy Oak™ (work wear)
1938	Jeepers® (shoes)	1893	Superior™
1946	J.C. Higgins® (sports eqpt. and uniforms)	1930s	Topline™
1986	Oakton Ltd.™	Pre-1960s	TradeWell™ (denim)
Early '40s	Nation-Alls™ (coveralls) —a sub-brand of Hercules	1930s	Vee-Line™ (undies)
Early '40s	Pacemaker™	1939	West Master™ (rubber footwear)
1940	Pas' Master® (billfolds & leather)	1961	Ted Williams®
1950	Perma-Pressed® (fabric treatment)		

If you find a garment with any of the above brand labels, the garment cannot be older than the starting date listed.

Sears label from the late 1960s, c. 1960s.
Photo courtesy of Dale Vest.

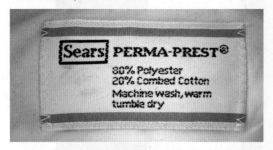

Post 1971 Sears label, c. 1970s.

Sears label used from 1983 to 1995, c. 1980s.

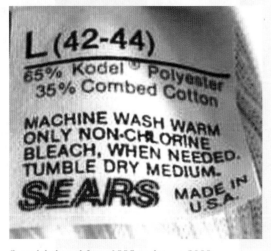

Sears label used from 1995 to date, c. 2000s.

Sewn in labels for men's and women's garments usually identify the company name in the following way:

Sears, Roebuck and Co., with the full name written in block print, was used on all labels beginning in the 1920s and ending in 1995.

DISCLAIMER: Many years ago, Sears provided label dating information on their website and has since been removed. At that time it was stated that their logo changed from full written name to just Sears with a box around it in 1974. This logo had been used for catalog print previously, and it was decided to utilize it for clothing.

Sears with a box continued to be used until 1983 when the box was deleted and the logo appeared as just Sears.

Since this information is no longer on their website, and repeated requests for verification remain unanswered, there must be some leeway provided for dating by just using the written name.

The upper left example is from two different shirts, the top label from the 1940s and the bottom label from the late 1970s.

Using the previous information, we note that both shirt labels in the above picture show the full written name. However, the Sears with a box supersedes this and dates that logo to 1974-1983. The wording on the Sanforized/size label of the top shirt dates it to pre-1994 (see Chapter Three for more information).

The Sears labels are known to be confusing, so be sure to check other dating clues like fabric content and fabric care labels to alleviate doubts.

Then a final design change in 1995 is still used today.

Note that Sears used the noted versions in various printed materials whose dates do not correspond with the clothing labels. Please double check dating by using other dating criteria.

{ J. C. Penney Company }

J. C. Penney Company did not enter the catalog business until 1962, but they have had a long history of store sales since 1902 when the first Golden Rule Store was opened by James Cash Penney. Penney incorporated and changed the store name to J. C. Penney in 1914.

Private label brands were, and always have been, a major reason for Penney's success, as customers liked the controlled quality and cheaper prices over brand names available at the time.

Some of the J. C. Penney private labels and their first date of use through the 1980s are:

DATE	BRAND NAME	DATE	BRAND NAME
1981	Action Master Naturals™	1982	Quail Run™
1971	Action Master™	1946	Ranchcraft®—this brand stopped in the 1940s then revived in the 1960s with a different label containing fabric content and / or different Penneys logo.
1983	Austin Manor®		
1922	Big Mac®		
1964-71	Bruce Crumpton™	1980	Rio Grande™
1983	City Streets®	1981	Royal Comfort®
1982	Comfort Suited Separates®	1982	Rugged Gear®
1927	Compass™	1930s	Sportclad™
1985	Dividends™	1982	St. Johns Bay®
1978	Finish Line™	1981	Stafford™
1924	Foremost™	1930s	Sterling Outdoor Clothing™
1920	Gentry Clothes®	1980	Suited Separates®
1940	Glenshire®—purchased from Aldens in the 1970s	1975	Super Cord® cotton/poly fabric for clothing
1976	Great Connections™	1972	Superdenim®
1940s	Highland Plain™	1964	Surf Breaker®
1920s	Honor Brand™	1987	Surf Rags®
1961	Hunt Club®	1940s	Swimaway®—existing brand purchased by J C. Penney in the 1940s
1941-46	Jim Penney®	1971	The Fox® (sport shirts)
1977	Lunada Shirts®	1983	The Fox Collection®
1930s	Majestic™ (braces & belts)	1978	The Fox Sweater®
1974	Man Mates®	?	Town Clad™
1914	Marathon™ (hats)	1927	Towncraft®
1922	Nation Wide® (work shirts and overalls)	1985	Towncraft Socks®
1989	Original Arizona Jean Co.®	1936	Travel Cool®
1930s	Ox Hide®	1920	Union Leader™ (denim)
1980	Par Four®—purchased from Cluett Peabody	1920s	Waverly™ (hats)
1922	Pay Day®	1980	Windsor Bay®
1930	Penco™ (shoes)	1978	Young Gentry®
1964	Penn-Prest® fabric treatment for clothing		
1959	Pima Prince® (underwear)		
1976	Plain Pockets® (jeans)		

If you find a garment with any of the above brand labels, the garment can not be older than the starting date listed. So, if you have a pair of overalls with the Oxhide label, they cannot be older than the 1930s—when the brand was introduced.

"A Nation Wide Institution" dates this J.C.Penney label to earlier than 1955, c. 1920s.

J.C.Penney label, using the full company name and written in cursive, was used in the 1930s.

J.C.Penney label featuring the full company name and written in block letters was used from 1930 until 1946, c. 1930s.

J.C.Penney label variation employing the full company name and written in block letters was used from 1930 until 1946, c. 1940s.

Penney's label variation shows the ® and was used from 1946 to 1957, c. 1950s.

Most labels will also include the J.C. Penney logo, which can be dated using the following information corroborated with a member of the JCPenney Archives Collection at DeGolyer Library, Southern Methodist University, Dallas, Texas.

The 1920s labels will state "A Nation Wide Institution". This phrase was dropped from the labels in the mid-1930s.

The 1930s labels used the full company name written in cursive.

From the 1930s up to 1946, labels still used the full company name, but generally only in block lettering form with variations.

For the 1946 – 1957 labels, Penney's redid their logo to be in block style capital letters all the same size and dropping the J.C. as well as adding an apostrophe S. This same logo was used no matter what the house brand might be.

The 1958-1963 label shows another revamping of the logo, which kept the all capital block lettering, with a larger P than the other letters. Given their similarities, you have to be extremely careful not to confuse this logo and the one from 1946-57.

The 1962-1963 label is the same logo as above, but with the addition of the fabric content and percentage.

Unique 1960s limited use label appeared. Note that these logos are of the few that were registered and / or had a WPL number pointing to Penney's partnership with select manufacturers and importers.

The 1964-1971 labels show that the Penney's logo was once again redrawn after the launch of their catalog. The "Atomic P", as it was known, is quite distinguished and easily recognizable. This logo also dropped usage of an apostrophe.

A 1971 to present label is written as one word with no periods and no spaces. The death of founder James Cash Penney in 1971 at the age of 95 prompted the company to return to its early name and roots with this new logo.

The 1971 and newer label will correspond with the U.S. regulation issued that same year for fabric care labels to be attached to every garment. Every label with this logo should also have fabric content and fabric care either attached with it or on a separate label close by.

Garments with the JCPenney logo and International Care Symbols on the care label will then be newer than 1997.

Through the years, the garment care label has moved from its usual place in the back neck to the side seam or even more towards the shoulder in some newer garments.

When using this logo guide to date vintage garments, please remember to use other basic label data previously stated.

Please note that the Penney's clothing logo's and printed versions for advertising do not match for dating.

When a logo was changed, all existing labels with the old logo were more than likely still used in garments instead of throwing them out. So, a garment made in 1964 may still have the 1958-63 label logo.

Penney's labels dropped the J.C. and added and apostrophe S in 1946 and continued with capitalized block lettering all the same size. This logo was used, no matter what the house brand was, and continued in use until 1957, c. 1950s.

Penney's label was revamped in 1958, continuing to use block lettering, but making the P larger than the other letters. This label was used until 1963. Be careful not to confuse this label with the other label showing the same size block letters, c. 1950s.

Penney's label variation of the 1958 to 1963 label shows fabric content % making it after 1962, c. 1960s.

Unique Penney's limited use label written in a back slant cursive and used throughout the 1960s. Note the WPL #, c. 1960s.

Penney's limited use label written in a back slant cursive and used throughout the 1960s.

Penneys logo revamp in 1964 corresponded with the launch of their catalog two years earlier. Known as the "Atomic P" logo, it is quite distinguished and easily recognizable because of the P and the dropped apostrophe. It was used until 1971, c. 1960s..

Penneys Atomic P logo was used from 1964 to 1971, c. 1960s.

Revised JCPenney logo with no periods or spaces and used from 1971 to today, c. 1970s.

JCPenney final revised logo was initiated after the death of James Cash Penney in 1971. The name is written as one word with no periods and no spaces and is still used today, c. 1970s.

It is uncertain whether this Penney's label actually belongs to J. C. Penney Company, c. 1960s.

SECTION

2

IT'S ALL IN THE STYLE

I once read that the cumulative Needle Trades in pre-WWI America produced and sold as many as 932 million wearable garments per year. Considering that the 1910 Census says that there were 93 million men, women, and children living in the U.S. at that time comprising 20 million households of 5 to 6 family members, that works out to an average of 10 new garments per year, per person. The average yearly family income was $1200 in 1910, and families spent between 12-15% of that income to purchase their clothing.

We can only assume, because of the different lifestyles that people led a century ago, that they wore their clothes, repaired their clothes, remade their clothes to fit another person, and then used the tattered remains for patchwork quilts or rag rugs. Men and women were helping to "save the planet" and "be green" decades before the terms had even been thought of or used.

I really don't feel that I have to give you a year by year, or even decade by decade overview of each specific style. I will, however, be noting specific style changes and when they took place, giving a glossary of terms with some corresponding illustrations, and providing other pertinent information that I deem necessary. So, let's delve into the world of style basics category by category.

So, let's delve into the world of style basics category by category.

{ Casual, Sport, and Work Shirts }

{ Overview }

Do you date vintage shirts by buttonhole orientation or collar style? By color or pattern? By fabric? You may find a few surprises or affirmations in this part of the guide.

In the nineteenth century, normal shirt sizes were 14 1/2 to 17 and today, more than a century later, these sizes are still considered the norm and measured in exactly the same way: by neck and sleeve. There were also men's extra sizes available in 17 1/2, 18, 18 1/2, and 19, the king-sized shirts of their day.

Work shirts, knit shirts, and sport shirts have evolved on their own, or mirrored dress shirts in their style features. Already a wardrobe staple for many decades, work shirts had attached soft collars unlike their dressy counterparts with detachable collars.

Men's shirts had always been long sleeved for protection, until a detachable sleeve appeared during WWI, along with an actual short sleeved version.

■▫ Catalog example of removable sleeve shirt. Sears, c. 1916.

▫■ Catalog example of early short sleeved shirt. Sears, c. 1916.

Usually, if you wanted shorter sleeves when working in the hot summer months, you just rolled them up. For the first three decades of the twentieth century, casual attire for golf, tennis or other sports was a soft negligee shirt without a necktie and rolled up sleeves.

Chambray WORK SHIRT Bargains
We Pay Postage---Sale Ends Feb. 28

FULL 36-INCH LENGTH
Large and Roomy
TRIPLE STITCHED

FOR STOUT MEN

FOR TALL MEN

FOR BOYS

REGULAR SIZES

Closed Front | Coat Style

Coat Style Only 79¢

35 U 614—Blue only. SIZES: 17½, 18, 19, 20-inch neck. **State size.** Extra big—amply cut with larger sleeves, armholes and chest. **We Pay Postage** and ship same day.

Coat Style Only 79¢

35 U 613—Blue only. HALF SIZES: 15 to 17½-inch neck. **State size.** 36-inch sleeves and 38-inch body length assure utmost comfort. Low sale prices and **We Pay Postage.**

Just Like Dad's 59¢

35 U 924—Blue only. HALF SIZES: 12 to 14-inch neck. **State size. We Pay Postage.** Strongly made of tough blue chambray. Closed front. Full and roomy. Two button-thru pockets.

These Shirts Are Made Extra Full and Roomy
Size 17 Is 51 Inches Around the Chest

Extra Heavy Tupelo Chambray **89¢**

Blue or Khaki Color **85¢**

$1.48

Heavy Weight Fast Color—Full Cut

Men who work outdoors require strong, serviceable Work Shirts that will stand up under the hardest wear. So that every man may try these and be convinced of their superior wearing qualities, we are offering them at a special low price.
Made of heavy weight tupelo chambray, a shirting which has withstood our most strenuous tests for strength and wear. The cotton used was dyed before it was spun into yarn; that is why the color is so even and fast.

Each shirt is cut extra full and roomy throughout. Size 17 measures 51 inches around the chest, and all are full 34 inches long.
Made in four-button closed front style, with flat attached collar. Two large buttoned through pockets. Sleeves have continuous facing that safeguards you against rips. One-button cuffs.
HALF SIZES: 14½ to 17.
State size wanted.
35 B 629—Blue only......89c
Postage, 5c extra

Heavy Weight Khaki Jean

You could not get a better value than these oft-button snap style Work Shirts of heavy weight Khaki Jean. Will give you long service, for the material is one of the most durable made.
Flat collar is interlined to keep its shape. Stitched at of the comfortable extension style. One-button, interlined cuffs. Two large, buttoned-down flap pockets. All seams stitched closed on cuffs. Ivory buttons.
HALF SIZES: 14½ to 17. State size wanted.
35 B 712—Khaki color only.....$1.48
Postage, 5c extra

WWI military uniform shirts had soft attached collars and were so popular that Arrow introduced a line of attached collar shirts made of the same fabric. The actual khaki army shirts were worn proudly by veterans after the war with all patches intact or purchased new from a military surplus outlet.

Many work shirts into the 1920s were pull-over-the-head style about 35" long, with about a 14" long buttoning placket from the neck.

Catalog example of shirt styles available. Montgomery Ward, c. 1930.

Catalog example showing that shirts were pulled on over the head. Montgomery Ward, c. 1925.

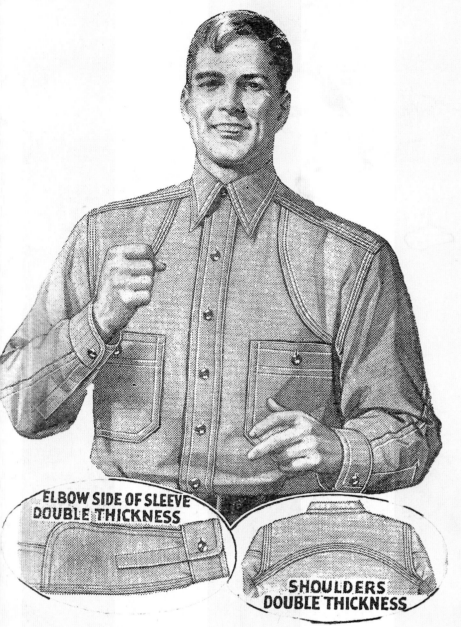

ELBOW SIDE OF SLEEVE
DOUBLE THICKNESS

SHOULDERS
DOUBLE THICKNESS

Catalog example showing oversized pockets. Montgomery Ward, c. 1928.

Catalog example showing that shirts were available in either open front or closed front styling. Montgomery Ward, c. 1928.

The 1920s brought about advertising and boasts of triple stitching, which had been started towards the end of WWI with overalls and spread to other work garments. Triple stitching and double anything, whether it was elbows or knees, were thought of as signs of good construction and long wearing. Check out and note the size of those pockets and their low placement, and the long collar points.

Some dress and work shirts featured small side gussets, which continued to be used into the 1960s. They were inserted to give a little extra room for movement, which had previously made the juncture of the side seams tear.

Denim, chambray, moleskin, twilled cloth, sateen, plaid chambray, Stifel polka dot, khaki twill, wool broadcloth flannel, wool flannel, corduroy, Army serge, and Buck Skein flannel were popular work shirt fabrics during this time.

Sanforized was trademarked in 1930 by Cluett Peabody® (Arrow® shirts) as a process to reduce shrinkage in their dress shirts. It was such a huge success that its use quickly spread to work shirts, then slacks and on to other cotton based fabric garments.

A "Tough" Shirt at a BARGAIN SALE PRICE

69c
Regular Sizes

Wards Sanforized Shrunk Double Elbow PIONEER
—Cut in Price!

We couldn't Find a Work Shirt Like it Selling for Less Than 79c to 89c

- Heavy weight Fine Yarn Chambray
- Sanforized 99¼% Shrinkproof
- Double Elbows add 58% More Wear
- Unbreakable Metal Buttons
- 2 Large Button-through Pockets
- Round Corner Double Stitched Cuffs
- All Main Seams Triple Stitched
- Interlined Dress Style Collar

To say that Wards famous Sanforized Shrunk Pioneer is one of the most serviceable Work Shirts made is an old story—but when Wards cut the price on this popular favorite—that's "big news"!

Men's Regular Sizes
Colors: Blue or gray. Regular Half Sizes: 14½ to 17-inch neck. State neck-size and color. Ship. wt. 1 lb.
35 U 3103—*Sale Price.* Coat style..............69c

Tall or Stout Sizes
79c
Blue. Ship. wt. 1 lb.
35 U 3104—Tall Half Sizes 15 to 18-in.
35 U 3105 — Stout Sizes: 17½, 18, 19, 20-in. neck. Each, 79c

Catalog example showing that a Sanforized shirt was 99.25% shrink-proof. Montgomery Ward, c. 1935.

Catalog example showing a shirt with a Talon slide fastener. Montgomery Ward, c. 1932.

Catalog example showing slide fastener or button front option. Montgomery Ward, c. 1935.

Catalog example showing zippered work shirt. Montgomery Ward, c. 1941.

Slide fasteners (later known as zippers) began showing up in work shirts by 1932 to make them easier to put on and take off. They previously had been used in overalls, coveralls, and shoes, but their application then began appearing in children's and women's clothing, along with men's sport shirts, trousers, and jackets.

Chambray Work Shirt—Talon Hookless Fastener

SUEDE CLOTH—Perfect Spring Shirts for Men and Boys —Reduced!

MEN'S $1.00 slide fastener

MEN'S 79c button front

Slide Fastener or Button Front
- Good Sturdy Weight Cotton Suede Cloth
- Interlined Collar . . . Non-rip Sleeve Facing
- Double Shoulder Yoke for Extra Wear
- 2 Button-pockets—Pencil Compartment
- Unbreakable Buttons . . . Triple Stitched

Sturdy Cotton Suede Cloth for rugged wear, with features that mean extra service and comfort. No wonder we sold thousands at a higher price in Wards General Catalog. State size and color. Ship. wt. Men's 1 lb. 4 oz. Boys' 12 oz.

Slide Fastener
35 U 3429—Men's Shirt. Colors: Tan or gray. Sizes: 15, 16, 17, 18-in. neck.............$1.00
35 U 4803—Boys' Shirt. Tan color only. Even Ages: 6 to 10 years. Half Sizes: 12 to 14½ in. neck............89c

Button Front
35 U 3415—Men's Shirt. Colors: Tan or gray. Half Sizes: 14½ to 17-in. neck.............79c
35 U 4801—Boys' Shirt. Colors: Tan or gray. Even Ages: 6 to 10 years. Half Sizes: 12 to 14½-in. neck.............69c

Boys' 89c

Boys' 69c

Men's and Boys' Sale, Page 91
ZIPPER WORK SHIRT 59c ea.

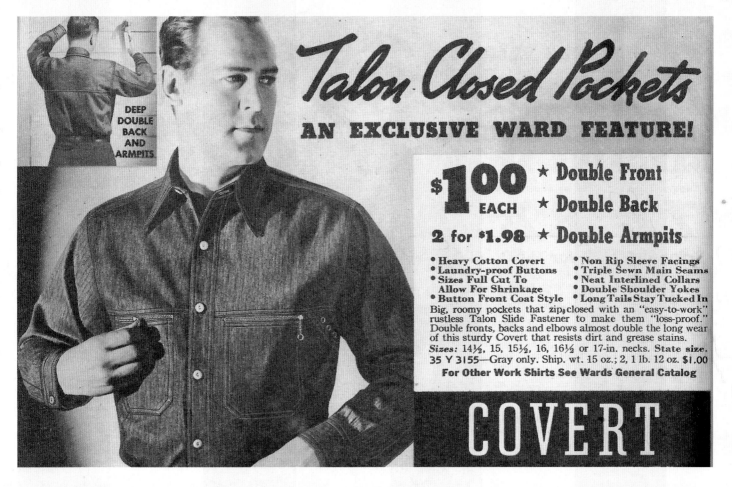

Talon Closed Pockets

AN EXCLUSIVE WARD FEATURE!

$1.00 EACH ★ **Double Front**

★ **Double Back**

2 for $1.98 ★ **Double Armpits**

- Heavy Cotton Covert
- Laundry-proof Buttons
- Sizes Full Cut To Allow For Shrinkage
- Button Front Coat Style
- Non Rip Sleeve Facings
- Triple Sewn Main Seams
- Neat Interlined Collars
- Double Shoulder Yokes
- Long Tails Stay Tucked In

Big, roomy pockets that zip, closed with an "easy-to-work" rustless Talon Slide Fastener to make them "loss-proof." Double fronts, backs and elbows almost double the long wear of this sturdy Covert that resists dirt and grease stains. *Sizes:* 14½, 15, 15½, 16, 16½ or 17-in. necks. State size. 35 Y 3155—Gray only. Ship. wt. 15 oz.; 2, 1 lb. 12 oz. $1.00

For Other Work Shirts See Wards General Catalog

COVERT

DEEP DOUBLE BACK AND ARMPITS

By the mid to late 1930s, slide fasteners were added as a decorative touch to pockets on shirts, sweaters, and even overalls.

To combat the dreariness as the Depression years rolled along, bright colored plaids replaced the plain colored fabrics of only a few years earlier for the working man.

Catalog example showing Talon zippered pockets. Montgomery Ward, c. 1937.

Catalog example showing bright colored plaid shirts. Sears, c. 1935-36.

AT ONLY **65c**

SELLING AT **$2.98**

BARGAIN **$1.19**

LOW PRICE **$1.98**

Cotton Domet Flannel   **13-Oz. All Wool Flannel**   **Woven Plaid Patterns**   **Part Wool Flannel**

Going! Going! GONE YOUR LAST CHANCE TO GET POLO SHIRTS AT CLOSE-OUT PRICES

▼ Catalog example showing early polo shirts. Sears, c. 1936.

▼ Catalog example showing early polo shirts. Montgomery Ward, c. 1937.

In 1936, John Wanamaker® introduced a sports shirt imitating the garment worn by sugar planters in Cuba called a Guayabera. Usually made of linen, they had long sleeves that were worn rolled up, unlined collars to be worn buttoned or open, side vents, and a panel back.

Then, a new kind of shirt came to the forefront of fashion for more than just the polo pony crowd. Frenchman Rene Lacoste introduced a white knitted pullover shirt with about a 5" opening at the neck, a turned-down collar, short sleeves, and a crocodile logo embroidered on the chest. This new spin on the polo shirt started showing up on tennis courts and golf courses. Polo knit shirts and khaki bush shirts were shown in the movies and gained even more popularity among the masses.

MEN'S COOL POLO SHIRTS *at Big Savings*

COOL TUCK STITCH
Ⓐ 3-Button Neck Ⓑ Lace Neck
44¢ 3 for $1.30
Wards new Cotton tuck stitch gives that heavy ribbed appearance that is seldom found at such a Low Price. The improved shirt type collar adds a new comfort. Sizes full cut to allow for shrinkage.
Colors: Light Blue, Corn, White. *Chest Sizes:* Small (34 to 36 in.); med. (38 to 40 in.); large (42 to 44 in.) State size, color. Ship. wt. ea. 10 oz., three 1 lb. 10 oz.
(A) 35 YA 5302—3-Button Neck 44¢
(B) 35 Y 5303—New Lace Neck 44¢

DEEP CUT PRICES
Ⓒ TALON NECK TUCK STITCH **64¢**
Wards best quality Cotton sports Shirts. Tufhast colors. *Colors:* White, Lt. Blue, Maize. *Chest Sizes:* Small (34 to 36 in.); med. (38 to 40 in.); large (42 to 44 in.). State size, color.
35 Y 2658—Ship. wt. each 8 oz. . 64¢

Ⓓ Sports Neck Celanese **77¢** 2 for **$1.50**
Woven-in stripes. Box pleat sports back with stitched on half belt. *Colors:* Blue, Tan, Wine. *Chest Sizes:* Small (34 to 36 in.); med. (38 to 40 in.); large (42 to 44 in.). State size, color.
Ship. wt. ea. 7 oz.; two 12 oz.
35 Y 5311—77¢; 2 for........$1.50

Save on COOL SPORT SHIRTS

You Need Plenty for Summer .. and You Can Buy Them on Time!

**A Hollywood Sports Sensation
You'll See Them Everywhere**

**Miracle Value! Rib Knit
With Handy Zipper Pocket**

**Spun Rayon In-and-Outer
Looks and Feels Like Silk**

At the same time, sport shirts walked away from the sports arena and onto the street. Straight bottomed sport shirts were introduced to be worn outside the trousers, although it was usually worn tucked in as was the custom of the time.

There was still controversy as to whether one had to wear a knit or casual shirt completely buttoned at the neck, or could wear it partially unbuttoned, and how far could it be unbuttoned. The best selling Prince of Wales style had a single button under the collar, which could be buttoned for a tie or left unbuttoned and worn plain or with a kerchief.

Some knit sport shirts used a draw-string at the neck, with cords threaded through eyes mimicking the style shown on western shirts of the day. Cowboy shirts of bright colors with trimmed pockets, edge piping, and three pearl buttons or snaps on the cuffs were a must to visit the newly popular dude ranches. The most used collar style was long & pointy.

Tee shirts came out of the underwear drawer in the late 1930s and became a fashion must for leisure time.

Stretchy Mesh Rib Knit   Long or Short Sleeves

Catalog example showing 1930s casual shirts. Montgomery Ward, c. 1939.

Catalog example showing '30s casual shirts. Sears, c. 1939.

CELANESE POLO SHIRTS

KEN-BUCK COMBINATION
Maynard Jones
$2.19

BRAND NEW!
No. 736 — We call this one the "Ken Buck" because it is a combination of our popular Ken Maynard and Buck Jones shirt. Notice the piping on the collar, shoulders, back yoke and front. The new inverted arrow pockets and the embroidered horse shoes. This shirt will go like wild fire. Sizes 14 to 17. Postage 6c

Body	Trim
Blue	Orange
White	Black
Red	White
Black	White
Orange	Black

LUSTROUS TWO-TONE RODEO SHIRT
$1.69

COLORED LIKE A PINTO
Purple and Orange
Red and Yellow
White and Black
Cerise and Black

No. 746 — NEWEST two-tone rodeo shirts. It has the shaped 3-button tight fitting cuffs. Two pointed pockets, peaked shoulders and back yoke. The contrasting colors make this a HOT number. Sizes 14 to 17. Postage 6c extra.

TEXAS RANCHER SUPPLY CO.   310 Main St.   Fort Worth, Texas   Page 15

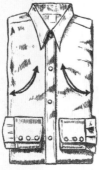

SILK SHIRTS - SNAP BUTTONS
The Classiest Ever Worn
Inverted Arrow Pockets   **$3.44**
9 Colors and Combinations
Blue Body with Gold Arrows
Orange Body with Purple Arrows and Snaps
Green Body with Dark Green Arrows
White Body with Black Arrows
Purple Body with Gold Arrows and Snaps
Red Body with White Arrows
Black Body with White Arrows and Snaps
Rust Brown Body with Dark Green Arrows
Wine (Maroon) Body with Light Tan Arrows
No. 728—Newest and most novel silk shirt. Postage 6c extra.

FREE   FREE
We are happy to present this INITIAL KIT FREE with every shirt purchased from us. Put these initials on whatever place you want them to stick. Press with a hot iron for half a minute. That's all! They are there to stay and all the washing will not get them off. There is extra material in every kit for additional letters, emblem, or your brands. Ask for this FREE KIT with your shirt order.

FREE WITH EVERY SHIRT

TEXAS RANCHER SUPPLY CO.   310 Main St.   Fort Worth, Texas

MEN'S AND BOYS'
SALE SPECIAL
"TEE" SHIRTS!

39¢ Values

Popular Crew Necks

MEN'S STYLE		BOYS' STYLE	
27¢ EACH	**3 FOR 75¢**	**25¢** EACH	**3 FOR 69¢**

Two-Way Collar   New Airy "Kool Kloth"   Derby Rib Crew Neck   Rayon .. Smooth, Cool

Catalog example showing '30s Western style shirts that polo shirts imitated at the neck closings. Texas Rancher, c. 1937.

Catalog example showing 1930s neck closings on polo shirts. Montgomery Ward, c. 1937.

Catalog example showing '30s Cowboy shirts. Texas Rancher, c. 1937.

Catalog example showing casual shirts. Sears, c. 1940.

Catalog example showing '30s t-shirts. Sears, c. 1939.

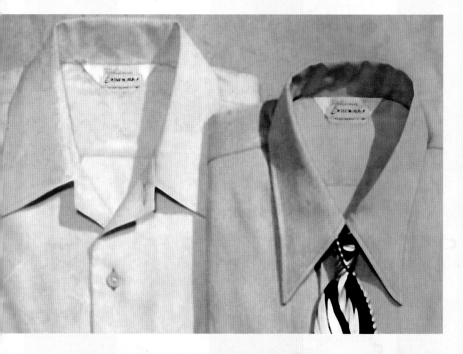

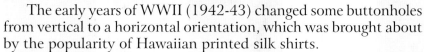

■ Catalog example showing convertible collar. Montgomery Ward, c. 1945.

■ Loop & button closure showing hidden button, c. 1950s.

■ Loop & button closure showing shirt as it would be worn for casual, c. 1950s.

■ Loop & button closure showing shirt as it would be worn for dress, c. 1950s.

The early years of WWII (1942-43) changed some buttonholes from vertical to a horizontal orientation, which was brought about by the popularity of Hawaiian printed silk shirts.

Casual shirts still sported fastenings up to the neck so they could also be worn with a necktie, or worn with the neck widely opened. The loop & button neck closures, introduced a decade earlier and coupled with horizontal buttonholes, gained acceptance during this time and would remain popular into the early Sixties.

After wearing starched uniforms and stiff wool military garb for years, men returning from the war wanted casual shirts that were soft all over and with no starch. They wanted a more casual look for their leisure time after work. They wanted unique shirts: Hawaii print patterns, fancy Western shirts, bold colors—even pink, and topstitching as a style detail.

Raglan sleeves

"Strike" insignia

E $4.88 Each

Pilgrim
THE RIGHT WAY TO SAY
MEN'S FURNISHINGS

F $3.88 Each

...ard to beat
...hem for comfort

"TEN-PIN" BOWLER   PLAID 'N' PLAIN

1. 2-TONE HAWAIIAN 2.98   2 RAYON 2-TONER 2.98   3. LUANA "CONFETTI" 2.49 up

4. CALIFORNIA STYLED 3.98   5 NEW! "AMERICANA" 3.98   6. CHECK TRIM LUANA 3.98

7. 2-TONE GABARDINE 4.98   8. JACKET STYLED! 3.98   9. PLAID 'N' GABARDINE 3.98

Catalog example of 1940s t-shirts. Montgomery Ward, c. 1945.

Catalog example showing colorful casual shirts. Sears, c. 1948.

Catalog example of colorful casual shirts. Montgomery Ward, c. 1950.

Catalog example of colorful casual shirts of the 1950s. Aldens, c. 1952.

Double sizing appeared in the very late 1940s. Previously, casual shirts and dress shirts were sized by neck and sleeve length, i.e. size 15 x 33. Casual knits had been sized S, M, L, or XL, so the two sizing methods were combined.

Despite the U.S. entering the Korean War and McCarthy looking for communists, the Fifties became a very colorful decade with cars painted pink & gray or turquoise & white, and home appliances appearing in colors other than white. It only made sense that fashion would continue as colorfully as it had been for the last few years.

The advent of more manmade synthetic fabrics meant that clothing could be laundered at home and needed little ironing. Guys just wanted to have fun by riding their motorcycles, or practicing and playing the guitar to become the next Rock 'n Roll star. Movies and celebrities influenced styles of the '50s.

For a happier YOU ...in '52!

Give yourself a HARLEY-DAVIDSON 125

Catalog example of colorful, casual shirts of the 1950s. Sears, c. 1956.

Catalog example of unique print shirts of the Fifties. Sears, c. 1956.

Chambray work shirts remained styled as they had been for decades. The only thing that ever varied was the length or shortness of the collar points.

As the Continental look, Ivy-league look, and beatnik styles surfaced in the mid-'50s and continued into the early '60s, unusual and atomic style prints appeared in fabrics, and everything remained colorful. Comfort was foremost in everyday and sports wear.

Many families now had TV sets, and television cowboys, including movie veterans Gene Autry and Roy Rogers, brought about a new wave of wearers for cowboy shirts along with jeans and boots.

Catalog example of Thunderbird style shirts of the 1950s. Sears, c. 1956.

Catalog example of cowboy shirts of the Fifties. Montgomery Ward, c. 1956.

■ Catalog example of knit sweater shirts. Sears, c. 1962.

■ Catalog example of knit casual shirts. Sears, c. 1962.

■ Catalog example showing Autumn colors for shirts and matching sweaters. Sears, c. 1968.

Button-down collars, open stitch knits, light colored madras plaids, and small paisley prints were the utmost of fashion for shirts. A change back to vertical buttonholes started in the mid-'50s, and collar points shortened more than ever. Oxford cloth button-down shirts added a hang loop at the back yoke.

Horizontal buttonholes and loop closures had continued as a fashion statement on most casual shirts, but the switch began to vertical buttonholes and collar points started to shorten by the last few years of the '50s.

The early to mid-'60s gave us easy care perma-press blends of cotton and synthetic fibers, along with light and comfortable Italian knit and Banlon® knit shirts—either banded or plain at the bottom.

Luxurious Ban-Lon® Sweater Shirts
Soft, absorbent nylon for strength and shape retention. It's mighty comfortable, too

Fleecy soft Orlon® in styled-for-action **Sweater Shirts**

① $3.90   ② $3.90 $5.90 ③

Clothing remained colorful in the 1960s, but the color palate had changed to Autumn shades of golds, greens, oranges, and browns. These colors would remain popular through the end of the 1970s.

The '60s brought remakes of certain styles from bygone eras, such as the chin strap style that had appeared in the very early 1900s, and then again in the late '30s and early '40s on work shirts. I found no entries for this style in any catalog, so the uniqueness of the earlier ones can make them desirable.

The early 1970s made the American flag and its red, white, and blue colors a part of apparel for both sexes as a sign of rebellion, or a salute to America's Bicentennial.

The '70s also brought body hugging polyester shirts to wear with leisure suits, an update of the Guayabera in Dacron & cotton, along with spirited paisleys, zigzags, skinny rib knits, tapestry prints, and Aztec designs for shirts to wear with bell bottom jeans.

{ Pendleton® }

Pendleton shirts are loved for their warmth, colorful plaids, and casual style, so I thought I would give them a little extra attention as to dating.

Pendleton Woolen Mills started in 1909 with woven fabrics and colorful Indian blankets. Since men's woolen shirts were only available in gray and possibly a few other plain colors, the company decided to use their plaid fabric to perk up men's fashion with colorful wool shirts in 1924. They expanded to a full line of woolen menswear by 1929.

Retro style chin strap shirt of the 1960s. $50-60.

Label for retro style chin strap shirts of the 1960s.

Advertisement showing Pendleton plaids and offerings. Unknown magazine, c. 1950.

Pendleton suggests five Tartan Gifts in virgin wool

With a deep sense of pride you give— or receive—a Pendleton. You know so certainly that no gift could be finer. New and exclusive for this season's giving is the rich authentic Kilgore Tartan—virgin wool through and through, soft and luxurious, Pendleton-spun, dyed and woven.

(Illustrated, top to bottom)
Topster Jacket $18.95,
Regular Shirt, $15.35,
Sport Shirt, $15.35,
Lounging Robe, $29.00,
Clans Robe-in-a-Bag, $25.00.

ALWAYS VIRGIN WOOL

Pendleton®

PENDLETON WOOLEN MILLS • PORTLAND, OREGON

The shirts were marked 100% Virgin Wool through the 1950s and into the early 1960s.

The year 1956 brought about the Sir Pendleton® line, and 1958 introduced Pendleton Plaidmaster Jackets.

Consumers could purchase fabric from the Pendleton Woolen Mill Store to take home and make their own garments. In some cases, they were given actual Pendleton labels to sew in these garments.

Pendleton introduced washable wool in 1960 and started sewing care instructions for the new fabric in the shoulder of the garment. These early care labels have a 1960 copyright symbol. Note that this is different from the post 1971 care labels sewn into the neck seam.

A label redo in 1964 added the International Woolmark symbol.

The "Authentic Scottish Tartan" labels on the front placket at the bottom date shirts from the 1970s through the 1980s.

In 1980, Pendleton introduced Pendleton Country Japan.

The first Pendleton Big or Tall shirts were introduced in 1984.

In 1996, Pendleton moved the assembly of men's shirts and jackets to Mexico, which should be shown on the label as "Made in Mexico".

Pendleton label used into the 1960s.

Pendleton label given out at their fabric store in the 1950s.

Pendleton sewn in label for washable wool instructions dated 1960.

Pendleton label showing International Wool Symbol used after 1964.

This label will mark your garment
as hand-tailored from the finest
woolens, styled and woven by

Pendleton

100% VIRGIN WOOL

signifying
Quality,
Beauty and
Originality

HAND TAILORED FROM
"**Pendleton**"
WOOLENS
PENDLETON WOOLEN MILLS
PORTLAND, OREGON
100% VIRGIN WOOL
MADE IN U.S.A.

NOTE: This fabric has been sponged and
shrunk and is ready to be tailored. See reverse
of card for suggestions on the care of
Pendleton woolens.

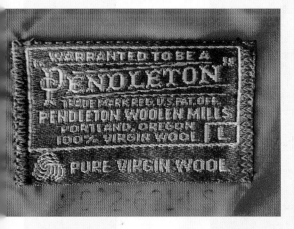

{ Denim Work Wear–
Jeans & Overalls }

{ Glossary }

I'm going to start this chapter with **vintage work wear terminology** so that you can see how many of the terms are interchangeable, and to provide some extra background for dating.

Band Top:
    A term used to mean a waistband on pants; or, band tops referred to waist overalls.

Bar Tacking:
    Reinforcement stitching in a tight zigzag repeated several times to fortify stress points in clothing.

Boilersuit or Slops:
    A protective coverall for dirty work.

Combination Suit:
    Band top or bib overalls with a matching jumper or jacket.

Combination Overalls:
    Another name for coveralls.

Corduroy:
    Durable cotton piled fabric with vertical ribs.

Coveralls:
    Usually referred to in plural—like a pair of trousers. Denim trousers with a bib piece held by straps covering the chest. The shirt and trousers are made in one piece to wear over clothing.

Denim:
    A course, durable weave of cotton fabric.

Double & Twist Denim:
    To resist shrinkage, yarns are doubled and then twisted before weaving; woven with 2 warp to 1 weft.

Dungaree:
    From the French word for denim.

Dungarees:
Pants made of blue denim.
Denim trousers with a bib and straps.

Engineer Jacket:
Collarless denim jacket with a bandless bottom.

Engineer Overalls:
Coined by Levi's for their bib overalls

Fabric Weight:
Denim is graded by its weight per yard, so if a yard of denim weighs 13 oz, it is considered to be 13 oz denim.

Hickory Stripe:
A durable twill weave fabric showing a stripe and used mainly for work clothes.

Jean:
Twill cotton fabric for work clothes.

Jeans:
Pants or trousers made of denim.

Jumper:
Another word for a denim jacket or denim shirt.

Khaki:
The fabric used for British Army Regiments in the 1880s of a closely twilled cloth of linen or cotton and named for the color of the fabric.

Levi's or 501's:
Trademarked name of denim pants by Levi Strauss Co.

Moleskin:
A heavy, durable cotton fabric.

Overalls:
See Coveralls

Railroad Suit:
An outfit comprised of overalls and a matching jacket; also called a combination suit.

Shop Coat:
Shorter version of 1920s Duster or knee-length jacket to wear over clothing for protection; constructed of durable fabric; appeared after WWII.

Stifel:
Maker of cotton denim, drills & calico fabrics from the 1840s to the 1930s.

Stifel Drill:
Fabric woven by Stifel with a strong bias in the weave.

Triple Stitching:
Three rows of detail stitching / topstitching.

Twill:
A diagonally woven fabric.

Waist Overalls:
Denim trousers without a bib.

Waist Band Pants or Band Top Overalls:
Term used post WWI into the 1950s for denim work pants; *also see Waist Overalls.*

Warp & Weft:
The two directions that the yarn runs in weaving; in denim the warp runs longways with the selvage and is dyed indigo blue and weft is across the fabric from selvage to selvage and is undyed.

Whipcord:
Fabric with a bold twill weave.

White Back Denim:
Early denim fabric showing "white" or light color on its backside; made with brown or blue warp with a white filling.

Work Pants:
Pants constructed of heavy duty fabrics to withstand the rigors of manual work.

{ Overview }

We've all heard the comment that "men's wear really doesn't change", and I think it is most true of the overalls style. With this, I am speaking of bib overalls, not band tops that would later become what we know as jeans.

Minor variations of the basic style include a loose hanging bag sewn across the front waist for carrying tools, a hammer loop added to the side of the leg, and double fabric sewn to the knees and thighs for better wear.

Worn since the 1800s, for the most part overalls are still constructed in the same style as they were then; they are still worn larger than an actual waist, have wide, roomy legs for bending and squatting, and come with either a solid high back or detachable suspenders with or without elastic.

Overalls and jeans have always been preferred work wear. In the 1800s and into the early 1900s, they were constructed of duck cloth, canvas, moleskin, or denim, where today we mainly think of them as blue or striped denim.

Catalog example of early coveralls and overalls. Sears, c. 1916.

■□ Catalog example showing overalls came in black duck, blue denim, and Everett black and gray striped denim. Sears, c. 1902.

□□ Advertisement showing introduction of hickory stripe denim. *Locomotive Firemen and Engineers Magazine*, c. 1912.

Sweet Orr®, founded in 1873, was the first denim work wear company to have their garments Union Made.

Cone® (brand) Denim started in 1895 and patented their denim in 1921.

Sweet Orr patented the Ace of Spades process to control shrinkage pre-1908; It was used on their Ace of Spades brand until the 1960s.

In the 1910s, a person could buy a pair of Levi's waist overalls at J.C. Penney's for 58 cents.

In 1912, Headlight introduced Hickory Stripe Overalls with the blue and white stripe design woven into the fabric. Previously, stripes had been painted on the fabric. Other striped fabrics had been available earlier, such as the Everett black and gray stripe denim dating to 1902 or earlier, but they never attained the popularity of denim stripes. More stripe patterns were added in the 1930s.

PLAIN OVERALLS.
Leader Overalls.
Made from 6½-ounce Blue Denim, fine weave, washable goods; double stitched seams; patent buttons; two front and one hip pocket.
No. 41R698 Price, per pair.....................30c

Black Hussar Overalls.
Made from full 8-ounce Black Duck, warranted not to break or rip; made double stitched at all vital parts; taped crotch; extra stayed fly piece; two front and one back pocket.
No. 41R700 Price, per pair.....................40c

Everett Overalls.
This Overalls is made from the Everett Black and Gray Striped Denim, a very neat pattern; double sewed throughout; continuous fly piece; patent buttons; extra well stayed. Two front, one watch, one hip pocket. This is one of our best selling numbers.
No. 41R702 Price, per pair.....................50c

Our 50-Cent Hercules Overalls are 75-Cent Value.

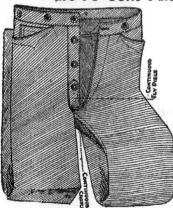

This is really one of the best overalls for 50 cents ever offered; there are none superior and few equal. Made from full 9-ounce York denim; double sewed throughout; reinforced and continuous fly piece; two front, one hip and one watch pocket. Warranted to wear longer and give more general satisfaction than high priced goods usually retailed at 75c and $1.00 per pair.
No. 41R706 Price, per pair.....................50c

Double Wear Overalls for 75 Cents.

This Overalls is made from full 9-ounce Blue York Denim; front is double from waistband to below knee; patent, never rip continuous fly piece; reinforced crotch stay; two front, one hip, one watch pocket; double sewed throughout. No better blue overalls can be had at any price.
No. 41R708 Per pair.....75c

Our New Woven Stripe Headlight is Sweeping the Country.

THE SECRET:
The stripe is *woven---* not printed or extracted.

Overall wearers have been quick to see that it will wear longer than any other striped overall made.

Made either style---
High Back or Elastic Suspender Back.

If you prefer the high back style, ask your dealer for Lot 5.

If you prefer the elastic suspender style, ask your dealer for Lot 33.

"A Smile of Satisfaction with ev[ery] [pair]

HEADLIGH[T] OVERALLS
Larned Carter & Co.
Detroit Mich.
World's Greatest Overall Makers

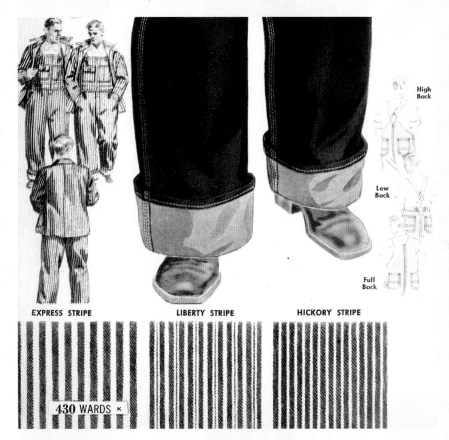

EXPRESS STRIPE   LIBERTY STRIPE   HICKORY STRIPE

430 WARDS K

High Back

Low Back

Full Back

■ Catalog example of available stripe for overalls. Montgomery Ward, c. 1941-42.

□ Catalog example of new overalls worn with a dress shirt and tie. Montgomery Ward, c. 1928.

During WWI, overalls came in a 36" inseam to account for shrinkage and be able to turn up the bottoms for cuffs or fit taller men. Turned up cuffs would remain a popular style until the 1950s—many times being used as an ashtray indoors.

In 1920, men joined "overalls clubs" or "old clothes clubs" to protest the high prices of clothing after WWI by wearing the overalls they already had—regardless of the number of patches.

It is thought that men wore their new overalls only to church. As they got "broken in", the overalls were then worn to town, on errands, or visiting neighbors. After much more wear, the overalls were then worn for work.

Overalls and jeans were common work wear for farmers, miners, railroad men, or factory workers. Overalls were available in two different styles of backs while jeans utilized suspenders, belts, or both. A third style of back, the full back, would be added in the late '30s.

SHAPED SLEEVES TO FIT THE ARM LARGE, NEAT COLLAR

⊞ Catalog example of the two styles of overalls backs available in the 1920s. Sears, c. 1929.

⊞ Catalog example of the three styles of overalls backs available after the mid-1930s. Montgomery Ward, c. 1938.

⊞ Catalog example of jean cloth work trousers. Montgomery Ward, c. 1925.

⊞ Catalog example of denim band overalls, which would later be called jeans. Montgomery Ward, c. 1934.

Detachable Suspender | High Back

SEARS, ROEBUCK AND CO.

LOW BACK | HIGH BACK | FULL BACK

Wards Have a Size for Every Man in Sanforized 8-oz. Blue Denim Pioneers 95¢ 2 for $1.85 Regular Sizes

Send Your Order Early

Montgomery Ward & Co.

Strong, Reliable Jean Trousers

Men who do rough work prefer jean cloth Work Trousers because of the strength of the fabric and the long service it gives. Firmly woven material with hard finish. All strain points reinforced. The oxford gray color will not show soil easily. Full size garments. The price is low enough for you to order several pairs.

SIZES: Waist, 30 to 44 inches. Inseam, 30 to 36 inches.

State waist and inseam measurements wanted. "How to Order" on Page 209.

42 B 5137— Oxford Gray only.
PRICE, Postage, 8¢ extra $2.19

MEN'S 2:20 Denim Band OVERALLS 88¢

BUCKLE BACK STRAP

- Cut full . . . and plenty long, to suit tall men
- Triple stitched main seams; bartacked at strain points
- 6-pockets, belt loops and suspender buttons

2:20 white back blue Denim Band Overalls at this price are a real buy. Very serviceable for farm and factory work.

Even Sizes: 30 to 42-in. waist. Even inseam 30 to 36 in. (The 30 and 32-inch waist furnished in 30 to 34-in. inseam only.) State waist and inseam measurements. Ship. wt. 1 lb. 8 oz.
42 AM 6166—Ea......88¢

In the 1920s, the majority of overalls and waist overalls were made by cheap prison labor, which had been utilized in clothing manufacture since the last half of the 1800s.

Lee introduced the 401 Jacket in 1925.

White duck overalls and overalls with added pouches on the front were available in the late '20s. Note all the pockets to keep everything you might need with you when you work. White duck overalls and pants are still favored by painters today.

As an interesting note, overalls cost about $1.75 a pair after WWI (because of inflation), about $1.50 a pair in 1927, or you could buy 28" wide good quality 8 oz denim fabric for 16.5 cents a yard that same year. The cost dipped to $.65 a pair in 1933 with Union Made overalls costing about twice as much. People wanted quality and long wearing clothing.

Catalog example of white duck overalls and the added front pouch. Sears, c. 1929.

Catalog example showing work pants construction. Sears, c. 1929.

Catalog advertising showing well made, long wearing denim garments and their prices. Montgomery Ward, c. 1925.

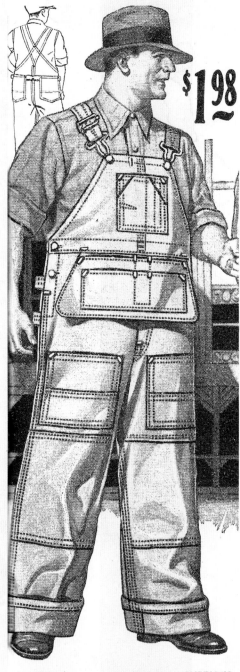

$1.98

Built Strong for Wear

How to Order

Overalls See Page 209

TWICE THE WEAR

Double Duty
CLOTHES FOR RUGGED WEAR

AMERICA'S FINEST WORK PANTS

Every Hercules Pants Guaranteed Not To Rip
A NEW PAIR IF THEY DO

Many companies used Sanforizing, a process patented in 1930 for shirts and quickly utilized for other cotton garments, in their denim wear to minimize shrinkage. See more about Sanforized in Section III of this book.

Other forms of shrinkage control were also used. In the ad, we don't know if the fabric was washed to pre-shrink it, if the garment was washed to pre-shrink, or if there was a secret process for preventing shrinkage.

Catalog example of 99.25% shrinkproof (Sanforized) denim overalls. Montgomery Ward, c. 1934.

Catalog example showing method of shrinkage control. Montgomery Ward, c. 1932.

Catalog example showing the three weights of denim available in garments with Sanforized or mill shrunk fabric. Montgomery Ward, c. 1938.

99¼% Shrinkproof White Back Blue Denim

MEN'S
89c
Either Garment

BOYS'
69c
Each

Mill Shrunk!!
Pure Indigo Dyed

Full 2:20 Weight
1st Quality White
Back Blue Denim

All Seams Triple-
Stitched—Rust-Proof
Buttons—Bar-Tacked
Strain Points
EXTRA FULL CUT

BLUE DENIM 3 QUALITIES

Stock up now on Wards famous Copper Riveted 101's. Bulldogs for strength ...Full cut in he-man sizes. Choice of 3 weights. Now Bargain Priced!

Regular Sizes: Waist 30, 31, 32, 33, 34, 36, 38, 40, 42 in.; inseam 30, 32, 34, 36 in. State both sizes.

Sanforized 10-oz. Wt.
WAS $1.13 **98c**

Regular Sizes as Above. Ship. wt. 2 lbs. 4 oz.; two, 4 lbs. 4 oz.
42 UB 6169—Each 98c
State sizes. Two for $1.90

Sanforized 8-oz. Wt.
WAS 89c **77c**

Regular Sizes as Above. State sizes. Ship. wt. 2 lbs. 2 oz.; 2, 4 lbs. 4 oz.
42 UB 6164—Each ...77c
Two for $1.48

Mill Shrunk Med. Wt.
WAS 69c **63c**

Regular Sizes as Above. State sizes. Ship. wt. 1 lb. 13 oz.; 2, 3 lbs. 8 oz.
42 UB 6181—Each ...63c
Two for...........$1.20

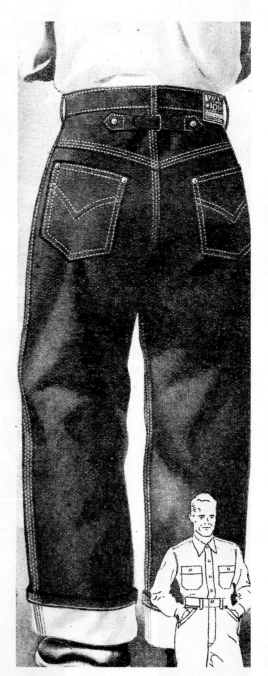

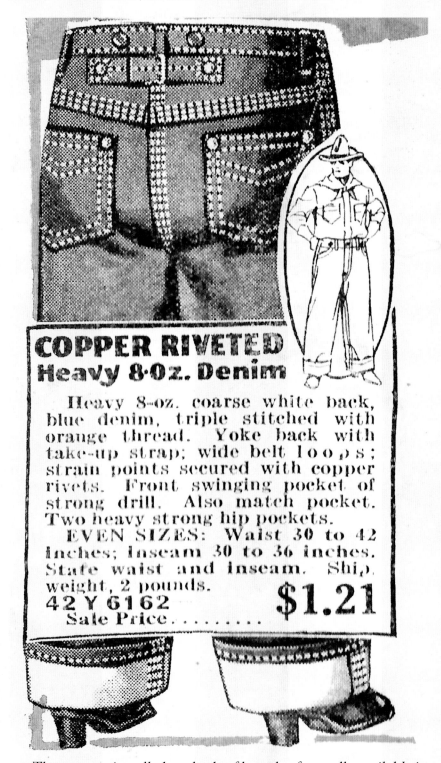

COPPER RIVETED
Heavy 8-Oz. Denim

Heavy 8-oz. coarse white back, blue denim, triple stitched with orange thread. Yoke back with take-up strap; wide belt loops; strain points secured with copper rivets. Front swinging pocket of strong drill. Also match pocket. Two heavy strong hip pockets.

EVEN SIZES: Waist 30 to 42 inches; Inseam 30 to 36 inches. State waist and inseam. Ship. weight, 2 pounds.

42 Y 6162
Sale Price......... **$1.21**

Catalog example showing jeans with copper riveting. Montgomery Ward, c. 1928.

Catalog example showing jeans with a martingale. Montgomery Ward, c. 1932.

There were virtually hundreds of brands of overalls available in the '30s with every company wanting to have the strongest, longest wearing garments. Previously, the cloth mills had sold to jobbers, jobbers sold to cutters, and cutters sold to sewers or manufactured the garments themselves. The Depression cut out the "middle man" and many small clothing enterprises added overalls to their garment production list

Copper riveting lost its original glamour from the 1870s, but with the late 1920s bringing about the need for tough wear and long lasting garments, rivets were revived on some brands of jeans. Copper riveting and a martingale, the back buckle for waist adjustment, reappeared and would be used until fabric rationing in WWII. Both were popular selling features for jeans.

Lee® introduced the Slim 101J Jacket in 1932 as a jacket without a baggy, blouson fit.

Lee introduced the "Storm Rider®" jacket, a blanket lined version of the 101J in 1933.

Cone Deeptone Denim® was patented in 1936.

Cowboys, whether they could sing or not, and their Western movies brought about a look at life away from the industrialized cities, the popularity of Dude Ranches, and the desire to wear jeans. By 1938, Levi Strauss had introduced a line of Western shirts for the Dude Ranch visitors and actual working cowboys.

Catalog example showing Cone Deeptone Denim for work garments. Montgomery Ward, c. 1939-40.

Catalog example of '30s Levi's ad for jeans and shirts. Texas Rancher, c. 1937.

Hard riding IS EASY IN LEVI'S

FOR THE ENTIRE FAMILY

Two Horse Brand

A new pair FREE If they Rip

10 oz. Blue Denin

Leather Label

Copper Riveted

Men's or Ladies' **$1.75** Per Pair

LADIES' LEVI'S No. 802—Sizes 24 to 34. Postage 10c extra.

MEN'S LEVI'S No. 800—Sizes 29 to 46. All lengths to 36. Postage 10c extra.

LEVI STRAUSS JUMPER $1.80

No. 801—Pleated front. Patented buttons that will not come off. Waist band and adjustable back. Buttoned cuffs. The famous Levi Strauss guarantee, your money back if you are not satisfied, goes with this blouse. Sizes 34 to 46. Postage 10c extra.

BOY'S LEVI'S

No. 803—Sizes 23 to 29. Lengths to 29 only. Postage 10c extra. **$1.50**

Handy Zipper Watch Pocket

Neat Zipper Fly Front

Western Style Yoke Back

Zipster

Reg. $1.39 Value.
...89c in Wards
Big Fall Catalog

SALE PRICED

79c
EA.

Sanforized

8-oz. Blue Denim

Best Boys' Bandtops. Western style yoke back, Buckle strap. Zipper fly, zipper watch pocket. 2 deep copper riveted front pockets. 2 back pockets thread riveted, can't mar chairs. Sanforized to 1%.
Even Sizes: 6 to 18. State size. Ship. wt. 1 lb. 7 oz.
42 UB 6060—Each. .79c

94 WARDS CB AS

From the late 1930s on, movie star John Wayne loved wearing Levi's in his movies. It is told that before shooting started on a movie, he would go out and buy several pair of new Levi's. He would then go down to the local river, tie the jeans to the bridge, and let them hang and beat in the water for several weeks. Then they would be ready to wear on set.

Slide fasteners (zippers) were added to jeans for men and boys in about 1940, and a overalls zip bib became available at the same time.

Denim overalls and jeans were some of the most popular clothing during the Depression.

Gene Autry songbook to capitalize on the western / cowboy trend, c. 1937.

Catalog example of zippered fly jeans. Montgomery Ward, c. 1941.

Catalog example of zipping bib pocket on overalls. Montgomery Ward, c. 1941.

New-

Loss-Proof Bib Pocket ZIPS SHUT!

OVERALLS ONLY

95c
EA.

Blanket Lined Denim Jacket **$1.55**

• Extra Heavy, Extra Strong 8-oz. Blue Denim.
• High, Wide Bib with New Zipper Pocket.
• Sanforized — less than 1% Fabric Shrinkage.
• Full Cut Sizes for Better Working Comfort.
• Rust-proof Buckles and Riveted Buttons.
• Bar-tacks Anchor All Points of Strain.

With the onset of WWII, most men were wearing military garb and denim clothing sales almost came to a standstill. That is, until the war put women in the workplace wearing overalls, short or long sleeved coveralls, jeans, or denim work uniforms.

After the war, overalls were still available, but changing American taste in clothing switched to service work clothes, a uniform of matching shirt and pants or jacket and pants and usually available in khaki, gray, green, blue and brown.

By the late '40s, jeans had become more than just trousers to work in; they became a garment for leisure wear. The legs narrowed and cuffs disappeared.

Levi Strauss re-introduced women's jeans with a side zip in the 1950s by adding Jeanies® and Jeanies of the West lines of clothing as the popularity for jeans for gals picked up momentum.

James Dean wore Lee jeans in the 1955 movie, *Rebel Without a Cause*, even though he personally wore Levi's off set. A company would later come out with James Dean Jeans® based on the Lee's he wore.

Levi Strauss introduced the slim fitting 557XX Trucker Jacket in 1962 to replace the two pocket 507. It only came in pre-shrunk denim.

The introduction of the jumpsuit for men in the early '60s changed the face of coveralls. Jumpsuits were lightweight, made of fabric other than traditional workwear fabrics, and could be worn anywhere—for work or leisure.

Denim jeans were firmly established as a unisex garment in the last half of the '60s, and the skinny cut legs of the jeans rivaled the skinniest cut slacks.

Catalog example showing jeans were acceptable for work. Sears, c. 1949.

Catalog example showing narrowed leg jeans for leisure. Montgomery Ward, c. 1950.

BAND OVERALLS AND WESTERN DENIMS

The late 1960s gave the fashion conscious person hippie bell bottoms and low rise jeans.

Not only had jeans become a unisex garment by the '70s, but also a garment to all ages of people to wear and enjoy their comfort.

Leg twist was pretty well eliminated by the late '70s with adjustments to weaving and manufacture. Leg twist occurs with laundering and causes the leg side seams to twist toward the front and back of the leg.

The late 1970s saw the introduction of "Designer Jeans" with the makers brand boldly placed on the back pocket.

Stonewashing denim jeans started in the late 1970s.

Jeans of stretch fabric started in the late 1970s.

Acid Wash jeans started in the mid-1980s.

"Shotgun" denim (where jeans were actually blasted with shotgun pellets) gained popularity in the mid-1980s.

In the mid-'80s, Levi Strauss launched a European campaign for their 501 jeans.

Cone Mills switched to new, more efficient, wider looms in 1986, which eliminated the selvage edge on denim.

"Cat Whiskering", now known as "hige" and used to make a pair of jeans look worn, entered the market in the mid to late '80s.

Japan entered the "vintage style" jeans market in the late 1980s.

The eruption of "vintage style" jeans' popularity caused a new rash of denim companies by the early 1990s.

The button fly closure has remained constant and is still used.

Today, there are Bib Overall Shows where you can show off your collections and possibly swap pairs or buy more.

A Word about Shrink to Fit Jeans

The fabric used for Levi's jeans was untreated for shrinkage, unlike Lee jelt denim with Sanforizing.

Shrink to fit jeans were made to have up to 10% fabric shrinkage. If you are buying a pair of NOS shrink to fit jeans, be sure to add 1" to 2" to your normal waist size and 3" to 4" to the inseam length.

For proper fit, shrink to fit jeans must be soaked inside-out in plain warm water (no detergent, no nuthin') for at least thirty minutes. Leaving them inside out, take them out of the water, DO NOT WRING, smooth them, and hang to dry. Before completely dry, put on your jeans and wear them, letting them dry on you. Be sure to rinse out the washer or soak tub to insure that no indigo color remains that might bleed on the next articles to be washed.

A Word about Repros

By the late 2000s, many companies like Stronghold, Blue Bell/ Wrangler, and Levi Strauss had started new vintage lines that are really hard to tell at a glance from the originals. One of the best ways, other than using specific dating criteria, is a fabric care tag—which became mandatory on U.S. sold goods in 1971. True vintage overalls and jeans will not have a care tag if they were made and sold before this date. Please see the chapter on garment labels for more information.

Catalog example showing jumpsuits, a lightweight version of coveralls that could be worn anywhere. Sears, c. 1962.

Catalog example of skinny legged jeans that rivaled trousers. Montgomery Ward, c. 1968.

{ The Jeans and Overalls Company List }

Many U.S. companies have made and sold overalls, coveralls, dungarees, and jeans through the decades since the first Levi's in 1873. Below are the brands / companies that I have located and their approximate date in business, if known.

Please note that when jeans gained popularity in the late 1960s, hundreds of new jeans wear companies were formed. None of these companies, nor any companies started from the 1970s on, have been included in this list.

This is the most all-inclusive list of work wear companies that I have been able to put together. There are probably others that I'm unaware of, and I did try not to include companies that specialized in work uniforms.

DATE	COMPANY NAME & NOTES
1936	110 Per Center®: by Sweet Orr
1920	999: by Sweet Orr
1910	ABC Blue Steel®
1908	Ace of Spades: by Sweet Orr
About 1946	Aldenbilt: by Aldens Catalog
1910	Anvil Brand: by High Point Overalls
1880s	Axanox
1922	Atlas Overalls®
?	Baker
1885	Bartel: by Perfection Brand Work Clothes
?	Beehive Brand
1935	Ben Davis®
?	Big 3
1919	Big Ace®
?	Big Allied
1915	Big Ben®
1908	Big Buck®
?1930s	Big Chief
?1950s	Big Dam Wear-Ease Overalls: by Irwin Phillips Co.
1920	Big Jack®
1922	Big Mac®: by J. C. Penney
?1960s	Big Man
?1940s	Big Mike
1949	Big Murph®
1909	Big Smith®
1908	Big Winston®
1926	Big Yank®
?1940s	Big and Tuf
1929	Biltwell®: by New England Overall Co.
1880s	Blackbear or Black Bear
1919	Blue Bell™
1912	Blue Buckle™: by Jobbers Overall
Late 1950s	Blue Gem
1899	Blue Ridge®
1935	Blue Wing®

DATE	COMPANY NAME & NOTES
1880	Boss™: later became Boss of the Road
1935	Boss of the Road™
?	Boy Blue
?	Brookfield: by J.A.White & Co.
1891	Brotherhood Overalls™
?	Bubble
?	Buckeye
1929	Buckhide®: by C. R. Anthony Co.
Late 1950s	Buddy Lee Jeans: by H.D. Lee
?	Bull's Eye
?	Burbank
?	Burlington Overall
?	Buss & Proud PA
1876	Can't Bust 'Em®: purchased by H.D. Lee in 1946
?1940s	Cantripum
Pre-1891	Carhartt®: by Hamilton Carhartt & Co.
?	H. W. Carter & Sons
1859	Carter's™
?1940s	Casey Jones
Pre 1935	Chieftain™: by Sears, Roebuck & Co.
1938	Circle S™: by Sears, Roebuck & Co.
?	Comes Bass
?	Comfort Brand
?1950s	Compass
1927	Copper King
1924	Cow Boy Special
?	Cowden®
Late 1890s	Crown Overalls or Crown Special Overalls
1880s	Cuvverem
?1940s	Dickies®
1880s	Dixie King
1962	Dixie Pal®
Pre-1905	Double Header®: merged with Signal

DATE	COMPANY NAME & NOTES
1880s	Dozfit
?	Dressy Dan
?1920s	Drum Major™: by Sears
1880s	Dubble Ware®
1866	Duck head®: name changed from O'Bryan Bros. in 1940s
1919	Dura-Bilt
?	Eagle Brand
?	Elk Brand Overalls
1956	Elvis Rock & Roll Platinum Brand Jeans or Elvis Presley Jeans; remakes in 2003
?	Engineer
?	Excelsior
1902	Finck's, Finck's Detroit Special, Finck's Red Bar
?1940s	Five Brothers
?	Flint Hills
1924	Foremost™: by J.C. Penney
?	Fort Brand
?1940s	Free Land®
1924	Frisko Jeens®: by Eloesser-Heynemann
Early 1960s	GAP Jeans
1929	(GWG)® Red Strap
?	Galesburg
1899	Gladiator: by National Bellas Hess (catalog)
1889	Globe: merged with Blue Bell in 1936
1927	Gold Label: by Eloesser-Heynemann
?1960s	Gold Star
?	Granite Overalls
?	Grant Brand
?1950s	Grants WTG: by W. T. Grant (Five & Dime)
?	Great 6
?	Green Hood
?	H-R Mfg. Co.
1950s	Happy Jim
Post WWI	Harlen Bros & Williams™: changed to Red Kap in 1939
?	Hawk Brand
1897	Headlight™: by Crown & Headlight
1908	Hercules®: by Sears, Roebuck & Co.
1920s	Homesteader®: by Montgomery Ward
?	Honor Bright
?	Hoo-sier
1904	Hudson Overall Co: many changes later became Wrangler
?	D.W.J. Hutton
1880s	Iron King Overalls
1880s	Ironalls
Pre-1905	J & C Overalls: by Oshkosh Clothing
Mid-1950s	JBS Jeans: in the style of James Dean's jeans in pants in *Rebel Without a Cause*
?	J.R. & B. Woolrich
1903	Jack Rabbit®
?	Jobbers Overalls

DATE	COMPANY NAME & NOTES
?	Jumbo Make
?	K.R. & Co.
?	Kast-Iron
1941	Key Imperial®
Pre-1905	Keystone: by Cleveland & Whitehill
?	King Kole
1880s	Kumfort
1899	Lee®: by H.D. Lee
1873	Levi's®: by Levi Strauss Co.
?	Lewis's
1927	Liberty
?	Lion Brand
1936	Madewell®
?1950s	Mansize
Pre-1908	Market Brand: by A. Lewin & Son
?	Meyer Brand
Pre-1920s	Mogel Overalls: by Swoffords
?1940s	Montgomery Ward®
?1940s	N & W
1930s	Nation-Alls®: by Sears, Roebuck & Co.
1921	NationWide®: by J.C. Penney
?	Never Rip
?	Never Wear-Out
?	Non Pariel: by Murphy Grant Co.
1889	O'Alls: by Carhartt
1892	O'Bryan Bros.: changed to Duck Head name in the 1940s
?	Ohio Overall Co.
?1940s	O'Kay
?1930s	Old Glory
Early 1960s	Old Kentucky
1910s	Onorbilt Overalls: by Philipsborn Dept. Stores & Catalog
1895	OshKosh B'Gosh®: by Oshkosh Overall Co.
?	Our Wheeler
?	Ox Horn
1930s	Oxhide®: by J.C. Penney
?	Panama Mobile
1933	Partridge®
1922	Pay Day or Super Pay Day™: by J. C. Penney
1885	Perfection Brand Work Clothes
?	Pettibone Bros.
1920s	Pioneer™: by Montgomery Ward
?1950s	Plainsman
1964	Plenty Tough®: by Ben Davis
1913	Pointer
1929	Powr House™: by Montgomery Ward
1930s	Rail Chief
Pre-1902	Railroad King
1946	Ranchcraft™: by J.C.Penney; only produced a few years; brought back in the 60s
1932	Red Axe: by Blue Bell
?	Red Ball
?	Red Diamond
1924	Red Kap™

DATE	COMPANY NAME & NOTES
Pre-1904	Red Seal Overalls
?	Reindeer Brand
?	Rip Proof
1949	Roebucks™: by Sears, Roebuck & Co.
1922	Roomy Richard®
1903	Round House®
?	Royal: by G. & F. Co.
1880	Sampson
?1930s	Santa Fe
?1940s	Seafarer Jeans
Pre-1917	Sensible: by Johnson & Larimer Mfg.
?	Shenandoah
?1940s	Shenk & Tittle
1919	Service Suits & Overalls®: by Cowden
?	Show Me Overalls
Pre-1905	Signal: by Hilker-Wieders Mfg.
?1940s	Silverbloom
?1940s	Smith
?	Snag Proof
?	Stag Trousers
?	Star or Star Union Overall
?1960s	Steel Klad
1947	Steer Buster®
1926	Stone Cutter®
1925	Stone Mountain Shirts & Overalls®
?1960s	Strong Reliable
?	Strong Brand
?	Stronger Brand
?1920s	Stronghold
1930s	Sturdy Oak™: by Sears, Roebuck & Co.
?	Summit: by Guiterman
1873	Sweet Orr®
?	Ten-Point
?1940s	Test
?	Texas Brand Overalls
?	The Clearfield
1896	The Engineer
?	The Flyer
?	The Lightner Brand

DATE	COMPANY NAME & NOTES
?	The Mack
?	The R. R. Brand
?	The Railroad
?	The Train Love Brand
?	The Winner
?	Thoroughbred
Pre-1905	Tom Roberts Overall
?1950s	Topcraft: by Montgomery Wards
?	Tri-State
1880s	Tuf-Nut®
1922	Tug-O' War®: by Sweet Orr
1921	Uncle Fuller
1940s	Uncle Sam: by Chicago Mail Order
?	Under Hill
?	Union Brand
1920	Union Leader™: by J. C. Penney
1914	Union-All®: by H.D. Lee
1918	U.S. Overall: later became Williamson-Dickie, maker of Dickies
1924	Universal Overall®
?	Utopia Union Made
?	Victor
?	Victory
1910s	Wa Bash
?	Want More
?	Ward Wear™: by Montgomery Ward
1930s	Wards Homesteader™: by Montgomery Ward
?	Washburne
1914	Washington Dee Cee®
?	Watch Wear
?	Watch the Wearz
?	Wauk Wear
?1950s	Wear Well
?	Winner-Thomas Co.
?	Wooster's Overalls
?1940s	Workmaster: by Spiegel Catalog
1947	Wrangler®

I also found that many overalls were produced for specific railroads like:

Ann Arbor, M&IT, The Penn, C&NW, SO&CO NY, MRR, NKP, MWofΛ, THI&E, and Overy just to mention a few.

Since the railroads were unionized, their clothing was mandated to be manufactured by union clothing manufacturers.

THE GUIDE TO HIGH GRADE FOODS

CONTENTS   1 LB. 4 OZ.

Lee

TRADE MARK
REG. U.S. PAT. OFF.

SIFTED
EARLY JUNE PEAS

THE H.D. LEE MERCANTILE CO.
DISTRIBUTORS
KANSAS CITY, MO., SALINA, KAS.

CALVERT LITHO. CO. DETROIT ·

▣ H.D. Lee started as a mercantile and then expanded into clothing, c. 1900 to 1938.

▣ Advertisement showing Lee Union-Alls and the placement of the label on the outside. *Locomotive Firemen and Engineer Magazine*, c. 1917.

Listed below are more specific dating criteria for the three biggest jean producers in America: Lee, Wrangler, and Levi Strauss.

Please be advised that this information does not include jackets or other styles of pants other than jeans (except as noted), and does not extend beyond 1971.

{ H.D. Lee Company }

Lee Jeans and Their Dating

In 1899, Lee Mercantile Co. started producing dungarees for sale alongside their fine foods, many which carried the H.D. Lee name.

1911: Lee added bib overalls for work under the name Union-Alls®. A line of coveralls came two years later under the same name.

1914: Lee introduced khaki Union-Alls for her.

The U.S. Army wore Lee Union-Alls in the latter part of WWI.

1917: H.D. Lee was the first apparel manufacturer to launch a national advertising campaign for their Union-Alls. Note where the label is located in the earliest Union-Alls.

1919: Klondiker® Pants were introduced.

Buddy Lee, a doll made for in-store displays, was introduced in 1920 to model miniature versions of the company's clothing.

TRIPLE STITCHED SEAMS

LEE LABEL IS STITCHED ON THE BACK

FOR YOUR OWN PROTECTION

Beware of the "just as good." The *best* is cheapest in work clothing. To get real wear and satisfactory service demand your one-piece work suit by name

Lee Union-Alls

There is but one UNION ALL that's the LEE. Insist upon having Lee Union-Alls.

The name is embossed on the button; the trademark is stitched on the back. Lee Union-Alls are first in appearance, fit and quality.

Buy Lee Union-Alls, the standard one-piece work suit, because it is best for

WEAR
SERVICE
COMFORT
SAFETY

UNION   *Lee*   MADE
Union-Alls
INSIST ON THIS TRADE MARK

Lee Union-Alls are made in Khaki, blue denim, express stripe, pin check or white drill. **Lee Union-Alls** for children are made "just like Dad's."

1922: brought the introduction of Campus Cords® (trousers).

About 1924, Lee called their new version of jeans 101 Cowboy Pants or 101 Cowboy Waistband Overalls. They had the same basic cut, copper rivets, and double arcuate back pocket stitching as Levi's.

Lee would later have a deeper yoke and a u-shaped saddle crotch to merchandise more toward cowboys.

There would also be a 131 version of jeans and overalls made of 8 oz denim rather than a heavier weight.

1925: Lee introduced Lee Jelt Denim (from Cone Mills), a lightweight and durable fabric. Previously, Lee had produced its own denim for its jeans and chose a green line in their selvage edge opposed to Blue Bell™ using gold and Levi's using red or blue.

In 1926, Lee started offering jeans in custom sizes stated by waist and inseam.

1927: Lee introduced the Hookless Fastener (zipper) to a line of overalls for easy access during bathroom breaks. A national contest named the new overall garment with a zipper the Whizit. With the advent of barnstorming on the horizon, Whizit's would become the perfect flight suit.

A zipper fly version of waist overalls was called the 1010—later renamed the 101Z.

Advertisement showing Lee Union-Alls.
Locomotive Firemen and Engineer Magazine, c. 1917.

Advertisement showing Lee Whizit.
Frisco Employees Magazine, c. 1928.

1929: the #91 overall featured a 4 in 1 pocket on the bib.

Lee is rumored to have tested Sanforizing for shrinkage control in the late 1920s before it was patented in 1930.

1931: Lee Union-Alls featured Treg Twill, an exclusive Lee herringbone pattern, and Korm Stripes.

1935: Lee introduced and trademarked the name Lee Riders (waistband overalls).

1936: Lee used a Hair On Hide patch branded by hand on its jeans. This lasted into the early 1940s.

Lee tags say Sanforized and union made from 1936 to 1972.

1937: Lee brought out color match shirt and pants for service workers.

1944: The Lazy "S" became the official back pocket stitching for Lee.

1944: Lee 101 Cowboy Pants were renamed Lee Riders to go with their existing line.

1946: Hip pocket rivets were eliminated as they were known to scratch saddle leather.

1946: Lee buys "Can't Bust 'Em"™, Frisko Jeens®, and Boss of the Road® work clothes lines.

1951: Lee still used the term dungarees.

1951: Introduced Lee Chetopa® pants.

1953: Introduced Storm Rider jackets.

Advertisement showing Lee features for their garments. *Country Gentleman*, c. 1949.

Advertisement showing hinge-back Lee Union-Alls. Unknown Magazine, c. 1940s.

1915: Levi's s
1922: Belt lo
suspender button
1923: Single s
on the leg hems.
1928: Levi's t
1936: The rec
could spot a genu
1937: Suspen
rivets at back poc
1941: Remove
WWII: Durin
sometimes painte
abolished, and th
1944: The mic
off-set position.
1947: Rivets v
1950: ® (regis
1953: Levi's c
because of the co
1954: Zipper
502's. Scovill or C
Late 1950s: L
1958: Red tal
written on both s
1961: Levi's i
1965: Levi's r
brass rivets to bra
1967: Bar tac
at back pockets.
1969: Levi's i
The Levi's nar
when it changed t
Little e tabs after
Red tabs have
such at white or c
jeans in the late 1
Because of the
coming out with r
have the leather
criteria of the olde
the fabric care ta
pre-1970s.

Things to che

(Example is a
which are someti
the 1990s.)
Single sided I
to single sided ta
1958 to 1971.

1958: Introduced Lee Westerner®, a line of pants & jackets.
1959: Introduced LEEsures®, a line of work pants.
1959: Introduced Lee Tropics® (lightweight trousers).
1959: Introduced Cactus Casuals® (slacks).
1959: Introduced a line of white jeans & jacket called Lee Whites™.
1960: Introduced Lee Tacks® (slacks).
1960: Introduced Lee Trims® (slacks).
1961: Introduced Lee Leens® (trousers).
1963: Introduced Fastbacks® (trousers)
1964: Introduced Lee-Prest®, a version of no-iron permanent press fabric.
1965: Lee narrowed the shape of the leg on the 101's.
1965: Introduced LTP™ (slacks).
1966: Introduced Tech Twill® (slacks).
1966: Introduced Master Classic™ (slacks).
1967: Lee introduced their line of bell bottom jeans.
1968: Introduced Hipster™ (jeans & slacks).
The company was sold to VF Corporation in 1969.

Lee final notes:
The hip pocket label just said Lee until 1960 when the ® (R in a circle was added); MR was added in 1970; The Black Tag was used until the mid-1970s; Union Made was removed from the tags in 1972.
The 101-J is a reprint of Hickory cloth; 91-B represents jackets; 191 LB represents lined jackets; 91-J represents coveralls.
Lee pre-washed jeans were introduced in 1973.

{ Blue Bell Company }

Wrangler® Jeans and Their Dating

Because of its checkered past of sales, mergers, and name changes, Wrangler's are probably some of the hardest to date.
The firm started as Hudson Overall Company in 1904.
The company became Blue Bell Overall Company in 1919.
It merged with Big Ben Manufacturing in 1926, but kept the name Blue Bell.
To keep the denim orders straight, Blue Bell was supplied fabric with a gold selvage edge.
Blue Bell merged with Globe Superior Corp. in 1936 and kept the Blue Bell name.
The company started using Sanforizing in 1936 on its Super Big Ben Jeans; they introduced Super Big Ben Overalls with Sanforizing that same year.
1943: They purchased the H. D. Bob Company, then purchased Casey Jones Work Clothes (who called their jeans Wrangler). Again, the company kept the Blue Bell name.
1947: Introduced Wrangler Blue Jeans, which were marked as 13MWZ for 13 oz denim and men's with zippers. Designed with working cowboys in mind, these jeans had widely placed front belt loops to accommodate oversized rodeo buckles.
1950: Introduced black denim.
1950: The 11MWZ Wranglers had its middle back belt loop moved to the exact middle of the jeans. Previous versions have an offset middle back belt loop.
1964: Added the ® (registered trademark) to the label.

NEW GIFT IDEAS:

Lee "Junior" Riders, Chetopa Twill shirts and pants

Lee Riders authentic western cowboy pants or blue jeans

Advertisement showing Lee Riders— authentic western cowboy pants or blue jeans. *Ladies Home Journal*, c. 1954.

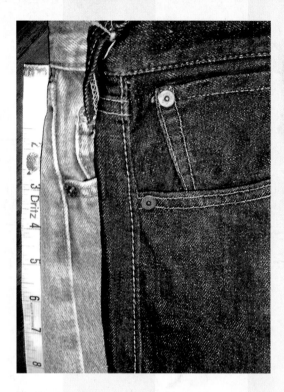

Example of Levi's watch pocket and front pocket placement, c. 1990s & 1930s.

Example of Levi's watch pocket selvage edge, c. 1930s.

Example of Levi's selvage edge at leg seam, c. 1930s.

Early watch pockets had a selvage edge inside; 1930s to 1940s watch pocket measured 3.5" to 4" wide, getting narrower in the 1950s. There is also a difference on how high the watch pocket is placed as the earlier ones almost met the waistband.

A selvage edge should show on inside leg seam. A redline (red line) will show against the white unless it has been laundered away. Selvage edge construction was used through the 1980s.

Example of Levi's plain back top button, c. 1930s.

Example of Levi's four button fly front, c. 1930s.

Example of Levi's stitches per inch, c. 1930s.

Example of Levi's changes in stitching color and overcast seaming, c. 1990s & 1930s.

The top button should be plain (as shown) on the backside, or have a single digit stamped on the backside until 1971. The most common single digit stamp is a 6, followed by 2, 5, or W. Three digit stamps on the button backs started in the '70s. Reproduction 501's will have "555" stamped on the back of the top button.

This 1930s pair of 501's only has four buttons for the fly. A fifth button was added later. Also note that the top button was "donut hole" style until into the 1930s, then it became solid.

Shown is stitching on a '90s pair of 501's (left) compared to late '30s stitching (right) to show the thread color difference, overcast difference, and more stitches per inch. Older jeans averaged about 7 stitches to the inch as shown in the bottom picture.

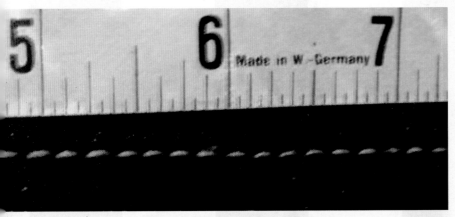

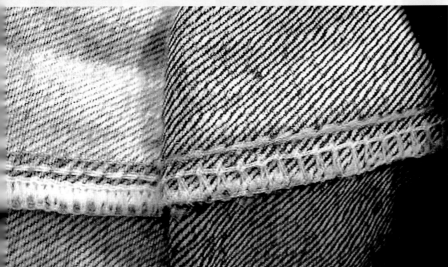

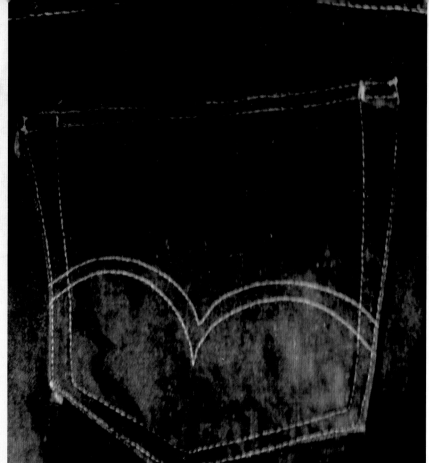

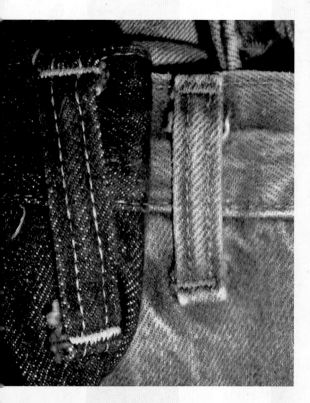

The arcuate (stitching pattern) on the back pocket helps date these jeans to the late 1930s. Each line is deep and done freehand while little "e" jeans will be done mechanically with a double needle.

A subtle difference that is often overlooked is the size change in belt loop lengths.

Brass rivets and buttons were changed to silver colored rivets (left and top) in the late 1960s.

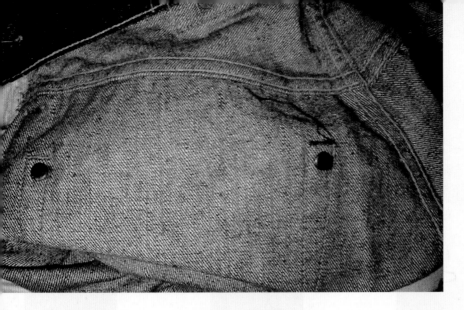

Hidden rivets on the back pockets started in 1937. This was later replaced with bar tacking. Hidden rivets can be seen from the inside, but not on the outside back pocket.

Watch pockets were about 3" wide at the interior stitching on older jeans and narrowed in the 1950s. Hip pockets were about 5" wide at the interior stitching in the 1930s and 1940s on 501's and narrowed in the 1950s.

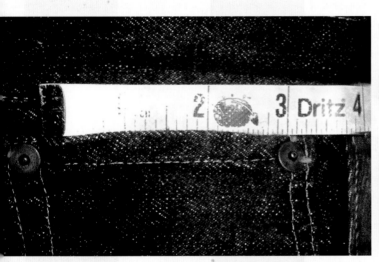

The coveted martingale / buckleback was removed during WWII to conserve fabric.

Example of Levi's hidden rivets, c. 1930s.

Example of Levi's watch pocket width, c. 1930s.

Example of Levi's hip pocket width, c. 1930s.

Example of Levi's martingale, c. 1930s.

For more dating information visit:

www.vintagemotorcyclejackets.com

www.vintagefashionguild.org

www.redcloud.co.jp

www.levisguide.com/patch/patches.html

And, finally, if you like the vintage work wear look, but don't want true vintage, check out these stores or brands for retro styling of new clothing:

Abercrombie & Fitch®	Barney's®	J.Crew®
Target™	Eddie Bauer®	Gap®

Places that sell:

Red Wing® boots	RRL by Ralph Lauren®
Dickies®	Levi's®

You will have to know the styles that you are looking for, and need to search for the items because of limited availability.

These online companies also
have vintage inspired work clothing:

waltontaylor	tinhouse	e-workers.net
riverjunction	dappers.jp	pickbrothersshop
wwiiimpressions	atthefront	

{ Sweaters }

Knitting is the process of turning thread or yarn into cloth. Women have been knitting by hand since the time Cleopatra lived in ancient Egypt and this tradition has passed through the centuries and across the continents.

The first knitting machine was introduced about 1600, while crude machines for home knitting appeared in the 1850s. Knitted garments have moved forward since then.

Commercial knitting had improved considerably with the invention of new machinery by that time, and Americans loved the comfort and warmth of wearing a cotton, Rayon or wool sweater for outdoor activities.

The 1920s introduced machine knit clothing which the younger generation fell in love with. Sweaters came in many styles and available in wool, cotton, and Rayon knits. Short sleeved or sleeveless sweaters in plain, checkerboard, diamond or jacquard patterns were worn over a long sleeved shirt with suspenders worn over the top of the sweater.

Sweaters weren't just for guys. Unisex goes back to the turn of the twentieth century, way before the word was even coined and has continued onward through the decades.

Catalog example of pattern pull over sweaters. Montgomery Ward, c. 1928.

A Worthwhile Saving!

Crew Neck All Wool

Was $4.49 Now Only $3.59
Shaker Knit Slipover

Comfortable Medium Weight

Reduced from $3.98

Now Only $2.49

Price Cut $1.49!

Novelty All Wool Sweater

111

The young Prince of Wales Edward VIII, who would later abdicate the throne as the King of England, was known for his style setting ways of dressing. When he showed up for a golf game in the 1920s wearing knickers and a Fair Isle knit sweater, a new style trend was set in motion. He was also known to have hand knitted some of his own mufflers.

Sweaters were worn for golf, skiing, hockey, cricket, and other sports, and came in both long and short sleeved versions. Many sweaters of this era were made with a 5-6" matching ribbed band at the waist, and the shawl collar was the most popular for cardigans.

In a couple of years, knitting mills were outdoing themselves with new innovations like the "saddle shoulder" sweater, and U necks instead of V necks for something a little different.

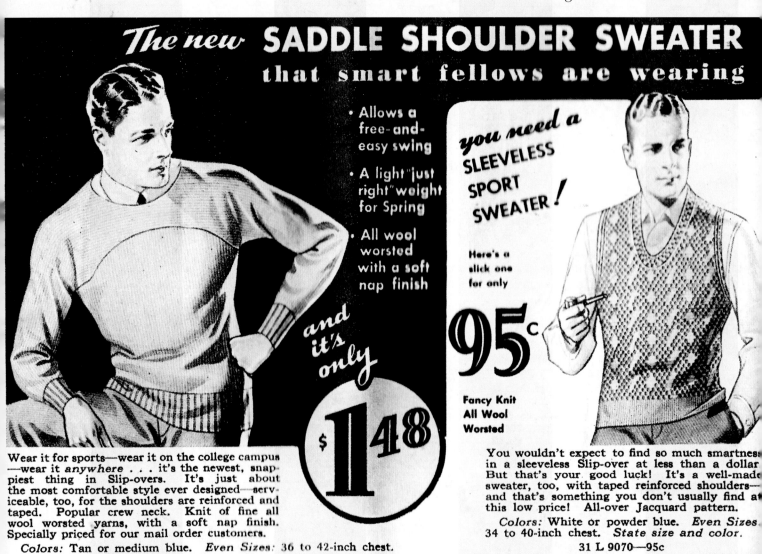

The new SADDLE SHOULDER SWEATER
that smart fellows are wearing

- Allows a free-and-easy swing
- A light "just right" weight for Spring
- All wool worsted with a soft nap finish

and it's only

$1 48

Wear it for sports—wear it on the college campus—wear it *anywhere* . . . it's the newest, snappiest thing in Slip-overs. It's just about the most comfortable style ever designed—serviceable, too, for the shoulders are reinforced and taped. Popular crew neck. Knit of fine all wool worsted yarns, with a soft nap finish. Specially priced for our mail order customers.

Colors: Tan or medium blue. *Even Sizes:* 36 to 42-inch chest.

31 L 9069—*State size and color. Postage 10c*

you need a SLEEVELESS SPORT SWEATER!

Here's a slick one for only

95c

Fancy Knit All Wool Worsted

You wouldn't expect to find so much smartness in a sleeveless Slip-over at less than a dollar. But that's your good luck! It's a well-made sweater, too, with taped reinforced shoulders—and that's something you don't usually find at this low price! All-over Jacquard pattern.

Colors: White or powder blue. *Even Sizes* 34 to 40-inch chest. *State size and color.*

31 L 9070—95c

Postage 8c

Catalog example of saddle shoulder and U neck sweaters. Montgomery Ward, c. 1933.

Sweaters continued in popularity with features such as raglan sleeves and zip front necks, with pockets for cardigans, newly styled vests and sweaters that pulled on over the head, and twin sets. Many sweaters previously boasting 100% Virgin Wool were replaced with wool blended with Rayon, wool and mohair blends, Zephyr Wool, and reprocessed or reused wool during the Depression.

LOW PRICED SPECIAL

$**1**29

- Medium Weight
- Abt. 1/3 Wool Mohair
- Talon Fastener
- Side Tabs, Rings

TALON FASTENER

$**1**77

- Baby Shaker Knit
- 50% Virgin Wool
- Rib Knit Collar
- Shirred Sports Back

Catalog example of zippered neck sweaters. Montgomery Ward, c. 1937.

During WWII, there was a trend towards hand knitting once again. Old sweaters were taken apart and the yarn re-used for a more modern style, as well as saving wool for the war effort. The ribbed band at the waist had shortened to about 4"—made shorter to conserve wool, two tones were popular, zip pockets had been added, and Raglan sleeves remained popular.

As men returned home, there was a new need for wool sports sweaters for skiing and other outdoor winter activities, which had been previously thought to be only for the leisure set. Sweaters and vests became popular for golfing and tennis to extend the playing seasons or to replace a jacket in mild weather.

The ribbed waist band continued to shorten and was only 3" by the mid-1950s, while the collar openings deepened. Sweaters were available in every color of the rainbow to match the colorful slacks of the decade.

Catalog example of wool sports sweaters. Sears, c. 1948

Catalog example of colorful array of sweaters. Sears, c. 1958.

...anberry	Turquoise	Light blue	Maize	Maroon	Medium blue	Camel tan	Medium green	Gray	Mint green	Charcoal heather	Med. gray heather	Lt. blue heather	T... hea...

The early 1960s gave cardigans a new look that buttoned or zipped all the way to the neck and were to be worn with skinny fit slacks. Colors switched to fall hues of golds, oranges, greens, and browns as the decade proceeded.

Catalog example of autumn hued sweaters. Sears, c. 1969.

{ Sweater Styles }

Cardigan: {01}
a sweater that buttons or zips the entire length of the front. These had the addition of suede fronts in the 1960s.

Shaker Cardigan: {02}
known for the large, loose stitches.

{ Sweater Styles }

Sports Cardigan: {03}
a two toned cardigan for school or sports.

V-Neck Pullover: {04}
a sweater with no buttons or zipper; collarless with a v-neck.

01 *(top left)* Catalog example of cardigan sweater. *Art in Knitting*, c. 1917.

(top right) Catalog example of cardigan sweater. National Bellas Hess, c. 1930.

(bottom left) Catalog example of cardigan sweater worn by actor, radio, and TV personality Ezra Stone. Unknown knitting book, c. 1940.

(bottom right) Catalog example of '60s suede front cardigan sweaters. Montgomery Ward, c. 1968.

02 Catalog example of a Shaker knit cardigan sweater. National Bellas Hess, c. 1930.

03 *(left)* Catalog example of a sport cardigan sweater. *Art in Knitting*, c. 1917.

(right) Catalog example of sport cardigan sweaters. Montgomery Ward, c. 1950.

04 *(top left)* Catalog example fancy knit V-neck pullover sweaters. Montgomery Ward, c. 1932.

(top right) Catalog example of wool U-neck pullovers. Montgomery Ward, c. 1934.

(bottom left) Catalog example of bandleader, radio and TV personality Fred Waring wearing a V-neck pullover sweater. Unknown knitting book, c. 1940.

(bottom right) Catalog example of classic V-neck pullover sweater. Montgomery Ward, c. 1950.

{ Sweater Styles }

Crew Neck Pullover: {05}
a sweater with no buttons or zipper;
collarless with a circular neck like a t-shirt.

Collared Pullover: {06}
a sweater with no buttons or zipper;
features a collar.

SLEEVELESS SWEATERS
FOR DAPPER COMFORT

All Wool Worsted   New Cable Stitch

05

06

07

{ Sweater Styles }

Sweater Vest: {07}
   a sleeveless sweater.

Sweater Vest with button front: {08}

Turtleneck: {09}
   a pullover sweater with a high band collar that folds over on itself. It was been worn since the 1800s and was extremely popular in the first three decades of the 1900s and again in the 1960s and 1970s.

08

2785

Robert Allen
OF THE STAGE, SCREEN AND RADIO

09

98c Here's Value to Shout About! ALL WOOL SLIPOVER

Turtleneck Style

Think of it! Less than a dollar for a good quality, good-looking all wool slipover! Thank Wards for such value. Neat all-over novelty stitch, contrasting color trimming. Rib-knit, snug-fitting cuffs and bottoms.
   Colors: Tan or maroon. **Even Sizes:** 36 to 44-in. chest. **State size and color.** Shipping wt. 11 oz.
31 N D 1146..........98c

05   Catalog example of crew neck pullover sweater. Montgomery Ward, c. 1950.

06   Catalog example of a collared crew neck pullover sweater. Montgomery Ward, c. 1950.

07   *(top left)* Catalog example of a WWI Army sweater vest. *Art in Knitting*, c. 1917.
   (top right) Catalog example of sleeveless sweaters / sweater vests. Sears, c. 1939.
   (bottom left) Catalog example of a sweater vest. Montgomery Ward, c. 1950.

08   Catalog example of movie start Robert Allen wearing a button front vest. Unknown knitting book, c. 1940.

09   *(left)* Catalog example of a turtleneck sweater. Montgomery Ward, c. 1933.
   (right) Catalog example of colorful turtleneck sweaters. Montgomery Ward, c. 1968.

Sweat or Training Shirt

Boys' Sizes, 83c   Men's Sizes, 97c Ea.

Good grade of cotton, fleece lined, gray color. Used extensively in all forms of sport. Helps the player to "warm up" before the game or for practice use. Even sizes. State size. Shipping wt., 2½ pounds.

6K2015 Men's sizes, 34 to 44 chest measure..**97c**
Team lots of **5** or more. Each..**92c**
6K2016—Boys' sizes, 26 to 32 chest measure **83c**
Team lots of **5** or more. Each..**78c**

Printed Design Sweat Shirt

Made of good grade cotton, fleece lined. Color of body is white with printed design in contrasting fast colors. This garment is strictly for athletic wear. Worn with or without a top shirt.

Even sizes. **State size.** Shipping weight, 2½ pounds.
6K2014—Men's sizes, 34 to 44 chest measure **$1.25**
6K2013—Boys' sizes, 26 to 32 chest measure **$1.10**

Sweat Pants

Made of fine quality cotton, fleece lined, same material as our 6K2016 and 6K2015 Sweat Shirts, gray color. Draw string at waist and ankles. Excellent for general training purposes. Small sizes, 32 and 34; medium sizes, 36 and 38; large sizes, 40 and 42 waist measure. **State size.** Shipping weight, 2 pounds.
6K2050 ....**$1.20**

Colored Sweat Shirts

Fine quality cotton fleece lined fabric. Knit cuffs and waistband of contrasting color. Even sizes, 34 to 42 in. chest. **State size.** Shpg. wt., 2½ lbs.
6K2011 Navy blue with white trimming.
$1.29
6K2012
Orange with black trimming....**$1.29**
6K2008—Red with white trimming **$1.29**

Catalog example of early sweatshirt and pants. Sears, c. 1927.

{ A Few Words About Sweatshirts }

I debated for some time whether a sweatshirt should be included with the casual shirts or sweaters. Worn alone or over a shirt, they serve the same purpose as a sweater—keeping warm.

When the fitness and sports craze hit young American men before the turn of the twentieth century, special clothing was needed, so we have the styling invention of the sweatshirt.

By the 1930s, zippered fronts had been added, as well as graphics.

69c

Look! Dizzy Dean
.. also Brother Paul

new! new!

Boys!

BABE RUTH
sweat shirt 49c

Organize a "Babe" Ruth team, and use these swell looking white Sweat Shirts as uniforms.

"Babe's" picture and autograph on the front in blue and red. Medium weight cotton knit cloth, fleeced on inside. Ribbed cuffs, bottom, and collar.

Even Sizes: 28 to 38-in. chest. *Order 2-in. larger than actual chest size. State size.*

60 L 5809—Postage 10c........49c

Catalog example of a graphic sweatshirt. Montgomery Ward, c. 1935.

Catalog example of a Babe Ruth graphic sweatshirt. Montgomery Ward, c. 1933.

Catalog example of various styles and graphics for sweatshirts. Sears, c. 1935.

Sport Sweatshirt **Pullover Sport Jacket** **Colored Sweatshirt** **"Me and Paul" Sweatshirt** **"M. Mouse" Sweatshirt**

OUTSTANDING BUYS IN FINEST SWEATSHIRTS MADE

Sweatshirts remained popular for leisure time with hooded sweatshirts introduced in the early '40s for warmth during outdoor activities without wearing a hat.

Fleece sweatshirts were warm and comfortable to wear, plus became stylish by the late '40s with the addition of collars, zip fronts and colors. Sweatshirts turned into fleece lined jackets in the 1950s and became a wardrobe staple.

By the 1960s, a front kangaroo pouch had been added to the front for carrying or storing gloves or other items.

And, they had been out of gray mode for almost ten years reflecting the popular colors of the decade.

Hooded Sweat Shirt

- 100% American Double Cotton Cloth.

$1 79 Each

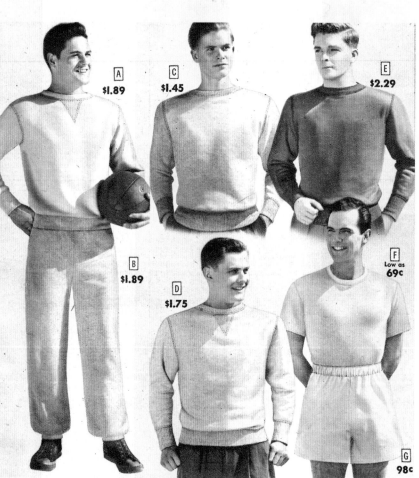

🔲 Catalog example of the first hooded sweatshirts. Montgomery Ward, c. 1941.

🔲 Catalog example of "V" neck insert and wide waist banding. Montgomery Ward, c. 1940.

🔲 Catalog example of how sweatshirts had expanded into jackets. Montgomery Ward, c. 1955.

🔲 Catalog example of '40s sweatshirts and pants. Sears, c. 1948.

A $1.89 C $1.45 E $2.29
B $1.89 D $1.75 F Low as 69c
G 98c

J. C. HIGGINS GYM CLOTHING for boys and men

Washable Cotton Sweatshirts designed two ways for comfort

Chill-stopping flat knit outside . .
Absorbent fleeced cotton inside

5 Raglan Sleeve Heavyweight Sweat-shirt. *State color* gray, navy, white.
83 K 4009—State small (34–36-in. chest), med. (38–40), large (42–44), ex. large (46). Wt. 1 lb. 8 oz. **$1.94**

6 Full Zipper Mediumweight Sweatshirt. Knit trimmed collar, cuffs, bottom. 2 slash pockets. *State color* black, gold, olive green or blue. Shpg. wt. 1 lb. 14 oz.
83 K 4023—State size as (5) above. **$2.94**

7 Hooded Heavyweight Sweatshirt. Hood is double fabric for double protection. Drawstring muff pocket. *State color* gray, navy, red, golden yellow. Wt. 1 lb. 14 oz.
83 K 4016—State size as (5) above. **$2.94**
Tall sizes. State medium, large, extra large.
83 K 4052—Shipping weight 2 pounds. **$3.40**

8 Sweatpants. Ribbed top. Adjustable drawstring. Matches 83 K 4016 above. *State* small (30–32-in. waist), medium (34–36), large (38–40).
83 K 4001—State red, gray, navy, white. **$1.94**

9 Half-zipper Short Sleeve Sweatshirt. Heavyweight. Knit collar, bottom. In blazing hot colors. *State* continental blue, tangerine, kelly green. Shpg. wt. 1 lb. 2 oz.
83K4084—State small (34–36), med. (38–40), large (42–44). Shpg. wt. 1 lb. 2 oz. **$1.90**

10 Half-zipper Long Sleeve Sweatshirt. Heavyweight. Self-fabric collar. *State size as* (5) above. Shpg. wt. 1 lb. 1 oz.
83 K 4003—State silver gray, navy, red, white. **$2.29**

SEARS 659

Catalog example of how sweatshirts had the front pouch added. Sears, c. 1962.

Catalog example of colorful sweatshirts and different styles. Montgomery Ward, c. 1968.

Catalog example of various style and colors of sweatshirts. Sears, c. 1968.

{ Coats and Casual Jackets }

Catalog instruction on how to measure for a coat. Sears, c. 1944.

HOW TO MEASURE FOR COATS AND JACKETS

Pull tape measure around your chest over the garment that you intend to usually wear underneath the coat or jacket—such as vest or sweater. Keep tape measure well up under your arms and over your shoulder blades in back. Keep tape snug, but not tight. The number of inches is your correct size. Measure carefully and make no allowances. Sears coats are all full cut. For Easy Terms, see inside back cover.

In flipping through decades of catalogs and my own research materials, I found references to the following **styles of coats:**

Automobile Duster:
A smock-like garment worn to protect one's clothing.

Bomber Jacket or Flight Jacket: {01}
A warm coat originally created for pilots in WWI since cockpits were not enclosed.

Chesterfield: {02}
A long, tailored overcoat, single or double breasted, usually of heavy tweed or wool, and always having a velvet collar.

Chore Coat or Work Coat: {03}
A casual, hip length jacket. Can be unlined or lined.

Hunting Coat: {04}
A coat or jacket with reinforced seams for durability which is usually waterproofed and lined, and specifically styled and worn for hunting.

AMERICA'S TOP FLIGHT JACKET STYLES
IN LUXURIOUS WOOL AND MOHAIR FABRICS

Leisure Jacket: {05}

Less structured and formal than a sports jacket, these garments were made to wear in a man's leisure hours, yet still be appropriately dressed with a shirt and tie.

Lumberjack Jacket: {06}

A jacket of wool plaid, a convertible collar, and knit cuffs and band at the waist.

Mac Farlane:

A topcoat or overcoat with an attached cape.

Mackinaw: {07}

A heavyweight wool plaid double breasted coat.

Motorcycle Jacket: {08}

A leather jacket adapted for riding motorcycles by an adjustable belt at the waist and zippered, tight fitting sleeves to stop air flow.

Norfolk: {09}

A single breasted coat or jacket with box pleats in the back and sometimes front, and having either a half belt or full belt.

01 Catalog example of a flight or bomber jacket. Montgomery Ward, c. 1941.

02 Catalog example of a chesterfield coat. Sears, c. 1929.

03 Catalog example of a chore or work coat. Montgomery Ward, c. 1940.

04 Catalog example of a hunting coat. *Outdoor Life*, c. 1923. Catalog example of a hunting or cruising coat. *Outdoor Life*, c. 1934.

05 Catalog example of a leisure jacket. Sears, c. 1944.

06 Catalog example of a lumberjack jacket. Montgomery Ward, c. 1925.

07 Catalog example of a mackinaw coat. Montgomery Ward, c. 1941.

08 Catalog example of a motorcycle jacket. Montgomery Ward, c. 1968.

09 Catalog example of a Norfolk jacket. Montgomery Ward, c. 1928.

Overcoat: {10}

A coat extending below the knee constructed of heavy wool to be worn as an outermost garment.

ShirtJac:

A heavy woolen shirt worn over another shirt as a jacket or coat.

Parka or Anorak: {11}

A heavy, knee length jacket with a hood for extreme cold.

Ski Jacket: {13}

A quilted coat or jacket.

Ranch Jacket or Barn Jacket: {12}

A western styled denim or duck jacket that is usually lined.

Slicker or Rain Coat:

A long, water repellent coat originally made of oilskin; a waterproof coat.

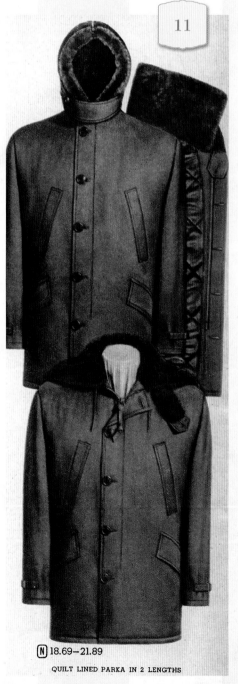

QUILT LINED PARKA IN 2 LENGTHS

Suburban Coat or Stadium Coat: {14}

A lined wool coat ending below the hip or 3/4 length at mid-thigh.

Toggle Coat: {15}

A mid-thigh length coat that has toggles for closure in lieu of buttons or zipper.

Top Coat: {16}

A coat ending above the knee and usually lighter weight fabric than an overcoat.

Trench Coat: {17}

An adaptation of heavyweight, rain resistant coats worn in the trenches during WWI. They usually include shoulder straps, which were added for rank insignia. Veterans loved the coats and wore them in civilian life where they became fashionable for both men and women.

Ulster:

A double breasted overcoat of heavy wool with a wide notched or fur trimmed shawl collar, completely belted or belted back only.

14

15

16

17

10   Catalog example of an overcoat. Montgomery Ward, c. 1935.

11   Catalog example of a parka or anorak jacket. Montgomery Ward, c. 1956.

12   Catalog example of a ranch or barn jacket. Montgomery Ward, c. 1930.

13   Catalog example of a ski jacket. Montgomery Ward, c. 1968.

14   Catalog example of a suburban or stadium coat. Sears, c. 1956.

15   Catalog example of a toggle coat. Montgomery Ward, c. 1968.

16   Catalog example of a topcoat. Sears, c. 1944.

17   Catalog example of a trench coat. Montgomery Ward, c. 1950.

GENUINE LEATHER MEN'S COATS

For BOYS and MEN *Genuine* **LEATHER-TEX**

Horsehide $5⁷⁹
Sheep Leather $4⁸⁹

Catalog example of styles and leather choices for jackets. Montgomery Ward, c. 1932.

{ Decade Overview }

Before the turn of the twentieth century, heavy wool shirts in bold buffalo checks with yokes in the front and back were introduced with sheepskin linings for extra warmth. These were worn over regular work shirts.

After WWI, the functional clothes that the military enlistees had been issued were still quite popular and guys clamored to find them. This desire prompted the birth of Army-Navy surplus stores.

The 1920s introduced leather jackets and coats in either horsehide or cowhide. Most had sheepskin lining for warmth, had button closures, and they ranged from stopping at the waist to being 30" long. These same style coats appeared in suede in the late 1920s.

Guys had discovered the warmth and comfort of leather for winter wear over plain wool outer garments, and an almost century long love affair was started. Perforated leathers and ostrich skin jackets were introduced for milder weather.

By the late 1920s, zip out linings were available in coats and even worn as a separate, collarless coat or vest.

As early as 1933, zipped waist jackets and coats were introduced, and by the late '30s, zipper closures would be common.

WATERPROOF SUEDE CLOTH
Rubber Interlining . . . Fleeced Inside

FLEECE LINING → ← **SUEDE CLOTH**

8 THIN LAYERS of RUBBER

Slide Fastener with Adjustable Cossack Bottom

$3⁴⁹

Button Front with Elastic Bottom

$2⁹⁸

Catalog example of early zippered waist jackets. Montgomery Ward, c. 1933.

$3 89

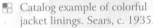
Catalog example of colorful
jacket linings. Sears, c. 1935.

Catalog example of color plaid coats worn during
the Depression. Montgomery Ward, c. 1939.

Catalog example of a letterman's jacket.
Montgomery Ward, c. 1939.

Catalog example of faux belted backs
on jackets. Montgomery Ward, c. 1939.

Not only were bold plaids popular in the '30s, but wild prints
and plaid linings became popular for plain colored outerwear.

Faux belted backs, which had become a style favorite for suit
jackets, crossed over into outerwear.

A wool and leather combination jacket was a new style sensation
in the late '30s. Within a few years, this style would be adopted
by high school and college athletes to sport their school logo or
initial. They would become known as letter jackets.

$4 49

Style Hit of the Season
WOOL WITH LEATHER SLEEVES
- Wool Body for Real Warmth with Fine Cape Leather Sleeves for Extra Strength where Wear is Greatest
- Slide Fastened Breast Pocket—Two Lower Pockets Trimmed with Cape Leather, Neater, Stronger
- Colorfully Striped, Rib Knit Collar, Cuffs and Waistband of about ⅓ Wool Keep Out the Wind

⑤ Easily Worth $4.98 **$3 39** 26 In. Long
⅓ Wool Diagonal Weave

⑥ Strong Leather Trim **$2 69** 25 In. Long
Rubberized Suede Cloth

Full Cut Wind-Proof Sports Jacket

On chilly days you'll need this water-repellent feather weight wind breaker Jacket for golf or any sport. Wind-proof Wamsutta Ski cloth, high count cotton twill usually called Balloon Silk. Action-cut for a full unhampered swing. Front zips full length; button tab at neck. Adjustable side straps. Large chest pockets. "Storm Cuff" elastic sleeve inserts keep wind out. Natural Tan or Navy Blue.

60 C 5952—State color and Chest size: 34, 36, 38, 40, 42, 44. Ship.wt. 1 lb. **$4.95**

Wind Proof jackets appeared and were quickly loved for their lightweight fabric and warmth.

Raglan sleeves, which were used in the '30s, continued to be popular for topcoats. Zip out linings, tall men sizes, and the introduction of a 3/4 length hooded parka were also part of the early war years.

The War Production Board limited the amount of fabric and how it was used in clothing during the war years. There were to be no silk ties, silk scarves, silk socks, or silk linings as silk was to be used for military parachutes. Clothing was even ordered to have fewer pockets, buttons, and buckles. Leather was also on the list, thus making shoe soles thinner and suspenders & garters extremely hard to find. Oddly enough, leather jackets were still sold as winter wear, but not in many styles or overly available supplies.

Post Wartime brought about the first light weight cotton jackets for golfing and other outdoor activities.

Catalog example of an early wind proof sports jacket. Montgomery Ward, c. 1938.

Catalog example of the first light weight cotton jackets. Montgomery Ward, c. 1945.

Catalog example of a two-way coat with zip out lining. Montgomery Ward, c. 1940.

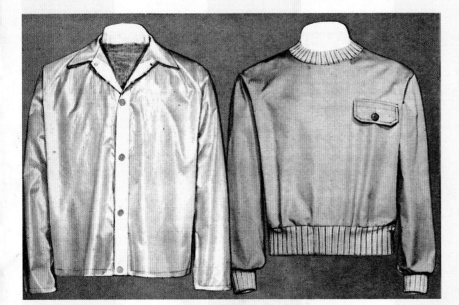

HERCULES fine quality, smartly styled leather Jackets

Reg. U.S. Pat. Off.

Regulation Air Force Jacket	Aviator's type capeskin Jacket	Cossack style capeskin Jacket
$16 50	$13 95	$10 98

■ Catalog example showing WWII jacket lengths. Sears, c. 1944.

■ Catalog example showing leather jacket styles. Montgomery Ward, c. 1949.

Leisure coats, casual coats, wrap-arounds, and loafer coats appeared as a casual style jacket to be worn with a shirt and tie, but for carefree hours. Some crossed over into sports coats to be worn with slacks in place of a suit.

The majority of short jackets hit at the waist or just below in the '40s and '50s, then lengthened to the front hip bend in the early '60s.

The 1948 Bold Look gave more stylish features to coats with large patch pockets, mouton collars, quilted linings, elastic waists, hoods, and placket fronts for hidden zippers.

Shirt Jacs had been introduced about 1940, but didn't gain in popularity until the early 1950s. They are a throwback to earlier decades when guys wore heavy wool shirts over their regular work shirts to keep warm. But, shirt jacs and wool jackets were for anytime wear, not just work.

Horsehide remained number one for leather jackets until the mid-1950s saw its replacement with steerhide for leather jackets and coats.

The mid-1950s also introduced garments of man-made fibers, such as a Nylon jacket with Orlon® fleece lining, Orlon® knit cuffs and waistbands. Short jackets were still popular, whether two-tone, wool or leather, and stadium or car club coats hit the fashion scene in the tweeds and windowpane fabrics.

Long-wearing, lightweight NYLON JACKETS shed wrinkles fast

- Catalog example of '60s windbreakers. Sears, c. 1969.

- Catalog example of early stadium jackets. Montgomery Ward, c. 1949.

A 10.98   B 9.98   C 11.89

E 12.89   F 12.89   G 12.89

ALSO IN
TALL
SIZES
3

A Western influence showed up in shearling lined Ranch jackets with the Presidency of L.B.J.

A word of caution: Foam bonded fabrics were popular in the '60s and '70s. They were used for clothing and shoes. Unfortunately, decades later, the foam usually starts to break down, flake, and become toxic if handled or breathed. There is nothing that can be done to stop this from happening, so please avoid the garments made with foam backed fabric.

◾▫ Catalog example showing the Western
influence of suede and shearling coats.
Sears, c. 1968.

▫◾ Catalog example of foam backed
fabric used for coats. Sears, c. 1962.

Nylon Knits bonded to FOAM

{ Dress Shirts }

{ Overview }

I once saw a 1910 advertisement stating that a gentleman should wear a striped flannel suit, a negligee shirt, and a bat wing tie to be well dressed. Almost sounds like a foreign language, but that was style speak at the time.

By proper definition, a dress shirt always has a collar and long sleeves. They were always laundered, starched and ironed. They were always worn with a suit or sports coat and slacks, and are always sized by neck and sleeve length.

When dating a dress shirt, please use additional label criteria. Even though popular orientation has been noted in the previous chapter, buttonholes have been placed both horizontally and vertically in every decade. Shirts with collar points of an approximate standard 2 7/8" have also been available in every decade.

As to a little background, in the early 1820s, a New York housewife was tired of having to freshly launder a shirt for her husband each morning. So, she simply snipped the collar off the shirt and washed it, then basted it back onto the shirt. Thus started the 100 plus year influence of the detachable collar for men's dress shirts.

📋 Advertisement showing detachable collars.
McClure's Magazine, c. 1902.

📋 Photo of unidentified gentleman wearing an
oversized detachable shirt collar, c. 1900s.

📋 Advertisement for Cluett shirts (pre-Arrow shirts).
*Brotherhood of Locomotive Firemen and Engineers
Magazine*, c. 1899.

In 1854, paper shirt collars were invented by pasting a sheet
of paper between thin muslin and then coating with shellac. This
collar could be wiped clean for days and cost less than laundering
a detachable fabric collar.

Dress shirts actually closed in the back as late as the 1900s, as
did formal shirts until the 1930s. Victorian dress shirts had pleats
in the front like we associate with tuxedo shirts, although they
were for everyday.

Once shirts started buttoning down the front, there were over
400 known distinctly different styles of collars to compliment them
and fit the owner's preference. A collar varied in height from front
to back with the most distinction being the points—which could
be as short as 1" or as long as 5".

By 1900, soft negligee shirts made of lightweight cotton fabric
were a full 36 inches long, about 6 inches longer than a dress shirt,
and usually had a full cut and pearl buttons. Some were a light
plaid or fancy stripe pattern, had detachable collars, and could be
worn for sleep or dress.

Many had attached soft collars and were made in chambray,
linen, percale, oxford, flannel, cotton, or sateen twill and were worn
by the masses for working. They also had vertical buttonholes.

Prior to 1915, the majority of manufactured dress shirts were
made by members of the Associated Shirt Manufacturers or the
Shirt Manufacturers Protective Association. Many of those union
members would become a founding section in ACWA in 1914.

MANY ADVANTAGES.

Perfect in fit, never ragged or uncomfortable. Very convenient, stylish, economical. Made of fine cloth and exactly resemble linen goods. Turn down collars are reversible and give double service.

NO LAUNDRY WORK.

When soiled, discard. **Ten collars or five pairs of cuffs, 25c. By mail, 30c.** Send 6c in stamps for sample collar or pair of cuffs. Name size and style.

REVERSIBLE COLLAR CO., Dept. 10, Boston.

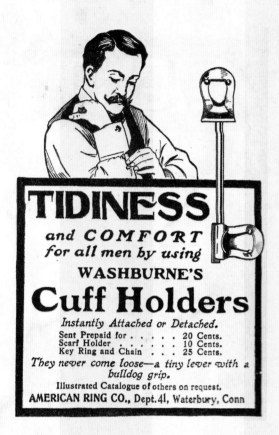
In a 1915 catalog, men's dress shirts were either placketed or unplacketed and had button cuffs or French Cuffs, which could be either attached or detachable.

Cuffs seemed to get dirty from rubbing on tables or from working, while collars got dirty from sweat and body oils.

After WWI, men began buying and wearing silk shirts in whites, colors, and stripes, with detachable collars available to match all of these. The returning Vets who had worn soft collared shirts during the war wanted to give up their stiff collars for comfort. With all the changes the 1920s brought to men and their clothing, the stiff, starched detachable collar vs. the soft attached collar almost brought men to blows.

Photo showing detachable collars, attached collar dress shirts, and a casual soft collar shirt. Shirt collar styles, c. 1920.

Advertisement for cuff holders. Unknown magazine, c. 1910s.

Catalog example of the new collar attached dress shirts. Montgomery Ward, c. 1925.

Collar Attached Dress Shirts

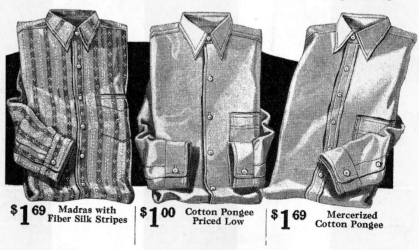

$1 69 Madras with Fiber Silk Stripes | $1 00 Cotton Pongee Priced Low | $1 69 Mercerized Cotton Pongee

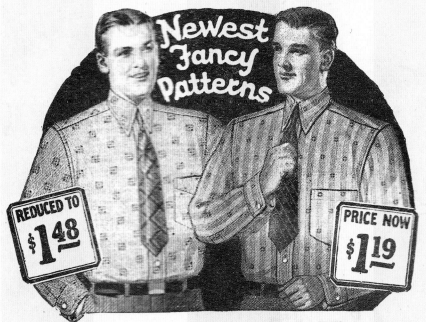

Latest Style Collars Attached—Longer Points

Shirts became available in tall sizes and fancy patterns prevailed.

Attached collar dress shirts outsold detachable collar shirts by the late 1920s. The more popular they became, the more readily available they became. Also came the introduction of the button-down collar, pinned collar, and tab collar. Button-down collars had shorter points to fit snugly over a necktie and not wilt or curl.

Many shirt collars had standard 2" to 2.5" collar points, but there was a fashion move towards longer points of 3" or more. These shirts were favored on college campuses in the late '20s, making long collar points and vertical buttonholes the norm.

Wilt-proof collars were invented to avoid the previous necessity of collar stays to keep the original long collars where they should be and prevent curling.

Catalog example of fancy patterned dress shirts. Montgomery Ward, c. 1928.

Catalog example of dress shirts in tall sizes. Montgomery Ward, c. 1928.

Catalog example of a wilt-proof attached dress shirt collar. Montgomery Ward, c. 1939.

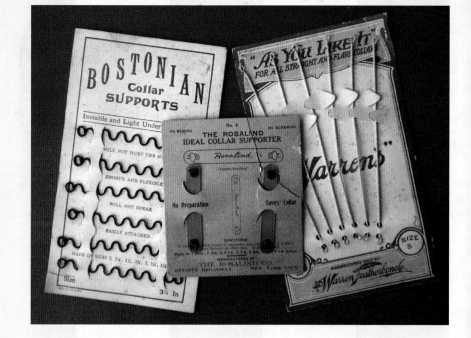

Example of Warren's, Bostonian, and Ideal collar supports for dress shirts, c. 1920s.

Example of side gusset construction, c. 1930s.

Example of two piece shirt sleeve construction, c. 1930s.

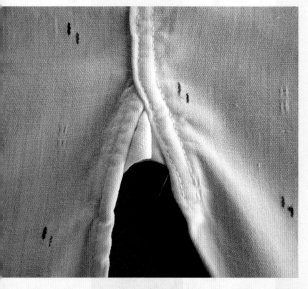

When collars became limp or curled, even when wilt proofed, there was always the collar stay. By the 1950s, stays or plastic bars were sewn into the backside of collars down to the point to keep them straight. Today, collar stays are removable from little pockets on the backside of collars.

Tiny side gussets, where the side seam ended and shirt tails began, ran from the late Victorian era into the early '60s. This was a revival of an idea used on shirts from the pre-1900s to provide an expansion area at a stress point and to prevent ripping.

The Thirties was one of the most fashion influential eras for men's clothing. Shirts were no longer just a garment with a collar and cuffs. They had convertible collars to be worn with or without a necktie; they could be worn tucked in or hanging outside the trousers or shorts; some were belted or had Norfolk backs; they came in all kinds of fabrics that could be shirred, pleated or tucked. Fabrics such as viscose and acetate brought forth the opportunity to print patterns that would stay brilliant. And the half sleeve had evolved enough be become a style staple.

The year 1930 brought the patent for Sanforizing to limit fabric shrinkage, and Zephyr broadcloths to repel liquids and hopefully stains.

There was also a two-piece sleeve construction that showed a seam down the back of the arm as well as under it, which had been used since the late 1800s. This feature was only done on select styles of shirts, and all shirts had gone to a single seam sleeve construction by the 1950s.

Pull over the head negligee shirts had been replaced by coat shirts that completely buttoned down the front.

SH**IRT** SALE!

SNAP CUFF BUTTONS
Are Laundry Proof and Look
Like Fine Cuff Links

WILT-PROOF COLLAR AND CUFFS

- Cotton Broadcloth
- Wards Full Cut Sizes
- All Pre-shrunk
- Pleated Sleeves
- Breast Pocket
- 7-Button Style

ONLY $1 09 **EACH**

Three big features that made them spectacular values at their former price! Smart-looking Wilt-proof Collar, Wilt-proof Cuffs (never need starch, always look neat) .. and Snap-fast Cuff buttons (can't crush, rust or come undone)! Exclusive with Wards!

SIZES: 14, 14½, 15, 15½, 16, 16½, or 17-in. necks. SLEEVE LENGTHS: Short, medium and long. *State size, sleeve length and color wanted.* Ship. wt. each 13 oz.
35 JF 2509—Plain White or vat dyed Blue Broadcloth. Each.....................$1.09
35 JF 2510—Blue or Tan Patterns. Ea. $1.09

Buy these Shirts on Wards Monthly Payment Pl

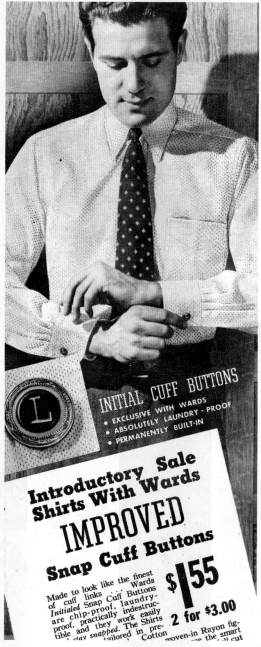

INITIAL CUFF BUTTONS
- EXCLUSIVE WITH WARDS
- ABSOLUTELY LAUNDRY-PROOF
- PERMANENTLY BUILT-IN

Introductory Sale Shirts With Wards IMPROVED Snap Cuff Buttons

$1 55
2 for $3.00

Made to look like the finest of cuff links ... Wards Initialed Snap Cuff Buttons are chip-proof, laundry-proof, practically indestructible and they work easily ... stay snapped. The Shirts ... tailored in pre- ... Cotton ... woven-in Rayon fig- ... the smart ... ll cut

Snap cuffs came out in 1934, some plain and some quite fancy like a pair of cufflinks, but most guys still preferred cufflinks or button cuffs.

Snap Fastener Cuffs
MAKE THESE FINE SHIRTS DISTINCTIVE

AND WARDS GUARANTEE THESE SNAP CUFF LINKS WILL NEVER RUST, CHIP OR TEAR OUT

WHITE

They open at the flick of a finger but stay tightly closed when snapped shut.

Two piece style, made with careful *Jewelers Precision* that guarantees long service.

MACHINE TURNED TO LOOK LIKE FINE JEWELRY

YOUR INITIAL SET IN CHIP-PROOF BLACK ENAMEL

Catalog example of snap cuffs on dress shirts. Montgomery Ward, c. 1934.

Catalog example of snap cuff buttons to replace cufflinks. Montgomery Ward, c. 1937.

Catalog example of snap fastener cuffs to replace cufflinks. Montgomery Ward, c. 1936.

- Smart Stripes
- Deep Tones
- Fancies
- Regular or Button Down Collars

YOU SAVE 30%

A

B   C

**Wards Fine Cotton
BROADCLOTH SHIRTS**

35 C 2943 — TRUBENIZED COLLARS
The collars will never wilt or wrinkle. *Asstd. Patterns:* Blue, Tan or Gray. Sizes and details below at left...$1.29; 2 for.....$2.50

35 C 2945 — BUTTON-DOWN COLLARS
Pearl buttons hold the points down. *Asstd. Patterns:* in Gray, Blue or Tan. Sizes and details below at left..$1.29; 2 for....$2.50

35 C 2958 — BUTTON-DOWN COLLARS   **35 C 2962 — REGULAR SOFT COLLARS**

⌨ Catalog example of dark dress shirts to go with light colored suits. Montgomery Ward, c. 1936.

⌨ Catalog example of dark dress shirts to go with light colored suits. Montgomery Ward, c. 1938.

⌨ Example of *Consumers Union Reports* (now just *Consumers Report*), c. 1940.

Gangster influence made monogrammed dress shirts (monogrammed on the breast towards the waist) popular. Lighter colors also provided a needed contrast for a dark suit, while the introduction and popularity of the light colored Palm Beach® Suit made contrasting dark shirts popular.

Consumers Union® of United States, Inc. was formed to give consumers information and advice on the goods they purchased. Their first booklet appeared in May 1936 and had over 37,000 subscribers by the end of that year. They are now known as *Consumers Report Magazine*®.

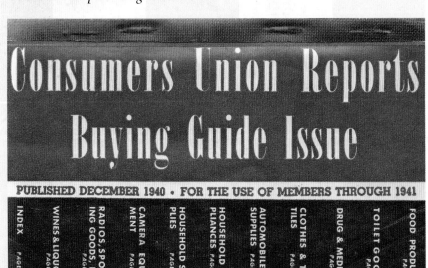

Consumers Union Reports
Buying Guide Issue

PUBLISHED DECEMBER 1940 • FOR THE USE OF MEMBERS THROUGH 1941

INDEX | WINES & LIQUORS PAGE 360 | RADIOS, SPORTING GOODS, ETC. PAGE 320 | CAMERA EQUIPMENT PAGE 305 | HOUSEHOLD SUPPLIES PAGE 258 | HOUSEHOLD APPLIANCES PAGE 226 | AUTOMOBILES & SUPPLIES PAGE 225 | CLOTHES & TEXTILES PAGE 175 | DRUG & MEDICAL PAGE 132 | TOILET GOODS PAGE 89 | FOOD PRODUCTS PAGE 15

MEN'S WHITE BROADCLOTH SHIRTS

Thread count of the material used in a shirt is in general a good indication of quality. The higher the count, the greater the strength is likely to be, and the better the appearance.

Broadcloth is woven with twice as many threads in the warp direction (up and down) as in the filling (across). Usual constructions are 128x68, 135x60, and 144x76 (the first number indicates threads per inch in the warp, the second in the

---

MEN'S SHIRTS 189

filling). Higher counts, found in more expensive shirts, range close to 180x85.

Another factor is the ply of the yarn—that is, the number of individual strands used in each yarn. In broadcloth they are 1x1, 2x1, or 2x2 in warp and filling respectively. 2x2 yarns make high sheen, pliable cloths and are stronger than 2x1 or 1x1 (count being equal). But a 1x1 cloth should prove satisfactory for general wear.

Sanforizing is still the best safeguard against excessive shrinkage. It does not, however, have anything to do with the wearing quality of the shirt.

Unless otherwise noted, the models rated are available with either soft or stiffened collars. Stiffened collars do not wear as well as the soft.

From CU *Reports*, January 1940. (Labor notes included.)

BEST BUYS

Towncraft (J. C. Penney Stores). $1.49. High count. Highest quality tested.

Scottville (Carson-Pirie-Scott & Co., Chicago). $1.65. Soft collar only. High count.

Conway (Marshall Field & Co., Chicago). $1.65. High count.

Wings (Piedmont Shirt Co., Greenville, S. C.). $1.65. Stiffened collar[1] only, of "genuine Aeroplane cloth guaranteed to outwear shirt." High count. Sanforized.

Super Hardwick (Allied Purchasing Corp., NYC). $1.65. High count.

Wanamaker's (John Wanamaker, NYC and Philadelphia). $1.35. Soft collar only. High count. Sanforized.

ALSO ACCEPTABLE

(In approximate order of quality without regard to price)

Frederick & Nelson (Frederick & Nelson, Seattle; div. of Marshall Field). $2. Soft collar only. High count. Sanforized.

Wilson (Wilson Bros., Chicago). $1.95. Soft collar only. High count. Sanforized.

Arrow Dale (Cluett-Peabody Co., NYC). $2.50. Stiffened collar only. High count. Sanforized.

AMC (distrib., Associated Merchandising Corp.[2]). $2. High count. Sanforized.

---

[1] Special collar fabric. [2] See Introduction, page 11.

(Cont'd next page)

MEN'S SHIRTS, SHORTS 191

ALSO ACCEPTABLE—CONT'D

Cameron Long-Life (Cameron & Co.; distrib., The Emporium, San Francisco). $1.69. Stiffened collar only. Medium count.

Arrow New Trump. $2. Soft collar only. Medium count.

Eagleson (Eagleson & Co., San Francisco). $1.65. Stiffened collar only. Medium count.

Emperor (National Dollar Stores, San Francisco). $1. Medium count.

NOT ACCEPTABLE

Wilson Picadilly (Wilson Bros.). $1.39. Medium count. Sanforized. Poor fabric strength.

Cameron Camo-dore (The Emporium). $1.49. Soft collar only. Medium count. Dimensions poor. Generally poor quality.

Needles Fruit of the Loom (Eclipse Needles Co.). $1.65. Stiffened collar[1] only. Medium count. Poor fabric strength.

Manro (New York Hat Stores; available in West only). $1.39. Medium count. Labeled "preshrunk," but shrank excessively.

Example of information for men's white broadcloth shirts from *Consumers Union Reports*, c. 1940.

Continuing example for men's white shirts from *Consumers Union Reports*, c. 1940.

Continuing example for men's white shirts from *Consumers Union Reports*, c. 1940.

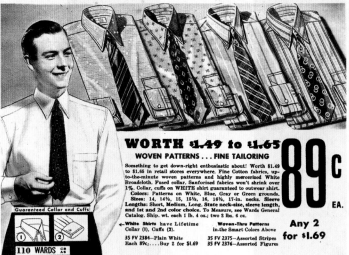

▣ Catalog example of dress shirt prints and woven patterns. Montgomery Ward, c. 1940.

▣ Advertisement showing detachable collars for military officers. Unknown magazine c.1910s.

There was also a movement in the late 1930s towards patterned, satin stripes, and tone-on-tone designs of lighter, sheer, and mesh fabrics for shirts for summer wear.

Wing collars, reaching an amazing 5" by the late '30s, scaled back slightly during the war to conserve fabric, and then lengthened again in the very late '40s. They stayed at about 4" until once again starting to recede around 1952 and reached a normal collar point length of 2.5" around the mid-'50s. Collar point length would keep receding into the mid-'60s and reaching its shortest length since the turn of the twentieth century. During all this lengthening and receding of collar points, standard 2 to 2.5" points were always available.

Rayon dress shirts appeared in 1940 and were quickly embraced because of the need for silk & Nylon for the war effort. Sanforset® was trademarked in 1941 for use on Rayon fabrics.

Detachable collar dress shirts were quite popular with naval officers during WWII. The collars were worn once, turned over, and worn again—then thrown away. The collars always looked fresh and clean and alleviated the need and cost for have a dress shirt laundered every day. Uncle Sam outlawed this practice and made shirts with attached cloth collars part of regulation dress for the Navy by late 1944.

By 1941, buttonholes on men's shirts had shifted to horizontal. After the war, checked material emerged for a "bold look" in men's dress shirts as the white collar workers went back to their jobs. Collars sported a line of bold stitching .5" in from the edge, as did the center placket which became about 2" wide. Buttons were bigger and easier to button. French cuffs were over 2.5" wide to showcase big gold disc cufflinks.

Just after the end of the war, button down collars with a bowtie became the choice for gentlemen of all ages. Many people were still in frugal mode from the Depression and World War II, which caused new ideas to emerge to get the most wear out of their clothing.

Du Pont Nylon

ALDENCREST BUY. REDUCED FROM 6.98! 5.98
Washes easily—dries quickly—needs little or no
ironing! Finest White 100% DuPont nylon—silky,
rich and smooth—outwears several cotton shirts.
1-button interlined cuffs, interlined long point soft
collar with stays. Long tails. Hand washable.
Neck Sizes: 14, 14½, 15, 15½, 16, 16½, 17-in.
Sleeve Sizes: 32, 33, 34, 35-in. State both sizes.
61 B 5533—Shipping weight 1 pound............5.98

Soft Collar Rayon

PINCHECK OR WHITE RAYON SHIRTS 2.98
Regular, interlined soft collar—removable plastic
stays keeps it neat. Rayon woven-through pinchecks.
Colors: Blue, or Maroon pincheck pattern. Hand wash.
Neck Sizes: 14, 14½, 15, 15½, 16, 16½, 17-in.
Sleeve: 32, 33, 34, 35-in. 1-button interlined cuffs.
61 B 5541—Ship. wt. 1 lb. 1 oz................2.98
WHITE RAYON CREPE—All sizes, features above.
61 B 5511—Ship. wt. 1 lb...................2.98

INITIALED SHIRTS—Luxury fabrics, most-popular medium-point collars **2.98** UP
Press-on initial included with each shirt (no X). Be sure to state initial when ordering.
Neck Sizes: 14, 14½, 15, 15½, 16, 16½, 17-in. Sleeve Sizes: 32, 33, 34, 35-in. State both sizes.

Monogrammed shirts remained popular, and it is interesting to note that monograms had moved from the lower chest in the 1930s, to the sleeve in the 1940s, to the pocket in the 1950s. In later decades, the monogram would be seen on a collar or cuff.

Nylon was used for clothing, not just Nylon stockings, after the war. Its popularity would spread past shirts and be used in underwear, socks, and blends for sweaters, slacks, and other garments.

In 1951, Van Heusen® introduced the Van Chick Shirt, which was the first shirt to not have any stitches showing on the collar, cuffs or front.

Wash 'N Wear shirts were introduced with the help of manmade fabrics in the early to mid-1950s. Sanforizing Plus® was invented in 1955 for wash 'n wear fabrics to hold smoothness and aid with crease recovery.

Small print dress shirts, like the print on a Foulard tie, were introduced in 1957. The Continental influence of the same year brought about smaller lapels on sport coats and shorter collar points to go with them.

Buttonhole orientation again shifted to vertical in the last half of the '50s into the early '60s, but horizontal buttonholes were still used. Note the vertical buttonholes on the 1956 shirts.

In 1964 easy care perma-press blends of cotton & synthetic fiber were introduced to replace Sanforizing and wash and wear fabrics. Button down collars and back pleats with little hangers attached at the yoke were "the" shirt of the times in the late '60s.

Once again, we witness extreme collar points in the late '60s and early '70s, which rivaled those of two decades earlier. The year 1971 ushered in the era of knit dress shirts in wild prints and stripes, and brought the mandatory garment care labels that we still find in our clothing today.

A side note concerning detachable collars for dress shirts: In 1862, Reversible Collar company was opened by Geo. K. Snow, who was the inventor of a machine to laminate cardboard and cloth. This was the start of the "Linene®" line of detachable collars. Sometime post WWII, the company became known as the Gibson Lee Collar

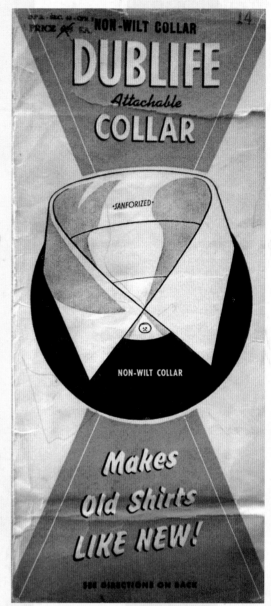

Catalog example of Nylon dress shirts. Aldens, c. 1952.

Example of a replaceable sew on collar to extend the wear of a shirt, c. 1940s.

Catalog example showing shirt buttonhole orientation as vertical. Sears, c. 1956.

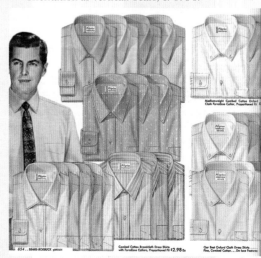

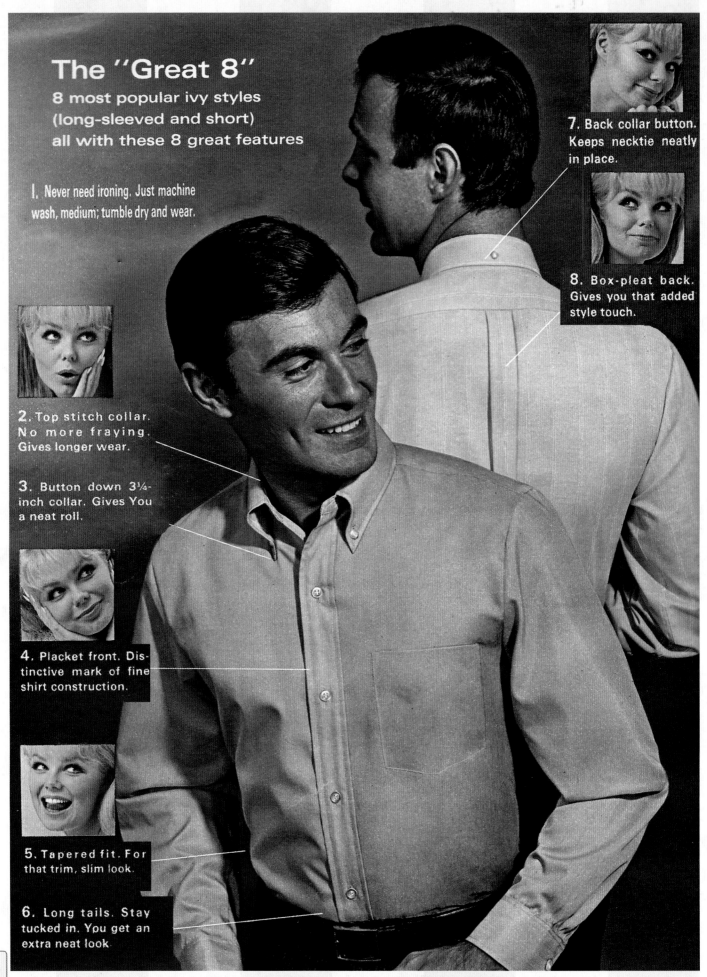

The "Great 8"

**8 most popular ivy styles
(long-sleeved and short)
all with these 8 great features**

1. Never need ironing. Just machine wash, medium; tumble dry and wear.

2. Top stitch collar. No more fraying. Gives longer wear.

3. Button down 3¼-inch collar. Gives You a neat roll.

4. Placket front. Distinctive mark of fine shirt construction.

5. Tapered fit. For that trim, slim look.

6. Long tails. Stay tucked in. Ypu get an extra neat look.

7. Back collar button. Keeps necktie neatly in place.

8. Box-pleat back. Gives you that added style touch.

Catalog example showing button down collars and back pleats on dress shirts. Montgomery Ward, c. 1968.

Pilgrim Neckband Shirt $2.98 each

Fine Sanforized, mercerized combed cotton broadcloth; maximum shrinkage 1%. French cuffs. White. Shpg. wt. each 1 lb. *State neck size, sleeve length from chart below.*

33 G 133G—Shirt..Ea. $2.98; 2 for $5.90; 4 for $11.60

VAN HEUSEN MEDIUM POINT WHITE COLLAR in ¼ sizes 14 to 17¼. *Please state neck size wanted. Postpaid.* (Shipping weight each 1 ounce).

33 G 15—Order today. Collar............Each 65c

Tall, Stout Men's Sizes $3.98 each

Tailored to fit tall or stout men. Combed cotton broadcloth; mercerized, Sanforized. Max. shrinkage 1%. Medium point fused collars. Collars on whites are guaranteed to wear as long as the shirt. *State neck, and sleeve sizes.* Shipping weight each 1 pound 2 ounces.

FOR TALL MEN. Shirt body 3 inches longer. *Neck sizes* 14½, 15, 15½, 16, 16½, 17, 17½ inches. *Sleeve lengths* 35, 36, 37 inches. *State sizes.*

33 G 302G—White
Each shirt.........$3.98
2 for only........ 7.86
4 for only........ 15.50

FOR STOUT MEN. *Neck sizes* 17 inches (53 inches at chest, waist); 17½ (55); 18 (57); 18½ (59); 19 (61). *Sleeve lengths* 33, 34, 35 in. *State sizes when placing order.*

33 G 303G—White
Each shirt.........$3.98
2 for only........ 7.86
4 for only........ 15.50

Also Order Collar

Stout and Tall Men's Sizes

B₂ PAGE 655..MEN'S SHIRTS

Co. This company is still in business (as of 2010) using the same machine that Snow invented, and still sells detachable collars to individuals, movie costumers, and theatre productions.

Victorian reproduction shirts, along with detachable paper collars and cuffs, are also available through Amazon Dry Goods Company.

Detachable collar shirts showed up in catalogs well into the 1950s.

Catalog example showing that detachable collars were still available long after the 1920s. Sears, c. 1956.

{ Shirt Collars }

Band collar:
Found on a shirt with only a band at the neck. Sometimes men wore their dress shirts without the detachable collars; thus, they show like a band collar.

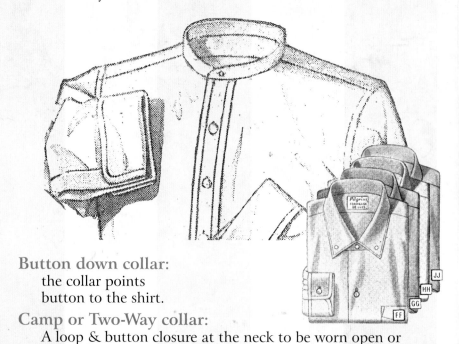

Catalog example of a band collar on a shirt. Montgomery Ward, c. 1928.

Catalog example of a button down collar on a shirt. Sears, c. 1956.

Hang tag example of a two way collar, c. 1950s.

Hang tag backside example of a two way collar, c. 1950s.

Example of a continental collar on a shirt, c. 1950s

Button down collar:
the collar points button to the shirt.

Camp or Two-Way collar:
A loop & button closure at the neck to be worn open or buttoned with a tie.

DOUBLE shirt satisfaction with dress'n'play® because_

COLLAR OPEN... you're set for a game of golf, a drive in the country or a Sunday walk in the park with the family.

CLOSE THE COLLAR, with your favorite Manhattan tie, you're set for the office or wherever the occasion calls for more formal dress.

dress'n'play® the convertible collar designed for both style and comfort

You'll get **DOUBLE** shirt satisfaction with your *Manhattan*® **LONG SLEEVES** dress'n'play® shirt

You'll get **DOUBLE** shirt satisfaction with your *Manhattan*® **LONG SLEEVES** dress'n'play® shirt

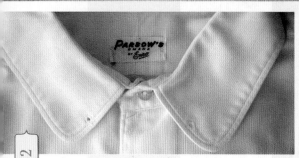

Continental collar:
The points are rounded off.

Pinned collar:

Finished holes on each collar point to accommodate a collar pin or tie bar; these cause a tie knot to be pushed up and out.

Spread collar:

A shirt with the collar points far apart. The spread collar was developed in the 1930s to be worn with a Windsor knotted tie.

Tab collar:

A small snap tab is sewn to the inside seam of the collar at about the height of the top button to hold it together when wearing a tie. It forces the tie knot up and out.

Catalog example of a pinned collar on a shirt.
Sears, c. 1962.

Catalog example of a spread collar on a shirt.
Montgomery Ward, c. 1950.

{ Shirt Pocket Trivia }

Almost every dress shirt pocket is a patch pocket.

A tuxedo or formal shirt will never have a pocket.

A dress shirt with French cuffs should not have a pocket.

A dress shirt with button cuffs can have a pocket.

Casual or work shirts usually have a pocket, or even two pockets, with the pocket being plain or flapped.

Did you know that a single pocket is always placed on the left side of a shirt?

Did you know that dress shirt pockets on vintage garments are usually smaller / narrower than pockets on casual or work shirts?

In the 1930s and '40s, many dress shirt pockets were as narrow as 3", with work shirt pockets being as wide as 5". The pockets were placed high on the chest because of the high waisted pants and trousers that were popular.

Pockets got smaller with the WPB regs on fabric usage during WWII.

By the end of the 1950s, shirt pockets had pretty well settled to standard sizing no matter the style of shirt.

{ Glossary }

Button or barrel cuff:
A band of fabric at the end of a sleeve that is fastened around the wrist with a button. This cuff can be 1 or 2 buttons wide. Some pre-1920s shirts with barrel cuffs needed cufflinks.

Coat shirt:
Nineteenth century term for a shirt that opened all the way down the front.

Collar band:
Where the collar attaches to the shirt.

Collar height:
The height of a folded down collar at the back of the neck.

Collar point:
The very tip of the collar.

Collar point length:
The distance from the collar point to where it attached at the band.

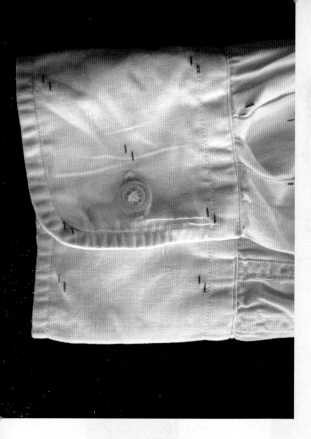

■ Example of a button or barrel cuff of a shirt.

□ How to measure the collar point length on a shirt.

Double cuff:
Also known as a French cuff.

Dress shirt:
A shirt that always has a collar and long sleeves.

French cuff:
An extra wide band of fabric at the end of a shirt sleeve that

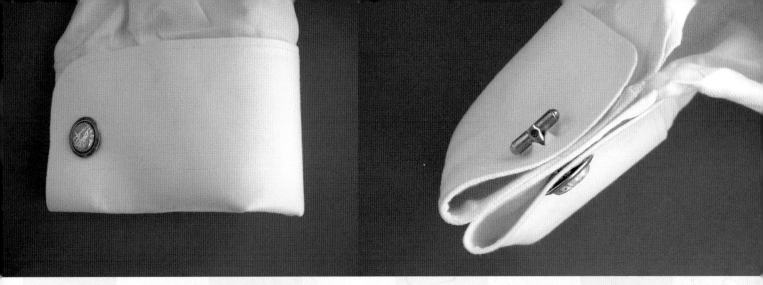

doubles back on itself and is held in place with a cufflink.

Hidden or covered placket:
A fold of fabric that hides the placket.

Negligee shirt:
A utilitarian shirt with a short placket that pulled over the head and had an attached collar and cuffs.

Placket:
The strip of fabric down the shirt front with the buttonholes in it.

Shirt tail:
The finish at the bottom of a shirt—dress shirt tails usually are shorter on the sides.

Spread or collar spread:
Distance between the shirt points at their tips.

Example of a French cuff on a shirt.

Example of a cufflink fitting into a French cuff on a shirt.

Catalog example of a hidden placket and placket on a shirt. Montgomery Ward, c. 1925.

How to measure the collar spread of a shirt.

How to measure the tie space on a shirt.

Tie space:
Distance at the top of a buttoned collar to allow for a tie knot.

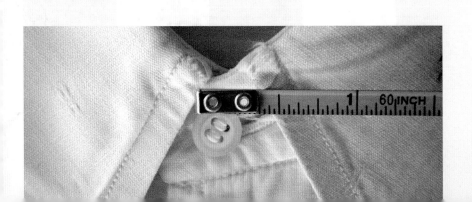

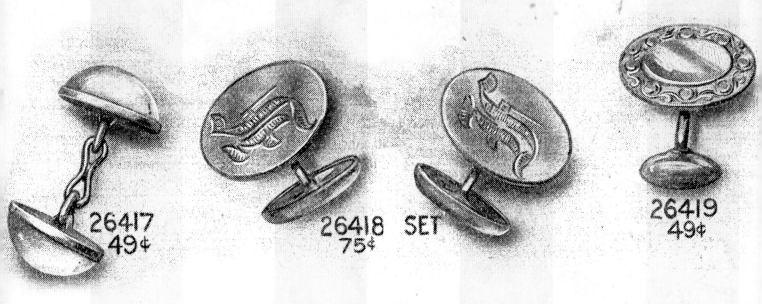

{ Cufflinks }

Cufflinks, worn on French cuffed shirts, have been around since the 1700s.

Cufflinks always come in pairs.

The simplest cufflinks are two buttons connected by a piece of string or a link of chain.

Cufflinks are used as a manly fashion statement and can range from simple metal to precious metal. They may also be set with precious stones.

The flip hinge post we know and still use today was invented in the 1920s.

Angled post cufflinks were a fad when invented in 1948.

A gentleman knows that the term "short-sleeved dress shirt" is an oxymoron.

— John Bridges

Example of button cufflinks, c. 1910s. $5-10.

Example of early swivel back button cufflinks, c. 1910s. $25-35.

Example of sterling button and chain cufflinks, c. 1920s. $25-40.

Example of sterling button cufflinks, c. 1920s. $25-40.

Example of angled post cufflinks, c. 1940s. $5-10.

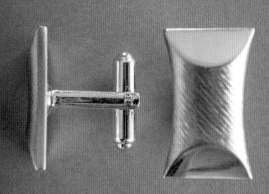

Example of straight post cufflinks, c. 1950s. $5-10.

Example of sterling and turquoise swivel post cufflinks, c. 1940s. $100-125.

Example of straight post cufflinks and matching button studs for tuxedo shirt, c. 1950s. $5-10.

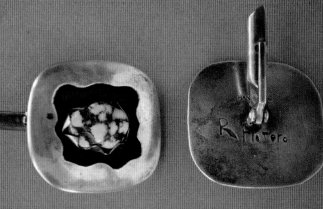

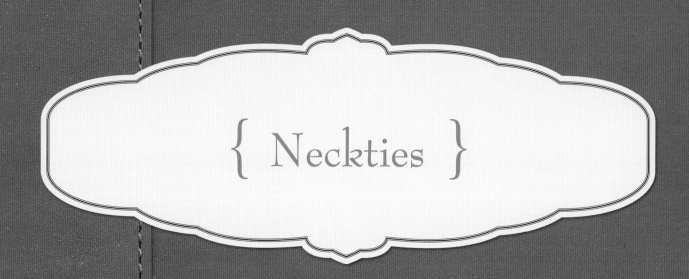

{ Neckties }

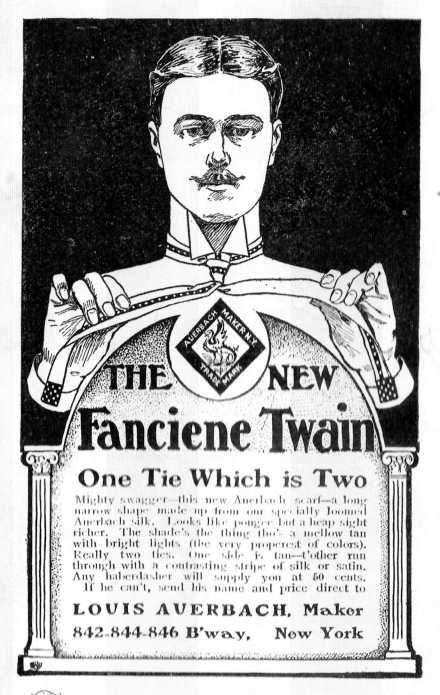

Collage of necktie labels, c. 1940s & 1950s.

Fat ties, skinny ties, loud print ties, subtle ties, Foulard ties, reversible fabric ties, hand-painted ties, screen printed ties, four-in-hand ties, bow ties, knit ties, square bottom ties, scarf ties, bolo ties, Western ties, clip on ties ... and the list goes on.

You see a big fat 5" wide tie and immediately think of the 1970s. You might think of wide ties from the late '30s into the early '50s, even though they almost never reached over 4" in width at that time.

You see a skinny 2" tie and think of the late '50s to early '60s beatnik or rockabilly era. But, they were also worn in the late '20s, and made an appearance in the '80s.

Neckties are usually the easiest vintage items to find, can be extremely affordable, don't take up much room to store, and become a quick and easy way to add a pop of color to your outfit or show a bit of individualism.

Postage, each, 1¢ extra

25¢ Ready Made Bow Ties 25¢

Good looking silk mixed Bow Ties, neatly made up. Elastic band with fastener. Bow ties are popular for wear with collar attached shirts.
COLORS: Plain black or fancy designs on navy blue, brown, green, purple or black. State color wanted.
35 B 355......25¢
Postage, 1¢ extra

Shield Bow Ties in fancy silk mixtures. Wire fastener hooks on collar button. This practical tie is very neat and of good quality.
COLORS: Figured design on navy blue, green, brown, purple, or black, also all black. State color wanted.
35 B 352......25¢
Postage, 1¢ extra

Teck Ties Adjustable Neck Band

45¢ Many men prefer ready made Ties because they can be put on so easily and quickly. This silk mixed Teck Tie is neatly made and with its attractive figured designs is very good looking. Easily adjusted. Priced low for such good quality.
COLORS: Figured designs on navy blue, purple, green, brown or black; also all black.
State color wanted.
35 B 346..............45¢
Postage, 1¢ extra

Silk Mixed Teck Ties With Shield

39¢ A very good value in Teck Ties. Well made of silk mixed material in pleasing patterns. Hooks securely on collar button, the wings fitting under the collar to keep tie in place. A tie that looks well and saves you the trouble of tying and untying.
COLORS: Floral and figured designs on navy blue, brown, purple, green or black; also all black.
State color wanted.
35 B 348..............39¢
Postage, 1¢ extra

$2.39

A New Style "Sportscloth" Shirt

One of the season's newest shirting materials—sportscloth—was used to make this good looking Shirt for men. Sportscloth is a fine, mercerized cotton shirting, with a soft, pleasing finish closely resembling light weight serge. Very rich in appearance and launders splendidly.
The shirt is made in coat style, and has a comfortable attached collar. Carefully finished throughout, with center plait front, buttoned cuffs and one neat pocket with a button-down flap. Through a very special purchase of these fine shirts, we are able to offer them to you at a remarkably low price. Order one today—when you see how fine it looks and feel its good quality you will want to get several more. Medium or long sleeve lengths.
HALF SIZES: 14 to 17.
State size wanted.
35 B 597—Cream White.
35 B 598—Blue.
35 B 599—Tan.
Each..............$2.39
Postage, each, 4¢ extra

Catalog example showing clip on ties. Montgomery Ward, c. 1925.

Catalog example showing how short ties were worn. Montgomery Ward, c. 1925.

Catalog example showing knit neckties. Montgomery Ward, c. 1925.

You don't even have to know how to tie a necktie, because ready-to-wear ties have been available for almost one hundred years.

Ties through the 1950s ended high above the waist and generally were tucked behind a vest or sweater neck, so ties didn't need to be longer than necessary.

In the 1920s, square bottom knitted ties cashed in on the knitting popularity of the era. Also shown are both a necktie of a sturdy open weave mesh and a loomed tie with unfinished edge from the '20s. Rose, taupe, and beige were preferred colors, and a broad knitted tie was a fashion staple in the '20s. Silks were ever popular with added silver or gold threads. Whether sedate or colorful, polka dots and stripes ruled over popular plain color or tone on tone ties.

Special Values in Attractive Neckwear

| Fiber Silk **49¢** Solid Colors | New Color **48¢** Combinations | Fiber Silk **39¢** Neat Stripes | Look Well **39¢** Wear Well | Heavy Weight **55¢** Pure Fiber Silk | Pure Silk **$1.00** Newest Colors |

Bow ties came in lengths of 30", 31", and 32", and mainly had to be tied by the wearer, although there were ready tied bow ties on adjustable elastic bands available.

In the '30s, neckties ranged from 2.5" to 5" wide and when tied were to end about 2/3 of the way between the top of the collar and the belt. For the most part, Rayon and silk were popular fabrics.

Woven wool ties and square end ties remained popular, washable ties appeared, and bar tacking helped eliminate loose stitching that unraveled—although many of the tie makers didn't use bar tacking. Colors in shades of browns, golds, blues, greens, and dull reds reflected the weariness of the Depression. A style trend of ties with matching socks emerged, polka dots from the 1920s got bigger on ties, and bow ties became more popular than ever.

Example of necktie blade in an open mesh weave, c. 1920s.

Example of mesh weave, loom weave, and knit neckties, c. 1920s.

Colors and patterns of neckties, c. late 1920s, early 1930s.

Catalog example of patterns for Rayon neckties. Montgomery Ward, c. 1935.

EXTRA VALUE 19c 3 for 55c

Fall Stripes—Figures
ALL RAYON

You'll be surprised at these values . . . at their quality, their good looking patterns and bright fall colors.
They're excellent for any occasion. All are of dull luster Rayon . . . the kind that ties into a small, smart looking knot. Good construction—they'll hold their shape remarkably well. Good weight, regular length and full shaped. Patterns like or similar to those shown. Don't fail to order a supply . . . each one we send will be different.
Colors: Grounds of blue, brown or maroon. State color choice.
35 ND 1776—Neat figures.
35 ND 1777—Contrasting stripes.
35 ND 1778—All-over patterns.
Each......................19c
Three for.................55c

HAND FINISHED 33c 3 for 95c

New—Better Quality
RAYON and SILK

Dull luster Rayon with small amount Silk . . . all hand made for shape-holding, resilient construction. Full cut, open at both ends, regular length, good weight, and all around finer quality. You'll be proud of every one. Wide assortment of patterns or plain colors.
Pattern Colors: Blue, maroon or brown. Plain Colors: Royal blue, navy blue, maroon, brown or black. State color choice. Ship. wt. each 3 oz.
35 ND 1779—Neat figures.
35 ND 1780—All-over patterns.
35 ND 1781—Fancy stripes.
35 ND 1782—Plain colors.
Each......................33c
Three for.................95c

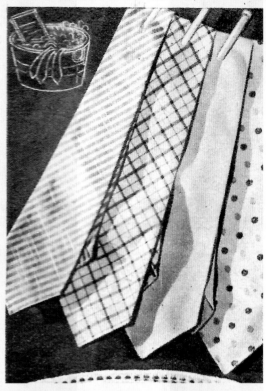

- Catalog example of patterns for washable neckties. Montgomery Ward, c. 1935.

- Catalog example of washable neckties. Montgomery Ward, c. 1937.

- Catalog example of colors and patterns for neckties. Montgomery Ward, c. 1938.

- Catalog example of colors and patterns for neckties. Sears, c. 1939.

- Example of woven plaid neckties, c. late 1930s. $5-10 each.

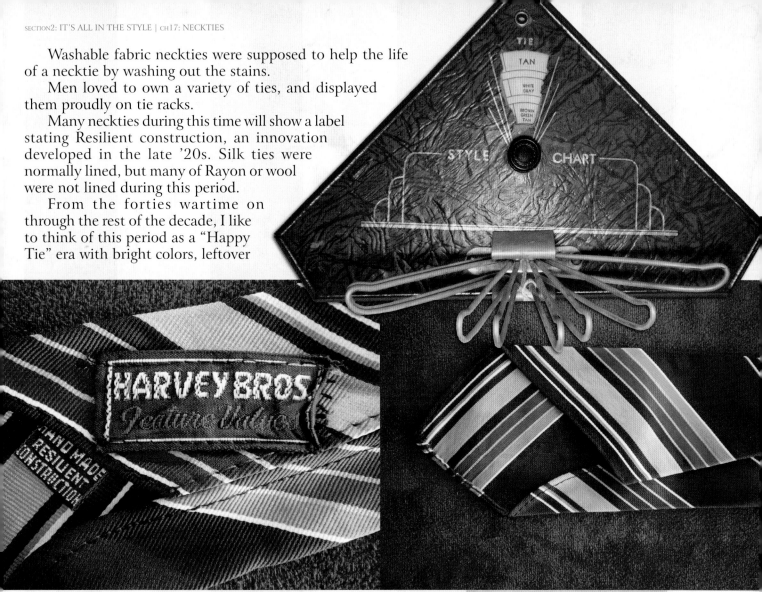

Washable fabric neckties were supposed to help the life of a necktie by washing out the stains.

Men loved to own a variety of ties, and displayed them proudly on tie racks.

Many neckties during this time will show a label stating Resilient construction, an innovation developed in the late '20s. Silk ties were normally lined, but many of Rayon or wool were not lined during this period.

From the forties wartime on through the rest of the decade, I like to think of this period as a "Happy Tie" era with bright colors, leftover

Art Deco styling, the up and coming Atomic patterned fabrics, and those marvelous hand painted and Hawaiian ties from the last half of the decade. Widths ranged from 3" wide to 5" wide, worn just little longer while the pants were worn higher on the waist, and linings were added.

Silk was used for parachutes in WWII, so companies relied on Rayon or wrinkle-free wool for neckties. It is interesting to note that maroon, wine, berry, burgundy, or other darker shades of red were prevalent in the 1940s with bright red only being used as an accent with other colors. What we consider "bright red", "cherry red", "fire engine red" or similar named reds did not appear as a background color until well into the 1950s.

◻ Example of Art Deco style tie rack, c. 1930s. Unknown value. *Courtesy of Cathy Mong.*

◻ Label showing resilient construction in a necktie, c. late 1930s.

◻ Example of unlined necktie construction, c. late 1930s and early 1940s.

◻ Catalog example showing colorful oversized patterns and the widening of neckties. Sears, c. 1944.

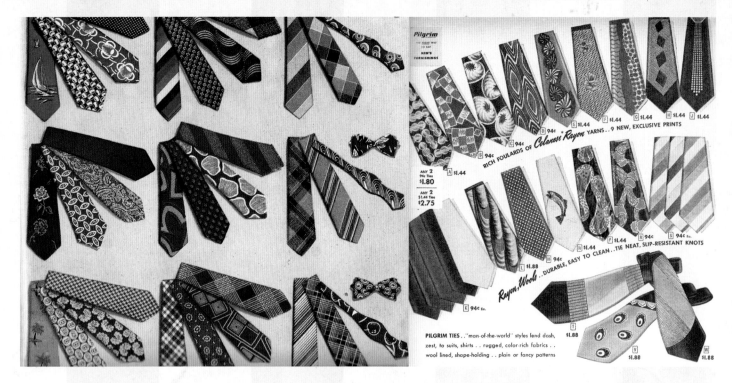

■□ Catalog example showing colorful ties, which are standard width. Montgomery Ward, c. 1945.

■□ Catalog example of wide ties with bold patterns. Sears, c. 1949.

After the war, putting on a bright colored tie lifted the spirits of the veterans returning home to their office jobs, lodge meetings, and churches. Any occasion could call for a fanciful necktie. In the late 1940s, screen printing added a new dimension to ties and quickly gained popularity for flamboyant styling. Peek-a-Boo ties appeared.

The 1950s continued with what had been done stylishly in the late forties until a big change came in the middle of the decade. As jacket lapels got skinnier, ties followed the trend. At that time, a well-dressed gentleman always wore a tie the same width as his jacket lapel. But, remember that 3" to 4" jacket lapels and ties were still offered along with the skinny trend.

Red and pink became popular colors for fifties neckties, which you wouldn't have seen in earlier years. The year 1956 reintroduced wash and wear all cotton neckwear, and ties were an average of 2 3/8" wide. The mid-'50s also presented ties of Dacron knits to prevent wrinkles.

In the late '50s and into the early '60s, neckties got as skinny as 1" and then widened as the sixties progressed. The year 1959 gave tie makers Scotchgarding to allow stains to be washed out with water.

The very late 1960s and into the '70s showed the return of the 5" wide tie, but in heavier fabrics and polyesters, and in wilder prints and bolder colors than had been seen before to be worn with wide lapel suits, and worn with wide brim hats and wide toed shoes of the day.

One of the best ways for dating neckties is the overall length:

1930s ties are approximately 44" long

1940s ties are approximately 47" long

1950s ties are approximately 51" long

1970s ties are approximately 55" long

1990s ties are approximately 58" long

To obtain the **overall length** of a necktie, measure from point to point.

To obtain the **overall width** of a necktie, measure at the widest spot just above the point of the blade.

If you use label dating clues along with length, width, color(s), and pattern, the job of dating vintage neckties should be much easier.

{ A Few Notes about Neckties }

A standard width of three to four inches for neckties has been available to match the standard lapel of the same width in every decade from the 1920s to today.

Clip on ties have been available since the late 1800s.

Bow ties that you actually tie have always been available in varying widths, so cannot easily be dated. Some clip on bow ties can be dated by the clips.

From the turn of the twentieth century to the 1930s, both men and women wore neckties.

Neckties were referred to as cravats until well into the 1950s, with some manufacturing companies retaining that term as part of their name.

At the height of the tie craze of the forties following WWII, there were over 600 manufacturers creating enough ties to sell over 200 million a year.

To be a well dressed gentleman, the rule was the width of the tie should match the width of the lapel on the suit with which it is worn.

■ How to measure the length of a necktie to determine age.

■ How to measure the width of a necktie.

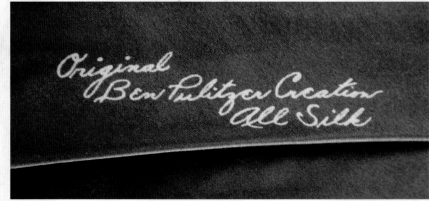

Be sure to check the back side of the necktie, not only for a label, but for screen printed information such as maker, hand painted notation, style, fabric, etc.

Also, sometimes a signature is hidden or incorporated in the design on the front.

Example of company maker's name screen printed on the back of a necktie.

Example of company maker and fabric screen printed on the back of a necktie.

Example of the pattern name screen printed on the back of a necktie.

Example of fabric and company screen printed on the back of a necktie. *Courtesy of Cathy Mong.*

Example of designer's name screen printed on the front of a necktie.

{ Tie Terminology }

Blade:
The pointed ends of a long tie.

Bow Tie:
A type of necktie consisting of a narrow strip of fabric which is tied symmetrically so that the opposite ends form loops. Bow ties usually have an adjustment for neck size to allow enough fabric to tie them properly. Bow ties also come in the clip-on variety.

Clip-on tie:
A bow tie or a long tie that clips onto the shirt collar while looking as if it has been actually tied.

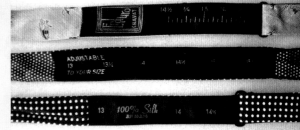

Example of two clip-on bow tie shapes, c. 1950s. $1-5 each.

Example of bow tie shapes, c. 1940s.

Example of how bow ties are adjustable to fit any neck size.

Example of bow tie and long tie clips, c. 1950s.

■ Example of hand embroidered bird and flower necktie, c. 1940s. *Courtesy of Cathy Mong.*

■ Example of hand embroidered floral necktie, c. 1940s. *Courtesy of Cathy Mong.*

■ Example of foulard patterned neckties, c. 1920s.

■ Example of hand painted neckties, c. 1940s.

Cravat:
Term for a necktie which started in the mid-1600s.

Embroidered Tie:
A tie that is decorated with a needle and thread design done by machine to resemble hand work.

Foulard design:
A symmetrical repeating pattern, often with geometrical shapes.

Four-in-hand:
A common knot used for tying a necktie.

Hand Painted Tie:
A tie with designs created with an airbrush, by dry-brushing, or actually painted.

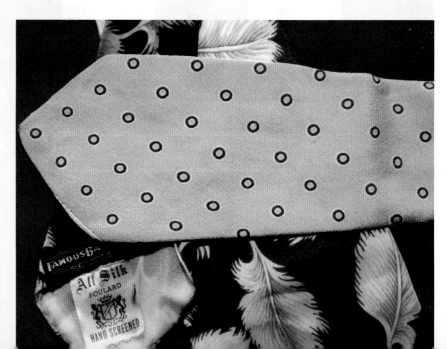

Jacquard Weave Tie:
A tie made of fabric that has a pattern woven into the fabric.

Long Tie:
A long piece of cloth that is placed under the shirt collar and tied into a specific knot at the tie space.

Narrative Tie:
Ties that tell of an interest, occupation, or show outdoor scenery.

Panel Tie:
Ties cut from printed fabric so that the design falls in the same area on each tie that is made.

Peek-a-boo Tie:
Nude or scantily clad images of women printed on a ties interior lining.

Sailors Knot:
A slip knot used by sailors to tie their neckcloths; adapted for tying a long tie at the turn of the twentieth century.

Screen Printed:
A process for printing a pattern on fabric using a stencil for the design.

Slip Knot:
The most common knot for tying a long tie; the knot is adjusted by sliding.

Western Tie:
Considered anything from a bolo to a string tie to a clip on that is worn with a western outfit.

Example of jacquard weave neckties, c. 1930s.

Example of jacquard weave necktie showing backside, c. 1930s.

Example of screen printed neckties, c. 1940s.

Example of embellished western tie, c. 1960s. $10-15 each.

Example of western tie with huge "knot" and 6" blades, c. 1970s. $5-10.

{ Necktie Construction }

In the late 1920s, bias cut woolen cloth was introduced as resilient construction to improve the stability and stop twisting.

From the 1930s through the 1960s and possibly into the 1970s, ties were made in two pieces. From the early 1970s on, neckties have been made in three pieces with a small section and seams occurring at the back of the neck when worn.

{ Tie Clips }

Tie clips and tie tacks are used to keep a necktie in a vertical line with the body and in its proper place. In the early decades, tie clips were small, about one inch, and clipped the edge of the tie and the shirt placket together. They elongated with time and reached two to three inches by the early 1950s to fit the wide ties that were being worn.

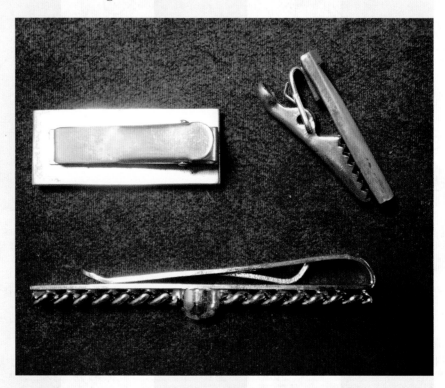

Tie tacks are needle-like and push completely through the necktie and shirt placket then are affixed in place with a backing. Unfortunately, they leave holes behind, especially in silk fabrics, so once a tie tack has been worn, you must always wear one and make sure to put it in the exact same place.

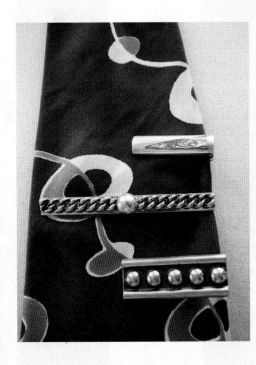

■□ Example of how tie clips fasten and
have lengthened through the years,
c. 1930s to 1950s. $5-10 each.

□■ Example of tie clip lengths,
c. 1930s to 1950s. $5-10 each.

{ Sports Coats and Suit Jackets }

{ Why Men Wear Black }

"Men wear black from custom, ignorance, indifference. Because other men do. Because it fogs in London. Because they don't know any better.

There are only four types to which black is becoming: rogues, fat men, undertakers, those bowed down with grief or disaster. Shall we take our choice?

Black is diminishing, depressing, forbidding, aging and—expensive. It makes a man look old, small, bilious, unfortunate, and either wicked or pious, says Edmund Russell in *Good Housekeeping*.

Watch two men going down the street—one in light overcoat and the other in black. Which of them will you have the impulse to want to know? Your interest and liking will all go out to the one in light clothes, unless for other overpowering differences. Even in business transactions you are more likely to win if you wear a light suit."

...an anonymous commentary from
McCalls Magazine, Dec. 1910

Display photo of two nattily dressed gentlemen. *True Romance*, c. 1923.

A sports coat is not just a suit jacket worn with odd slacks, although that's how it originally got its start.

Back at the turn of the twentieth century, most businessmen who wore a suit to work tried to make the most of what they had. They used the mix-and-match method to create different looks, moving away from wearing the same two suits daily, or in case one piece had to be cleaned. And, of course, a dark suit coat or blazer paired with white linen or flannel trousers in the summer was the "uniform" of choice that most men preferred.

The idea for a sports coat more than likely came in the early 1920s with suits made to be worn with a non-matching pair of plus fours to play golf.

By the 1930s, sports coats had come into their own and were colorful, bold plaids or tweeds, or colorful stripes to contrast plain trousers.

By the late 1950s, the summer uniform of a blue blazer and white pants remained as popular as it had been every decade since before the turn of the twentieth century. The white slacks would be replaced in the 1960s or '70s with khakis.

Please note that a man's sports coat or suit jacket will always button left over right—with the left side having the buttonholes and the right side having the buttons.

Before we really get started on this subject, I need to say that you can not always judge the age of a sports coat or suit jacket by the width of its lapel. A notch lapel will always set the standard for lapel width. In all decades from the teens on, a standard lapel width of 2.75" to 3" has been available even though style might have dictated them as skinny as 1" to as wide as 5.5 to 6". So, again, I have to stress using other criteria available for accuracy in dating.

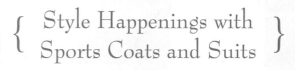

{ Style Happenings with Sports Coats and Suits }

The early 1900s showed men's suits with skinny legged trousers, and high buttoning jackets with no vest, patch pockets, and that landed at the leg bend of the lap.

INSERT PHOTOS 02-268 NEAR ABOVE PARAGRAPH

Just after WWI, jackets had longer styling with the hemline reaching fully to the fingertips, oversized patch pockets were still popular, and suits were always worn with a vest. The shoulders fit naturally with no padding, and the buttons were set high upon the chest to match the trousers' high waist.

Suit jacket pockets had been flapless until the Prince of Wales decided in 1921 to revert to an earlier style and have flaps added to the lower pockets of his suits. Although not the first to do this, his wearing flapped pockets sanctioned it for all.

Advertisement for Peck stylish clothing. *McClure's Magazine*, c. 1902.

By the early to mid-1920s, jacket lengths had shortened, the back vents omitted, lapels widened, and tapered waists remained high fitting. Jackets became fuller fitting in the late '20s, but would revert back to more fitted styling in the '30s.

The peak lapel on jackets, suits, overcoats, and tuxes was introduced and caused lapels to widen. Note that a peak lapel should only appear with double breasted styling. After being introduced a decade earlier, four button double breasted peak lapel suits gained popularity.

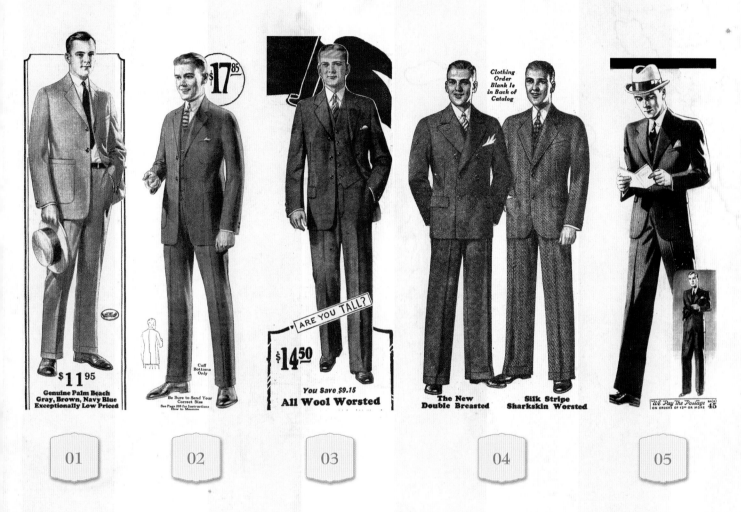

In the early 1930s, jackets were modified to create the illusion of an athletic torso. Shoulder pads were added to jackets for a square and widened silhouette to make a man appear larger and more muscular. Armholes were raised for a better fit and ease of movement, while sleeves that tapered to the wrist and peaked lapels made the chest look broader. The new style was shown with a more fitted waist and no back vent.

01 Catalog example of high waisted trousers. Montgomery Ward, c. 1925.

02 Catalog example of skinny trousers legs. Montgomery Ward, c. 1925.

03 Catalog example of three piece suit with widened lapels. Montgomery Ward, c. 1927.

04 Catalog example of the newly introduced and popular peak lapel on a jacket. Sears, c. 1929.

05 Catalog example that showed single breasted suits were still popular. Montgomery Ward, c. 1933.

Two trouser suits, which had started in the '20s, appeared to give the buyer more choices for wearing, as well as value during the Depression years.

Faux belted backs, a style borrowed from the Norfolk jacket, were also extremely popular for sports coats and suit jackets, but also extended to work jackets.

The Spencer jacket for formal wear was introduced in the mid-1930s. The first examples were white, cut short to the waist, and worn with black trousers having no back pockets. White dinner jackets were introduced at this same time.

Catalog example of broader shoulders and more fitted waist on suits. Montgomery Ward, c. 1935.

Catalog example of suit jacket with fitted waist. Montgomery Ward, c. 1939.

Catalog example of Depression era suit with two pairs of trousers. Montgomery Ward, c. 1933.

A New Spring Style – yet

SALE PRICED $11 65

$9 95 Your Choice

70₂ SEARS-ROEBUCK

Style AT A BARGAIN!

Your choice of All Wool Cassimere in the latest sport back models similar to style illustrated or All Wool Cheviot or Cassimere in our popular Hollywood model like the one pictured. Some of the Hollywoods have reversible vests. Colors are dark blue, gray or brown. We can't guarantee to furnish any particular color, but will send you one of the best looking, best wearing suits your money ever bought. Remember, we guarantee to please you.

SIZES: 34 to 42 in. chest; 29 to 39 in. waist; 29 to 35 in. inseam. State measurements; also age, height and weight. Shipping wt., 5 lbs. 7 oz.

45 W 17187
Sport Back Style 3
Piece Suit.....$9.95
45 W 17159
Hollywood Style 3
Piece Suit.....$9.95

The tradition of bygone eras for a different outfit for every task or occasion each day was replaced by more simplistic multi-task garments.

The loss of, or lack of, money required high style at more moderate prices. This forced American tailors to come up with their own inspirations and ingenious ways to achieve high style rather than to copy the Europeans.

Sanford-Goodall introduced the "Palm Beach" suit in the 1930s. It was designed with a Windsor lapel, either single or double breasted, and made of cotton seersucker, silk shantung, or linen.

Catalog example of broad shoulders and faux belted back on suit jacket. Montgomery Ward, c. 1935.

Catalog example of faux belted back on suit jacket. Sears, c. 1936.

Advertisement showing the Palm Beach suit. Unknown magazine, c. mid-1930s.

SETTING THE PACE

THE NEW PALM BEACH SUITS

Catalog example showing the introduction of sports coats to wear with coordinating trousers. Montgomery Ward, c. 1941.

■□ Catalog example of trousers and matching jacket set. Montgomery Ward, c. 1935.

□■ Catalog example of trousers and matching jacket set. Montgomery Ward, c. 1939.

Men's Corduroy Jacket or Slacks $2⁹⁸ EACH

For style and durability he'll want Corduroy—in either Navy blue or leather brown. JACKET—Cossack style with easy slide fastener front. Adjustable tabs on cuffs of sleeves and waist. Two slash pockets. Has smartly tailored back with three pleats for perfect fit. TROUSERS—Three-button high waistband style with 22-in. cuff bottoms. Side buckles and straps. The complete outfit makes a splendid gift because it's so practical. Thickset Corduroy.

Colors: Navy blue or leather brown. State size and color. Ship. wt. 3 lbs. each.
39 ND 1974—Jacket—32 to 40-in. chest..$2.98
39 ND 2051—Trousers. Sizes: 28 to 36-in. waist; 28 to 34-in. inseam.................$2.98
39 ND 1500—Jacket and Trousers.......5.89

2-Pc. Bush Coat Outfit
Bush Jacket — Trousers — 2-Pc. Outfit
$2⁸⁸ — $1⁹⁸ — $4⁷⁷

Colors shown match the actual colors of the Merchandise as closely as is possible with modern printing methods.

The year 1938 ushered in leather patches on the shoulders and elbows of jackets as a style. Patch pockets were shown on the dressiest of suits, even though flapped pockets were supposed to be the epitome of style.

Specifically constructed jackets and sport coats for wearing with coordinating slacks hit the style scene in the late 1930s. Made in different fabrics and styles than the normal suit jacket, they offered a fresh, new look to the businessman's wardrobe. They were still broad shouldered, with wide lapels, a fitted waist, and high buttoning for high waisted pants.

Pants and matching jacket sets formed a new kind of suit with a more casual look in the mid-'30s and continued in popularity into the war years.

Zoot suits of the late '30s and early '40s showed a different kind of flare than the usual suit. Their jackets featured large shoulders with as much as 6" of padding, a coat that was almost to the knees with a tapered waistband and wide lapels. This was paired with overly baggy, low crotch trousers that the legs tapered to very skinny at the ankle and a 3" wide waistband.

Consumers Union Reports Buyers Guide for 1940 had an interesting page about men's suits.

During WWII, the War Production Board not only limited style basics for clothing to conserve fabric, like trouser bottom circumference, inseams, no cuffs, no pleats, no tucks or overlapping waistbands, but also limited wool usage. Jackets sported a 24" overall length when they had been 30" only a few years earlier.

The majority of suits came with a matching vest until WPB regulations during WWII. Although three-piece suits returned after the war, they really didn't become a style staple again until the 1970s.

Double breasted suits were available in limited amounts, but now were made without a vest or second pair of trousers. Single breasted suits became the norm. Suit coat and overcoat lengths were shortened; cuffs disappeared and ankle widths were limited to 18.5" in circumference; patch pockets and front pleats disappeared. And, the more pronounced Athletic Cut jackets, which reduced fabric with their fitted waists, became popular.

Until the end of 1941, twenty-five million suits were produced in the U.S. annually. Then, suddenly, men were urged not to buy new clothes as it was thought that Uncle Sam might soon be providing them with khaki uniforms. This is somewhat of a misconception as many military officers and even enlisted men supplied their own clothing throughout the war. Clothing manufacturing facilities were switched to accommodate military clothing contracts.

As the war progressed, with so many men away from home, wives took their husbands' suits and cut them into warm suits for themselves or their children. The government even printed and distributed pamphlets instructing how to accomplish this.

For families of non-fighting or returning servicemen, the government encouraged economy and published "how to" booklets explaining how to re-use and / or save. The one below shows how to mend suits, while others told how to buy certain clothing items, how to make over knitwear, make-overs from coats and suits, and make-overs from leather, fur, and felt.

The regulations and restrictions were abandoned at the end of the war and fashion once again came into focus. While women's clothing designers dubbed their clothing "New Look", *Esquire Magazine* named the time following the war for menswear fashion "The Bold Look".

In the late '40s, lapels were basically 4" wide, narrowing to 3" by the mid-'50s, and then narrowing further to a mere 2" or less in the late '50s and early '60s.

Bold plaids for shirts, jackets, and sports coats appeared, ties got wider and more brightly colored, previously undesired colors for menswear began to appear, and two-tone clothing became more popular than ever.

With the trend towards more casual attire, many men opted for a single breasted sports coat and slacks rather than a suit for dress occasions or business. The less dressy appearance took on a life of its own after the war with bolder styles of two-tone combinations, and edgier plaid and tweed fabrics.

198   MEN'S SUMMER SUITS, SUSPENDERS

MEN'S SUMMER SUITS

The following summary is based on examinations and tests of a number of fabrics of many different types.

Tropical Worsteds. The best all-round fabric for Summer suits is still a good grade of tropical worsted, weighing about nine ounces per linear yard 58 inches wide, and made of fairly tightly twisted yarns. Such fabric suiting is light in weight and porous in structure, has adequate strength, and does not become clammy since it can absorb considerable quantities of perspiration without feeling damp. It holds its press and is by nature wrinkle-resistant.

Worsted and Mohair Tropicals. Worsted and mohair tropicals are generally the same in construction as the all-worsted fabrics, but they are slightly harsher to the touch.

"Palm Beach" Fabrics. "Palm Beach" cloth and similar fabrics follow tropical worsteds and mohair tropicals. "Palm Beach" cloth is a lightweight cloth of cotton and mohair, harsh to the touch; it retains its crease fairly well because of the presence of the mohair.

Rayon Fabrics. Crush-resistant spun rayons and rayon blends include "Rivercool," "Rivercrest," "Salyna," "Congo Cloth," "Cool-Long," "Teca Spun" fabric (acetate rayon), &c. Many of these fabrics contain acetate rayon, and, while some are among the best in the category, special care must be observed in cleaning and pressing, for some solvents used in dry cleaning, as well as high temperatures, may damage fabrics containing this type of rayon.

Cotton and Linen Fabrics. Fabrics which are made entirely of cotton or linen require too much maintenance: pressing, if they are not treated for "crush resistance"; and cleaning, if they are to retain a satisfactory appearance. Seersucker, a lightweight crinkly weave cotton fabric, may be cool, but its appearance and ability to hold its shape are very poor.

For further information and directions on the care of Summer suits, see CU *Reports,* June 1940.

▯ Example of men's suits ratings. *Consumers Union Reports Buyers Guide,* c. 1940.

▯ Example of USDA booklet on how to mend men's suits. Mending Men's Suits, c. 1943.

Mending **MEN'S SUITS**

UNITED STATES
DEPARTMENT OF AGRICULTURE
MISCELLANEOUS PUBLICATION
NO. 492

Suit jackets again sported broad, padded shoulders and up to 5" wide lapels just like they had at the start of the Depression. Peak lapels had remained wide on double breasted suit coats throughout the war, but regular lapels had been narrowed for fabric savings. The latter half of the '40s showed wide lapels on most suit jackets and sports jackets, but it is also worth noting that standard 3" to 4" lapels have always been available in every decade. Neckties widened to match the width of the lapels, but were also available in standard 3" to 4" widths.

By the early 1950s, jackets would lose at least 1" of shoulder padding for a slightly trimmer look. Although suits remained popular, a sport coat or leisure jacket with coordinating slacks had become acceptable business and special occasion attire.

All Dacron jackets and suits were first introduced in 1951. This was followed in 1954 with the introduction of (slubbed) (having a knobby, irregular surface) silk shantung from Italy, and within a couple of years the silk was blended with Dacron for new looking blends and weaves. These new fabrics heightened interest with the inclusion of slubs and nubs, flecks of color, small checks, and iridescent sharkskin.

NEW! 100%
VIRGIN WOOL
FLANNEL
Suits and
All-Occasion
Threesomes

NEW!
VIRGIN
WOOL
WORSTED
Late-style
Decorations

Catalog example of two tone jackets. Sears, c. 1945.

Catalog example of leisure jackets. Aldens, c. 1952.

Catalog example of fleck and tweed sport coats. Sears, c. 1956.

Catalog example showing skinny lapels and patch pockets. Sears, c. 1956.

For the man who had to wear a suit on a daily basis during the 1950s, various Hong Kong custom tailors offered quality garments in luxurious fabrics that were made to fit the owner. Representatives would show up in a city, take measurements, let you pick you style and fabric, and six to eight weeks later your suit would arrive.

The mid-'50s brought forth a two piece suit with matching walking shorts, and the Continental Suit with its shawl collar, straight shoulders, slightly fitted waist, shortened jacket, and tapered trousers without cuffs. These would set the stage for a most notable style change to skinny lapels, skinny ties, skinny legged trousers, and short collared shirts which would last well into the 1960s.

Catalog example showing skinny lapels in subtle plaids. Sears, c. 1962.

Catalog example showing sport coats in muted autumn colors. Montgomery Ward, c. 1968.

Part 1 of a chart for menswear color combinations. Montgomery Ward, c. 1941.

FOR SPORTSWEAR
You may use stronger contrasts and brighter colors throughout.

FOR CONTRAST
Choose Accessories that differ in color from the color of your Suit.

FOR HARMONY
Choose Accessories in various shades of the color of your Suit.

which

COLOR COMBINATIONS SHALL I WEAR?

SUIT	SHIRT	TIE	HANDKERCHIEF	SOCKS	SHOES	HATS
BLUE	White	Blue	Blue	Blue	Black, Dark Brown, or Burgundy Brown	Gray, Blue, Black, or Brown
	White	Maroon	Maroon	Maroon		
	Blue	Blue	Blue	Blue		
	Blue	Maroon	Maroon	Maroon		
	Gray	Blue	Blue	Blue		
	Gray	Maroon	Maroon	Maroon		
	Natural	Blue	Blue	Blue		
	Natural	Maroon	Maroon	Maroon		
GRAY	Blue	Maroon	Maroon	Maroon	Med. Brown, Dark Brown, or Burgundy Brown	Blue, Brown, Gray, or Gray-Green
	Blue	Blue	Blue	Blue		
	Green	Maroon	Maroon	Maroon		
	Green	Green	Green	Green		
	White	Blue	Blue	Blue		
	White	Green	Green	Green		
	Gray	Maroon	Maroon	Maroon		
	Gray	Blue	Blue	Blue		
BROWN	Green	Green	Green	Green	Med. Brown, Dark Brown, Burgundy Brown or Tan	Khaki, Brown, or Green
	Green	Brown	Brown	Brown		
	Tan	Brown	Brown	Brown		
	Tan	Green	Green	Green		
	White or Natural	Green	Green	Green		
	White or Natural	Brown	Brown	Brown		

Here's an Easy Guide to help you choose the right Tie, Socks, Shirts or other accessories to go with your Basic Suit-Color.

You may select your Accessory Colors to Harmonize with the color of your Suit or to Contrast with it.

For Harmonious Combinations choose shades of your suit color. For a Blue Suit wear a Blue Shirt with a Blue Tie, Blue Socks, Blue Handkerchief, Blue Hat and Black Shoes.

For Contrasting Combinations choose different colored accessories. For example, with a Blue Suit you may wear a White Shirt with a Maroon Tie, Maroon Handkerchief, Maroon Socks, Brown Shoes and Brown Hat; or Gray Hat and Black Shoes.

The Chart at the left shows examples of Harmonious and Contrasting Combinations. Use it as a guide to help you express your own taste and color ideas.

NOTE: Accessories shown on the Chart are described in terms of their Predominant Colors. For instance, a Tie with multi-colored figures on a predominant Maroon background is described as Maroon. This applies also to Shirts, Socks, Handkerchiefs.

Part 2 of a chart for menswear color combinations. Montgomery Ward, c. 1941.

{ Specific Dating Clues }

Note: Suit trousers dating should follow the same guidelines as the trousers dating listed.

1. Check the right interior jacket pocket for a Union Label.

Please see the section on union labels in this book for dating help.

2. Check the way that the jacket is lined.

Although some jackets were completely lined in the 1920s, '30s, and '40s, especially in formal wear, the usual lining was "petals" at the shoulders with additional lining of the front pieces and arms; This was common from the early '30s to the early '50s. Also, note if the seam edges are bound in fabric (usually pre-mid-'50s), not just turned under and pressed (post mid-'50s).

Skeleton linings, also called petal linings, were used until the early '50s when linings started going completely across the shoulder and were about 1/3 of the length of the jacket.

3. Look at and measure the size of the lapels.

Throughout the decades, notch lapels have had a common width of 2.5" to 3" wide and were available throughout every decade, but varied as styles changed. Peak lapels are almost always wider than notch lapels from the same time period.

In 1920, lapels ranged from 2.3" to 2.75", then went to 3.75" wide by 1925. The usually wide peak lapel of a double breasted jacket of about 4.75" gained popularity from the '30s into the late '40s when lapels were 4".

Skinny 2" lapels made their first short-lived appearance in the very early 1920s and would not reappear until the mid-'50s, when they stayed popular for nearly a decade. They also made a quick appearance in the '80s.

Wide lapels reappeared in the late 1960s and stayed until the late 1970s or even early 1980s. After a short reprieve, they came back to popularity again in the late 1990s.

Previously only on robes and sweaters, shawl collars on suit jackets and sports coats appeared as skinny lapels in the mid-1950s.

And, I'll make a quick point about collarless jackets: High button, collarless jackets first appeared at the end of WWII, but never really caught on. They reappeared in about 1960, with the Beatles first tour of the U.S. brought them to the forefront of men's fashion, but again they never became a style for the masses. They reappeared in the mid-'70s with lower mid-chest buttons and then again in the late '90s, where they have remained popular for certain ethnicities.

Nehru jackets appeared in the U.S. about 1969-70 and went away as fast as they came on the fashion scene.

Skeleton Lining

Inside of coat shows skeleton lining, which eliminates excess weight. It makes the coat hang well.

Dating clue: Check the label, c. 1910s.

Dating clue: Check the lining.
Montgomery Ward, c. 1925.

Dating clue: Lining example, c. 1940s.

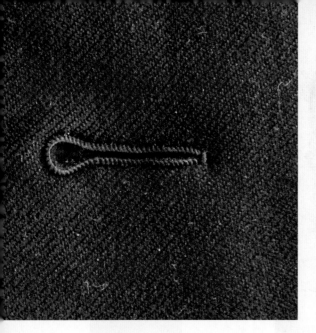

4. Look at the buttonholes.

Keyhole buttonholes (looking like a skeleton key should fit into them) are classic for men's suits from the 1920s into the '60s, at which time the sewn buttonholes changed to more of a loop than a keyhole. Tailored buttonholes (all fabric, not just sewn), like those found on coats, are more time consuming and tedious to make and weren't used very often until about the '70s.

5. And a few more quick clues:

Vents: Some jackets had deep vents to the waist for horse riding through the mid-'30s, but many jackets had no vents. By the late '20s, double side vents or no vents were the norm. No vents continued until the early years of the '50s when short 5-6" back vents appeared. By the mid to late '60s back vents were 11" to 12" long—going almost to the waist, and the mid-'70s vents shorted back to about 7" to 8".

▪ Dating clue: Buttonhole example, c. 1940s.

▪ Dating clue: Vent example, c. 1950s.

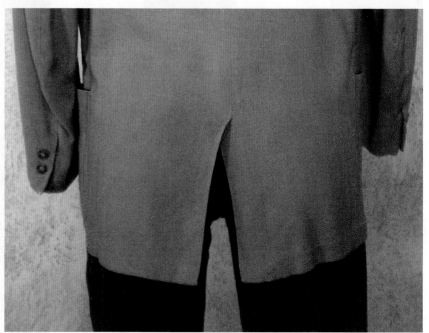

Check the trouser dating clues in the next chapter.

Check for a Woolmark, store labels, trademarks, and garment care labels. *Please see the Label chapter for more information.*

Any label in the back neck that is used as a hang loop or where the hang loop would be, whether it be Brooks Bros., Dry Clean Only, or Made in Canada, usually denotes 1970s or newer. This does not include labels placed in the back center at shoulder level—like the placement of Burberry's labels.

Fit & Measuring: *Please see the Everything Else chapter for more information.*

Pockets, pockets, and more pockets...

Pockets started as small bags worn on the outside of clothing to carry valuables, like money or jewelry. Since anyone could see your pocket, people started wearing them hidden inside their clothing to better protect their money. The problem was that the pockets were really hard to get to without undressing. So, not to let the pocket problem get the better of them, people cut a slit in their clothing to access the pocket. It was then only a matter of time until the pocket bag was sewn to the slit. Voila! A pocket as we know it today.

From this simple idea, designers have given us innumerable styles and manner of pocket placement.

Every man's suit jacket, blazer, sport coat, top coat, or jacket made after the turn of the twentieth century has pockets. So, I thought it might be helpful to talk about them a bit and show the different styles.

As a matter of outward style, the breast pocket, which is always on the left, should match the style of the side pockets. The top of the side pockets should always align with the bottom button on the jacket. Those are the only two style "laws" concerning pockets. Inside pockets are optional, but most suit jackets and sport coats have them in the front right lining.

In the early years of the twentieth century, many pockets were **jetted** or **flapless**. These are considered the most formal of pockets and are still used today.

Example of a jetted or flapless pocket, c. 1900s.

Example of a flapped pocket, c. 1900s.

Example of a double besom pocket, c. 1900s.

Flapped (or flap) pockets became popular in the 1920s when that fashion trendsetter, The Duke of Wales, had them added to his suit jackets. They are thought to be less dressy than flapless and should never be used on formal attire or tuxedo jackets.

Flapped pockets on better quality garments are usually **double besomed** with a narrow edge sewn above and below the pocket slit opening for a finished and tailored appearance. Thus the flap can be worn tucked in for a flapless look, or displayed on the outside.

Patch pockets are considered the most casual looking as a "patch" of matching fabric is sewn on the outside of the jacket to create a pocket.

In the '30s and '40s, it became a trend for movie stars to show a small change or **ticket pocket** above the right side pocket. This fad didn't really catch on, so a ticket pocket on the outside of a jacket is seldom seen. However, ticket pockets are commonly found on the inside right of a jacket and were used for carrying rail passage.

And, finally, there are **Norfolk pockets,** which are a variation on patch pockets with pleating. A variation on the Norfolk is **saddle bag pocket** styling that makes the pocket fuller and sometimes stand away from the garment. These are usually flapped.

▣ Catalog example of a patch pocket.
Montgomery Ward, c. 1949.

▣ Catalog example of a patch pocket.
Montgomery Ward, c. 1949.

▣ Catalog example of a ticket pocket.
Montgomery Ward, c. 1949.

▣ Catalog example of Norfolk pocket.
Montgomery Ward, c. 1949.

The CLASSIC Blazer

Color coordinated houndstooth check
Dress Slacks also available

{ Glossary }

Blazer:
A single or double breasted jacket inspired by similar coats worn on the HMS *Blazer* (ship) in the 1860s. The classic version is dark blue with peaked or notched lapels and brass buttons.

Catalog example of a single and double breasted blazer. Sears, c. 1968.

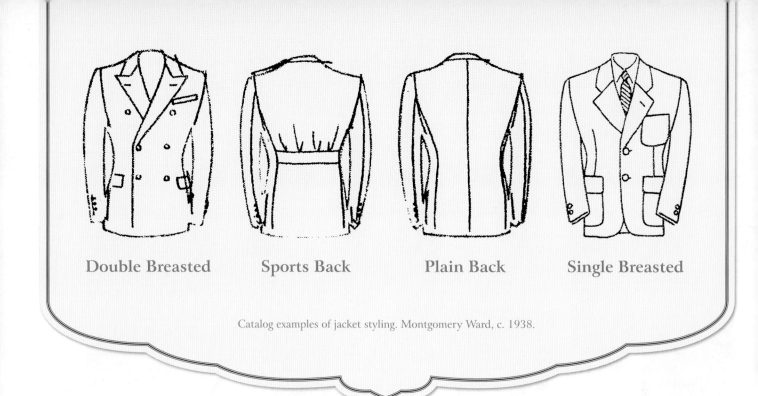

Double Breasted   **Sports Back**   **Plain Back**   **Single Breasted**

Catalog examples of jacket styling. Montgomery Ward, c. 1938.

Example of jacket lapel width, c. 1900s.

Double Breasted:
The jacket front pieces widely overlap and button in a horizontal plane. They can have 4, 6, or 8 buttons equating to 2, 3, or 4 columns on each set. The double breasted suit was introduced at the start of WWI, but it didn't gain in popularity until after the war.

Faux Belted Back or Sports Back:
The look of a belted back that is sewn into the back of the jacket rather than being loose.

Lapel Width:
The distance from where the lapel folds at the jacket front to the outermost edge of the peak or notch.

Nehru Jacket:
A hip length jacket with a stand up collar that, starting at the neck, buttons all the way down the front.

Norfolk Jacket:
Has shown decades of enduring style. It features an all around belt, two long vertical box pleats in front, and a single box pleat down the middle back. American tailors added front and back yokes.

Notch Lapel:
Where the suit collar meets the lapel to form between a 45 and 90 degree notch. Standard on a single breasted jacket, but quite rare with double breasted styling. (See example in single breasted.)

Peak Lapel:

The lapel forms a broad V shape that points up and outward and should only be shown on a double breasted suit coat, sport jacket, or tux. (See example with double breasted jacket.)

Plain Back:

A jacket back with no venting.

Shawl Lapel or Shawl Collar:

The collar forms a continuous curve by flowing into the lapel. Originally from the Victorian era and only shown on robes and sweaters until the 1950s.

Shoulder Padding:

Extra padding sewn at the top of the shoulder between the jacket and the lining to give the illusion of broader shoulders or being muscular. Padding usually ends where the sleeve starts and is hidden under the lining.

Single Breasted:

The jacket front pieces barely overlap enough to button. Can have 1, 2, or 3 button closure. Single breasted suits with double breasted vests were fashion forward in the 1920s.

Suit Jacket:

A buttoned jacket specifically made to be worn with its matching trousers.

Sport Coat:

A buttoned jacket similar to a suit jacket, but not worn as part of a suit.

Vent:

A vertical opening in the back of a jacket at the hemline. A single vent was originally initiated for sitting astride a horse, but also offers freedom for bending and other movement. A double vent is the English version showing a vertical opening toward each side of the jacket. And, a ventless has no vertical openings in the back of the jacket to interrupt the style flow.

Western Style Jacket:

A jacket characterized by front and back V shaped yokes, which are of a contrasting fabric or in some way made prominent, such as with piping.

Yoke:

An extra fitted or shaped piece at the shoulder of a garment. Can appear in just the back, or back and front shoulder areas.

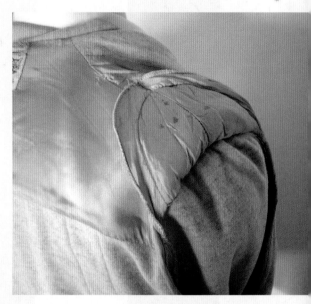

Example of jacket shoulder padding, c. 1950s.

{ Dress Trousers }

{ Trouser Terminology }

Button fly:
> The front opening of men's trousers is securely closed with buttons. Button flies are still used in many European countries and bespoke trousers would generally be replaced with zippers after WWII.

Example of a button fly on a pair of trousers, c. 1900s.

Style-world Stars Custom-look "Californians," full-draped. Many prices cut!

All Wool Worsted Sharkskin **12.89**

Sharkskin **7.89** up   Donegal Tweed **7.98**   Rayon Sharkskin **6.98**

California Conservative Slacks:

Have front pleats and dropped belt loops; made to fit slightly higher on the waist to give the appearance of a more athletic build.

Conservative Slacks:

Have no front pleats, regular placed belt loops, a zipper fly, and were made to fit slightly lower on the waist.

Conservatives Distinguished, all-occasion dress trousers Precision-tailored all wools, blends!

All wool or Wool Blend Gabardine **7.98** up   All Wool Serge **11.95** Wool Blend Serge **8.79**   All Wool Worsted Sharkskin **10.98**   Rayon-Nylon **5.98** Rayon Gabardine **3.98**

460 • •Aldens

Cuffs or Turn-ups:

Fabric at the bottom of a trouser leg that had been turned up.

Dropped Belt Loops:

The top of the belt loops are stitched about .5" below the top of the waistband.

Catalog example of California conservative slacks. Aldens, c. 1952.

Catalog example of conservative slacks. Aldens, c. 1952.

Catalog example of trouser cuffs. Montgomery Ward, c. 1949.

Example of trousers with no cuffs, c. 1900s.

Flat Front:
Trousers or pants that have no pleats.

High Waisted:
Trousers or slacks made to fit a couple of inches above the normal waistline; designed to give a taller, slimmer look.

Hollywood Waistband:
Created as part of the trouser rather than as a separate waistband. These trousers featured high waist styling via a longer rise and skinny, dropped belt loops with no sewn on waistband. They were always double pleated and full fitting.

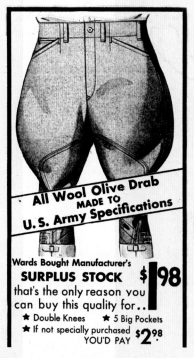

Ivy League:
Slim fitting, tapered trousers with unpleated fronts and either adjustable side buckles or a back buckle.

Jodhpurs or Riding Pants:
Fitted pants with a large thigh area that end between the lower knee and above the ankle with lacing at the hemline for a tight fit. Usually worn with knee high boots for riding horses or motorcycles.

Knickers or Knickerbockers: Loose fitting pants that end below the knee where they fasten with a band that buckles or buttons. Originally designed for golf, these pants became popular wear for other sports. Men's knickers will always have a button fly closure in the middle front; women's knickers will have a flap front closure or only button down the side.

Pants:
Coined from the word pantaloons, leg coverings similar to present day trousers.

Pleats:
Folded material stitched into place in a trouser waistband.

Plus Fours:
Knickers that extend 4" below the bend of the knee; also come in Plus Twos, Plus Sixes and Plus Eights.

Catalog example of Hollywood waistbands. Montgomery Ward, c. 1941.

Catalog example of jodhpurs or riding pants. Montgomery Ward, c. 1933.

Catalog example of knickers or knickerbockers. Montgomery Ward, c. 1928.

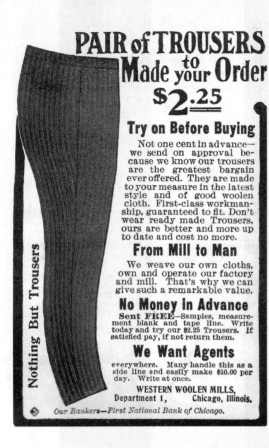

Catalog example of how trousers taper. *McClure's Magazine*, c. 1900s.

Advertisement for trousers with waist adjustors. *Munsey's Magazine*, c. 1902.

Example of trouser waist adjustors, c. 1900s.

Shorts:
Trousers ending above the knee; short legged garment for sporting activities. Appeared in the U.S. in the mid-1930s, but didn't become popular until after WWII.

Size:
Usually stated as the waist measurement and inseam measurement, example: 34 (waist) by 32 (inseam). See the measuring chapter in Section III of this book for more information.

Slacks:
Hagger™ coined the term "slacks" in 1940 for a pair of odd trousers to be worn during slack / leisure time.

Taper:
The way the legs of trousers narrow from the crotch to the hemline.

Trousers:
A garment covering the lower torso with the legs separated.

Zipper Fly:
Zippers placed in the fly to replace buttons were introduced to men's trousers in the early 1930s, but took special machinery and training to install—driving up the cost from a few pennies to about a dollar each.

{ Spotting the Style Trends }

In the early 1900s, men's trousers had skinny, straight legs with no cuffs, could be back or side belted for a waist adjustment, and generally worn with suspenders. Belts were worn at this time, but usually only with work trousers.

Wide legged trousers with wide waistbands dominated in the mid-thirties—some without belt loops or braces buttons. Bold plaids, stripes, and fabrics spread outside the college campuses and dominated the style for young men. Colors brought relief from the gray "Dust Bowl Days", and by the late '40s were relief from War khaki.

Bold plaids and colors remained through the '30s, but leg widths decreased. For the first time, trousers gave many choices to the wearers: pleated or flat front, regular belt loops or a Hollywood waistband, stovepipe or flared legs, button or zip fly, and plain colored or patterned fabrics.

Catalog example of 22" wide leg trousers. Montgomery Ward, c. 1932.

Catalog example of 22" wide leg trousers with wide waistbands. Montgomery Ward, c. 1934.

Catalog example of bold plaid trousers. Montgomery Ward, c. 1937.

Catalog example of bold plaids and available waistbands on trousers. Sears, c. 1939.

Catalog example of lounger outfits of matching fabric shirts and trousers. Montgomery Ward, c. 1939.

Catalog example of slack suits of matching fabric shirts and trousers. Sears, c. 1940.

PLEATED FRONT SLANTED POCKETS

POPULAR COTTON NUB CRASH

COOL COTTON WASH SUITING

Slack suits of matching fabric shirts and trousers were considered ultimate style for leisure time.

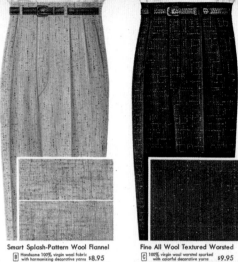

Smart Splash-Pattern Wool Flannel
[B] Handsome 100% virgin wool fabric
with harmonizing decorative yarns **$8.95**

Fine All Wool Textured Worsted
[C] 100% virgin wool worsted sparked
with colorful decorative yarns **$9.95**

▣ Catalog example of colorful trousers.
Montgomery Ward, c. 1956.

▣ Catalog example of flecked and textured
fabric trousers. Sears, c. 1956.

▣ Catalog example of slim tapered slacks.
Sears, c. 1962.

▣ Catalog example of slacks with jeans styling.
Montgomery Ward, c. 1968.

Mass WWII uniform distribution made manufacturers realize that not all men were created equal as to height. Manufacturers started adjusting the overall sizing of trousers to fit tall, average or short men, not just offering different inseams.

By the late '40s, trousers showed up in colors never before seen for men's garments, while flecks, tweeds, slubs, and textures were a bit more to the liking of the everyday man in the '50s.

By the mid to late 1950s, styles were dramatically changing with style elements growing skinny. Ivy League trousers came with a flat front and adjustable rear buckle strap, which by the end of the decade would be changed to side buckles. Perma-press fabrics and polyester blended fabrics invaded the clothing scene in the 1960s. And slacks took on jeans styling in fabrics of twills and corduroy.

{ Some Trousers and Slacks Facts }

Slacks have utilized zippers since 1932, but some jeans, most formal wear (tuxedo) trousers, and bespoke suits still used button flies past the late 1950s.

Slacks, trousers, and pants are always referred to in the plural because it takes two legs (a pair) sewn together to make them.

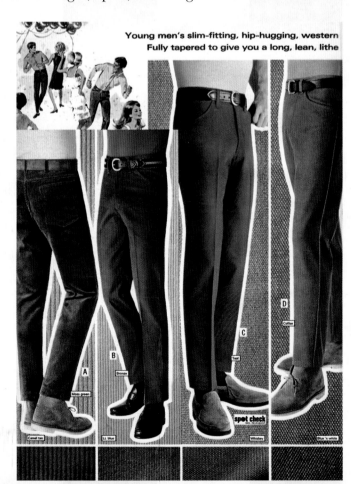

The average front rise on a pair of trousers or slacks is 13" with the back rise being 18". A couple of inches longer on both measurements will usually designate high waisted and are made to be worn above the natural waistline. This rise was stylish from the 1930s to the mid-1950s.

The size of a pair of trousers or pants is the actual waist measurement. So, if the waist measures 40", they are generally a size 40. Beware of vintage cotton or other shrinkable fabric pants being marked a certain size and may have actually shrunk with laundering; check the actual measurement.

Double pleated trousers have been a mainstay in fashion since the teens.

Trousers worn with a double breasted jacket are to have cuffs.

The taper of men's trousers changed through the decades, going from skinny and tightly fitted, to Oxford Bags in the 1920s with as much as a 40" hemline, to Continental slacks in the mid-'50s eventually narrowing to a 17" hemline.

The Daks Slacks, the first beltless trouser, was invented in 1932 for golfers.

Plus fours were replaced with slacks for golfing in the late '30s.

The slacks of the 1940s had broad hips and big seats, wide legs, and were usually only available in gabardine or flannel.

One of the most outstanding features of the early 1950s was the introduction of manmade fabrics, such as Acrylics and Polyesters, for garments. When mixed with wool, the garment would hold its shape better and didn't wrinkle as much.

Diagonal pockets first appeared in 1954 on casual slacks along with a renewal from the '30s of waistbands that didn't require a belt. These slacks had no belt loops and were called self-belt or beltless.

Stretch slacks were introduced in the late 1950s. Action stretch used vertical stretch fabrics for a 30-50% give. Comfort stretch used horizontal stretch fabrics to allow 15-30% give for comfort and body movement.

In the early 1960s, single front pleats were more popular than double front pleats.

The first hip riding, low rise pants and jeans appeared in 1963.

Perma-press fabrics were introduced in 1964.

Bell bottoms appeared on jeans and slacks in 1966. This gave men the choice of skinny tapers to huge bells.

{ Trouser Dating Clues }

1. The first thing is to **check the pants closure** to see if it is a button fly, metal zip or Nylon zip.

A button fly will usually date to anytime before the mid-'40s; zippers started being used in men's trousers in the '30s, but were costly to install. You will find button fly closures on WWII military trousers as well as men's suits and slacks until about the end of the war.

To qualify the button fly info above: Many men have suits tailored (bespoke) with button flies and it was also a style trend in the '60s and '70s. Button flies on trousers up through the late '30s would have a button closure to the waistband; large hook and bar closures for the waistband didn't appear until into WWII.

An invisible zipper, which was metal with the teeth covered in fabric, was patented in the late 1930s and used in men's trousers, but they are rare to find. The usual metal zipper will overlap the war years and be used consistently until the mid-'60s when the Nylon zipper came into vogue. There is a transition/overlap period between metal and Nylon zippers. The late '70s and '80s trended toward a '40s retro style and brought back metal zips to some extent, and some men's suit companies have never used anything but metal zips in their suit trousers.

Older trousers should have the waistband facing and pockets constructed of a fine linen fabric. This would change to cotton or a cotton blend in the 1960s.

2. **Check the belt loops** on the trousers. The actual loops should be about .25" wide for most pre-'60s trousers, going to as wide as 1" in the '70s. The length will vary with the popularity of belts during a certain period of time.

Hollywood pants appeared in the 1930s with no belt loops, but are usually shown from the 1940s on with drop loops—meaning the top of the belt loops started/dropped about .25" to .5" from the top of the waist. This style gained even more popularity after the war and stayed until the mid-1950s.

Note that in the late '40s and early '50s pants also had a sewn on waistband with dropped loops, know as modified Hollywood style, or a sewn on waistband with regular placed loops.

If the pants have braces buttons, they should be on the inside of the waistband. Outside placed braces buttons usually denote Victorian (into the teens or 1920s), contemporary 1990s, or bespoke.

3. **Check the knee and hemline width**. There have been distinct changes in trousers, although work pants have always been made roomier and with wider legs for comfort and ease of movement. -

{ Hats, Caps, and More }

Catalog example of fedora style hats.
Sears, c. 1935.

Back in the Golden Age of hats and caps, nearly every man wore one for any outdoor activity. Bowlers were for riding; Fedoras and Homburgs were for dress; Pork Pies for the new age and jazz musicians; Berets were for motoring; Skull caps were for college boys; Ten Gallon hats or Sombrero's were for outdoors or cowboys; Crushers were for casual; Golf caps and Newsboys were for outdoor casual. Need I mention Conductors hats, Baseball caps, Doctors surgical caps, meat cutters hats, Deer Stalkers, military hats and caps …? In fact, we shall just say that men and women were expected to keep their heads covered when out of doors—for protection from the sun, wind, and rain. And, indoors, hats were to keep their hair out of their faces.

First, you might want to identify the style of hat or cap that you prefer:

The **Fedora** style was invented in the final decades of the 1800s, and any hat resembling its style is also usually called a fedora—even straws or twills. Fedora's are the most popular style of hat and easiest to personalize by the pinch of the crown, addition of dimples, and the roll of the brim. The snap brim can be worn up, down, or down in front and up in the back.

Silk
Faced
Lining

**Snap Brim Bond Street
De Luxe**

Catalog example of a fedora style hat.
Sears, c. 1929.

Genuine Porto Rican

PRICE NOW $1.00

Until WWII, all basic felt hat styles, including fedoras, usually came in black, brown or gray. Then olive green and varying shades of the basic colors were added. After the war and into the '50s, hats in every color from pink to gold to blue became available to compliment the wearer's outfit.

The Panama Hat is straw hat with fedora styling.

The Trilby is the European version of the fedora with a typically shorter brim and a more distinctive upturn in the back. They are traditionally made with fur felt or tweed for a softer styling, and will always show a deeply indented crown.

The Homburg is also similar to a fedora, but always sports a center crease, no pinches, and the brim is turned up all the way around. Introduced in the 1800s, homburg's were made popular by the style setting Prince of Wales in the 1930s and Winston Churchill in the 1940s.

The Bowler, also known as a Derby, is constructed of a hard felt with a rounded, uncreased crown and a stingy turned-up brim. Since they are small and tight fitting, bowler's were invented in the 1800s as riding headwear that was less likely to be blown off than wider brimmed hats. By the last decades of the nineteenth century, bowlers were replaced by straw Panamas and western / cowboy hats with wider brims which offered more protection from the sun.

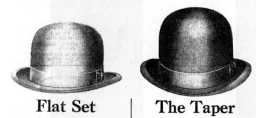

Flat Set | **The Taper**

Catalog example of a Panama style hat. Montgomery Ward, c. 1928.

Catalog example of a homburg style hat. Montgomery Ward, c. 1935.

Catalog example of derby or bowler style hats. Sears, c. 1916.

Advertisement for a derby style hat. *McClure's Magazine*, c. 1900.

Dempster Derby $3

Made for $5 Hat Buyers

Ask your dealer to show you the latest shapes. They are fashionably correct. This is the mark— it means a $2 saving and hat satisfaction you can't get short of $5.

CHARLES W. DEMPSTER & CO.

Manufacturers, 220 Franklin Street, Chicago

The **Pork Pie or Telescope** has a flattened top and a short crown with a characteristic indent all the way around. Also has a skinny snap brim and can be made of felt or straw.

Fancy Telescope

Drop Tip

Open Telescope

The **Boater** was introduced in the late 1800s and is always constructed of light colored, coarse straw with a flat crown and a flat brim. The straw is stiffened so the hat cannot lose its shape.

A **Crusher or Bucket** is a soft hat that can be rolled or crushed and still retain its shape.

A **Ten Gallon or Western** hat is a high crowned, wide brimmed hat which can be made of soft felt, hard fur felt, straw or leather. Invented by John B. Stetson in the 1870s, it is the second most personalized hat. A good western hat is sold with a tall rounded crown and flat brim meant to be customized for the wearer. Western hats are usually shown with decorative hat bands, and sometimes wing or stampede strings are attached.

$1⁹⁵ Excellent Quality Straw Hat

$3⁹⁸ Choice of Fine Quality Smooth Finished Fur Felt or Genuine Velour

Our Famous "Carlsbad" Hat

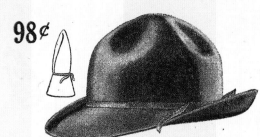

98¢

Inexpensive Wool Crusher

Catalog example of pork pie hats. Montgomery Ward, c. 1910.

Catalog example of a boater style hat. Montgomery Ward, c. 1925.

Catalog example of a crusher style hat. Montgomery Ward, c. 1925.

Catalog example of a western style hat. Montgomery Ward, c. 1925.

A **Golf Style Cap** can come in one-piece, four quarter, or eight quarter styling. It is a rounded cap with a small, stiff brim in front. Golf caps are also called flat caps, driving caps, skid lids, and newsboys.

Golf caps from the '20s and '30s will have a heavy leather sweatband about 1" - 1.25" high; many will have a snap on the bill to keep the front in place. Caps of the '40s will have thin leather sweatbands; thin leather will change to cloth sweatbands as the years pass.

Winter hats are worn during cold weather to keep the head warm.

Men's Leather Helmet

Reduced from $1.00 **75¢**

39 H 74—Black or brown. State color.
SIZES: Small (6¾, 6⅞); medium (7 to 7¼); large 7⅜ to 7⅝). State size. We Pay Postage.

Another big surprise bargain! Genuine sheepskin leather Helmet that shows its superiority, and after months of hard wear in all kinds of weather will prove its real quality. The leather is soft and pliable yet very strong. Full lined with thick flannel which is very warm. Adjustable snap fastens under chin. The practical thing for the coldest weather.

Aviator Style

Here are some basics about what hats are made of:

Fur felt is usually rabbit fur blended with wool for low cost hats, or beaver fur blended with wool for higher cost hats. The highest quality is beaver fur only.

Wool felt is made from sheep's wool.

Straw is dried stems of certain grains which are braided to form plaits that are then sewn together.

There are three basic edges for a hat:

Raw Edge is just the cut felt with no other finish.

Welted Edge is where the edge is doubled back on itself and turned in toward the crown; may or may not be stitched.

Bound Edge is where grosgrain is attached with a regular through stitch, a concealed stitch, or an ornamental hand done stitch.

Fedoras have remained popular for over a century with little change in style other than the brim width.

The oldest styles up into the 1940s will have a medium weight leather sweatband about 2" high with an average brim width of 2.625" to 2.75" and an outer grosgrain band width of about 2".

6½-Inch Crown
4-Inch Brim

OUR 1937 FEATURE
TWO SWELL SHAPES

Two Shades and Trims

Thin Leather Laced Edges

6-Inch Crown
3½-Inch Brim

Belgian Beaver (Light Sand)
Trim with Brown Band and Lacing
Black Hat Trimmed with Silver Band and Lacing

No. 1251 - 4-inch Brim $4.85 Postage 15c extra

No. 1252 - 3½-inch Brim Postage 15c extra

These two shapes will be the year's Sensation at all Rodeos. They can be creased in any shape. The thin leather lacing will help keep the shape and will give extra years of wear. Sizes 6¾ to 7½. Postage 15c extra.

Catalog example of a golf style cap. Montgomery Ward, c. 1933.

Catalog example of a winter cap. Sears, c. 1927.

Catalog example of a winter cap. Montgomery Ward, c. 1930.

Catalog example of a ornamental stitched brim western hat. Texas Rancher, c. 1937.

By 1935, brims had narrowed slightly and measured 2.25" to 2.5" and remained the same until after WWII. WWII years rationed leather, so the sweatband leather got thinner. Many '40s fedoras will show small buttons with elastic loops on the grosgrain bands—thus making them easy to date.

After the war and before the early '50s, brims widened slightly to late '20s dimensions of 2.625" to 2.75". The sweatband height shrank to about 1.5", with the grosgrain outer band shrinking to about the same height.

By the mid-1950s, suit lapels were starting to shrink in width, neckties got skinnier to match, and hat brims also narrowed to go along with this style trend, which would remain popular until the mid-1960s. That's when younger men gave up wearing Fedoras for the more casual baseball cap.

Baseball caps, which were actually worn to play baseball, appeared in the last decades of the 1800s. They were made of wool, had tiny bills, and were fitted to the head to keep them firmly on the head during a game.

The bills grew larger in the late 1930s and into WWII. By the 1960s, caps became adjustable instead of fitted and were made of cotton with mesh backs for ventilation, After that, we saw them made of cotton / poly blend fabrics, having padded fronts, and having screen printed logos applied to the front to advertise every person, place or thing imaginable.

Catalog example of the three styles of hat edges. Montgomery Ward, c. 1945.

Catalog example of a baseball cap. Montgomery Ward, c. 1945.

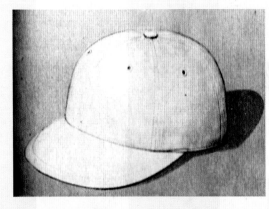

Find your hat or cap size

If your head circumference measured in inches is:	Then you wear a U.S. Hat size:
20 7/8	6 5/8 or Small
21 1/8	6 3/4 or Small
21 1/2	6 7/8 or Small
21 7/8	7 or Medium
22 1/4	7 1/8 or Medium
22 5/8	7 1/4 or Large
23	7 3/8 or Large
23 1/2	7 1/2 or Ex. Large
23 7/8	7 5/8 or Ex. Large
24 1/4	7 3/4 or Ex. Large
24 5/8	7 7/8 or XX Large
25	8 or XX Large

WARDS DRESS FELT HATS NOW COME IN ALL SIZES

READ ABOUT THIS NEW SERVICE BELOW

Regardless of the size you wear, Wards will fit you in any Dress Felt Hat shown on these two pages. They are stocked in the following *Standard Hat Sizes:* 6¾, 6⅞, 7, 7⅛, 7¼, 7⅜, 7½.

If your hat-size is one of these sizes, the hat you order will be shipped promptly. If your hat-size is smaller than 6¾ or larger than 7½, Wards will still fit you, for we will make a special hat to your individual measure. This special fitting service requires two weeks. For Men's Summer Hats, Dress and Work Caps only those sizes given under each hat are available. **Be sure the Summer Hat, Dress or Work Cap that you order comes in your size.**

Here's All You Have To Do To Insure Getting A Perfect Fitting Hat

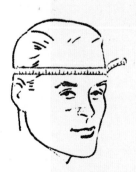

First—Tell us the size of your present hat (look for sticker under sweatband). **Second**—Measure your head as shown at left. Be accurate. Hold tape comfortably tight in position you regularly wear your hat. Take measure two or three times to be sure you have the right size. Send us the number of inches your head measures. **Third**—Compare this measurement with chart below. Send us hat size that corresponds to your head measure. If your head measures between two sizes, order next larger hat-size.

If Head Measures...	20⅜	20¾	21¼	21⅝	22	22⅜	22¾	23⅛	23½	24	24⅜
Order Hat Size......	6½	6⅝	6¾	6⅞	7	7⅛	7¼	7⅜	7½	7⅝	7¾

Catalog example of how to find your hat size. Montgomery Ward, c. 1938.

Some well known hat makers and brands

Bailey®—founded in 1922

Biltmore—founded in 1917 in Canada

Borsalina—founded in 1827 in Italy

Brent®—house brand for Montgomery Wards, started 1927

Cavanagh®—founded in 1928

Churchill®—founded in 1928 and bought in the '50s by Resistol but kept name

Dobbs®—founded in 1922

Knox®—founded in the 1830s

Marathon®—house brand for J. C. Penney, started 1914

Montecristi®—known for custom made hats

Pilgrim®—house brand for Sears, Roebuck & Co. 1905 - 1964

Resistol®—founded in 1927

Robert Hall®—house brand for Robert Hall founded in 1944

Stetson, John B.®—founded 1865

Stetson, Stephen—founded in 1920s or '30s

Stevens—founded 1917

Care of your vintage hat

Regardless of whether you have chosen a felt or straw hat, be sure to keep it clean. A good brushing with a soft bristle brush against the grain will benefit either, or you may want to simply wipe it down with a slightly moistened cloth.

Reshaping of straws or hard felts should be done by a professional to avoid permanent damage.

If your vintage hat happens to get wet, turn the sweatband down and let the entire hat air dry naturally. Do not place by an air vent or blow dry, as hastened drying can this will cause shrinkage or damage.

Store your vintage hat on a hat rack, or with the top of the crown down to avoid damage or misshaping of the brim. If you must place it brim down, make sure that the brim goes over the edge of a table rather than flat, snap the brim in an upward position before setting down, or place the hat over a tall appropriately sized bowl that is high enough to keep the brim up off the flat surface.

Finally, if you happen to have a haberdasher in your city or town, make their acquaintance as they can be one of your best friends. There are options for restoring vintage hats that have not been taken care of. Some hats can be reshaped, some stains can be removed, hatbands can be replaced, and minor repairs can be made.

If you can't find a "hat guy" locally, there are nationally known hatters like Hatman Jack's Wichita Hat Works on the web at: www.hatmanjacks.com.

Catalog example of youngster having fun wearing a hat. Montgomery Ward, c. 1925.

Advertisement for a hat crown ironing machine. *The Dry Cleaner*, c. 1935.

{ Background on Some of the Hatters Unions }

The different Hatters Union labels are some that just don't show up very often in a hat or cap.

The earliest Hatters Unions date back to the 1820s and they were some of the first unions to have a Union Label affixed to their wares. The very first known label was a 1" square of buff paper perforated around the edges like a postage stamp and sewn under the sweatband. As time passed, each particular union name was printed on their designed label by a Union Printer. All union labels should show the "Union Bug" somewhere to denote that they were printed by a unionized printing company.

Any Hatters Union labels were to be attached to the inside of the hat under the sweatband and should be stitched in such a way that the thread of the label must pass through the hat bow.

The *Hat Makers Union* and the *Hat Finishers Union* joined to form *The United Hatters of North America* (UHNA) in 1896.

The *United Cloth Hat & Cap Makers of North America (1901)* became *The Cloth Hat & Cap Operators Union* a few years later. The *Millinery Workers Union* merged with them in 1918 to form *The Cloth Hat, Cap & Millinery Workers International Union* (CHCMW).

Other unions working in 1917, but not part of the above, are the *Straw Hatters' Union*, the *Cloth Hat and Cap Blockers Union, Cap Makers Union (1902), Fur Cap Makers Union (1916), Chicago Cloth Headwear Manufacturers Association, The American Association of Wholesale Hatters, Boston Cap Manufacturers Association, Wool Hat Manufacturers Association, American Wool Hat Manufacturers Association (1914), National Association Men's Straw Hat Manufacturers of America (1916),* and the *Cloth Hat and Cap Makers Union*.

The *Cloth Hat, Cap & Millinery Workers International Union (CHCMW)(1918)* joined *The United Hatters of North America (UHNA)(1918)* in 1934 to form *The United Hatters, Cap & Millinery Workers International Union (UHCMW)* and operated under the American Federation of Labor *(AFL).* Its membership and manufacturing rapidly declined starting in the 1950s.

There was a big push in the early 1980s to add the existing UHCMA labels to all the hats they made. UHCMA also made women's hats through the 1960s, but the labels were different.

The *UHCMW* finally merged with *Amalgamated Clothing & Textile Workers Union (ACTWU)* in 1983 and labels were no longer added to caps and hats.

ACTWU merged with *International Ladies Garment Workers Union (ILGWU)* in 1995 to form the *Union of Needletrades, Industrial & Textile Employees (UNITE).*

There seems to be so many hat and cap makers unions that it is really hard to keep track of them. Just remember that if you find a label in a hat, it can only be as old as the union it is representing or as new as that unions merger date. Thus a CHCMW label would date the item to between 1918 (when it was formed) to 1934 (when it merged with another union).

■ CHCMW label used from
1918 to 1934, c. 1920s.

■ UHCMW label used from
late 1970s to 1983, c. 1980s.

{ Shoes }

{ Dress and Casual Shoes }

What can I say about shoes? Toe styles have changed from square, rounded or pointed to square, rounded or pointed, while some remain the same for decades. The major parts of a shoe are the upper, sole, and heel. And, according to the United Shoe Machinery Corporation (USMC), there are only two basic styles of men's shoes: the bal and the blucher, with unlimited variations on each.

Bal:

> a derivation of Balmoral, the Scottish castle where the shoes were first worn. The basic style stitches the vamp to cover the front edges of the quarters. We usually consider this shoe an Oxford.

Blucher:

> styled after a half boot designed by Prussian Army officer Gebhard von Blucher in the early 1800s. The ears of the quarters are on top of the throat of the vamp, or in simpler words, the side pieces lap over the top.

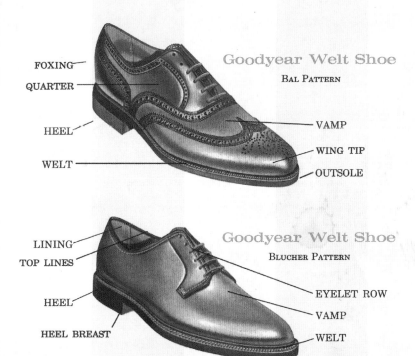

FOXING
QUARTER
HEEL
WELT

Goodyear Welt Shoe
BAL PATTERN

VAMP
WING TIP
OUTSOLE

LINING
TOP LINES
HEEL
HEEL BREAST

Goodyear Welt Shoe
BLUCHER PATTERN

EYELET ROW
VAMP
WELT

Example of Bal and Blucher styles of shoes.
How American Shoes are Made, c. 1966.

$2.98 PR.
Were $3.29

16-Inch

Molded Tap Sole

Metal Heel Plate

Black or Tan

Molded *Weatherproof* Welt

- Tough Double Tanned Grain Cowhide Leather Uppers.
- Special molded tap sole—a real mileage master.
- Wide, soft plain toe—designed for extra foot comfort.
- Extra heavy one-piece Wonderwear Composition rubber sole.

Catalog example of lace-up boots. Montgomery Ward, c. 1935.

Catalog example of engineer boots. Montgomery Ward, c. 1968.

Catalog example of cowboy boots. Sears, c. 1939.

Catalog example of work boots. Montgomery Ward, c. 1925.

Catalog example of fancy western boots. Texas Rancher, c. 1937.

4
18.97

3
13.97

Engineer boots with oil-tanned leather uppers resist moisture

11 IN. HIGH

Sizing has remained the same. I will qualify this statement with a notation by the USMC that in the late 1960s there were more than 300 sizes and widths of shoes available for the entire family. At that time, there were twelve widths of shoes ranging from AAAAA (very narrow) to EEEE (very wide), but these widths were not available in all sizes. Adult shoes were normally made in widths of AA, A, B, C, D, and E, which is still the norm today.

The "Standard Measurement of Lasts" was implemented in 1888 to set standard length, ball width, and girth for each size of last. The last is a wooden form shaped like a foot that a shoe is built on. Lasts lengthen 1/3" and increase 1/4" in circumference around the ball of the foot for each size.

The USMC estimates that in the mid-1960s there were 1,000 shoe manufacturers producing more than 630,000,000 pairs of shoes annually.

Basic shoe styles

Boots:

A closed shoe with uppers going above the ankle. Can have lacing or be pulled on.

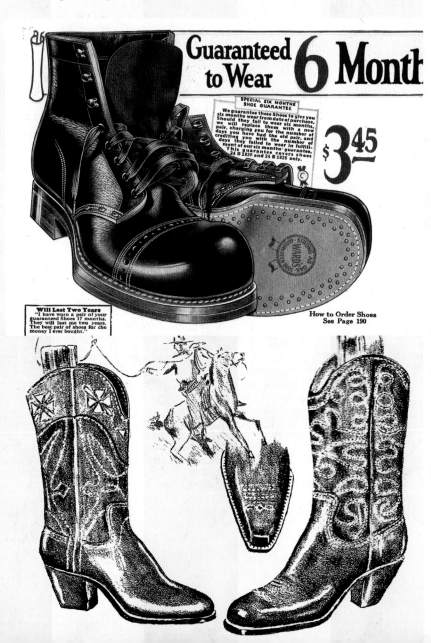

Guaranteed to Wear **6 Month**

SPECIAL SIX MONTHS SHOE GUARANTEE

We guarantee these Shoes to give you six months wear from date of purchase. Should they fail to wear six months, we will replace them with a new pair, charging you for the number of days you have had the old pair, and crediting you with the number of days they failed to wear in fulfillment of our six months' guarantee. This guarantee covers shoes 24 B 1820 and 24 B 1825 only.

$3.45

Will Last Two Years
"I have worn a pair of your guaranteed Shoes 17 months. They will last me two years. The best pair of shoes for the money I ever bought."

How to Order Shoes See Page 190

Brogues or Brogans:
An oxford style shoe with wing tips and usually trimmed with pinking, perforations or stitching.

CORDO-COLOR Wing Tip Brogues

Widths
D, E

A handsome Shoe with lots of character . . . patterned after an expensive British style. Rich-looking Dark Brown Cordo-style leather uppers with long sweeping wing tips; boldly punched medallion toes. Brass eyelets, so popular with the style-wise younger set. Finest Goodyear Welt oak tanned leather soles, leather heels. Sturdy counters; white drill cloth lined vamps; smooth leather insoles, leather lined quarters.

Men's Sizes: 6, 6½, 7, 7½, 8, 8½, 9, 9½, 10, 10½, 11. Widths D and E. Please state size and width wanted in your order. Ship. wt. 2 lbs. 12 oz.

24 C 1530—Dark Brown. Pair **$2.85**

Chukka Boots / Norwegians / Turf Boots:
Ankle boots with two or three eyelets for lacing or a buckle.

Loafers / Moccasins / Slip-ons:
Characteristically slip onto the foot and held on with pressure of the upper with no lacing or fastening.

[F] $6.95 [G] $5.50 [H] $6.95 [J] $7.95

A DOZEN RELAXING STYLES . . choose your favorites

Easy going slip-ons . . cool handwovens . . sporty saddle oxford . .

bold "buckle 'n' straps" . . spongy crepe soles . . tractor tread sole

Monk Straps:
A closed shoe held on by means of a strap across the instep.

Catalog example of brogue style shoes. Montgomery Ward, c. 1925.

Catalog example of chukka or turf boots. Sears, c. 1969.

Catalog example of loafer style of shoes. Sears, c. 1949.

Catalog example of slip-on shoes. Montgomery Ward, c. 1940.

Catalog example of monk strap shoes. Montgomery Ward, c. 1937.

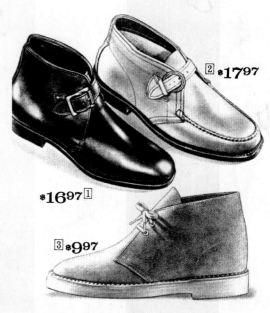

[2] $17⁹⁷

$16⁹⁷ [1]

[3] $9⁹⁷

BOOTS . . rugged he-man look

To Measure see General Catalog

the Most Popular Slipper Styles for Men

$198 PAIR

Fashion's Favorite Monk Style

Catalog example of oxford style shoes.
Montgomery Ward, c. 1945.

Catalog example of men's summer sandals.
Montgomery Ward, c. 1938.

Catalog example of spectator shoes.
Montgomery Ward, c. 1934.

Oxfords:
Shoes with enclosed lacing, aka Bal's or Balmorals.

Sandals:
An open shoe held on with straps or thongs.

Spectators:
Brogue or wing tip oxfords that must have two tone or contrast colors.

Brown and
Smoke

Black and
White

$2.00 PAIR

The LAST WORD in SPORT OXFORDS

Shoes by the Decade

Shoes for men and women with one short limb have been available since the last part of the 1800s, as has being able to repair your own shoes.

THE Ideal Extension Shoe

For all persons having one short limb.

Expert workmanship backed by years of experience.

Write for Booklet.

Past. Present.

Wilfred L. Miller Co., Room 61, 40 W. 28th St., N. Y. City

As we start the 1920s, oxfords were replacing high button shoes, but interestingly enough both basic styles were available in the Sears catalog through the 1960s.

17% stronger than any other dress leather upper

③ ④

KANGAROO $20⁹⁷ either style

Styles 3, 4, 5 are cushioned

5 Kangaroo 19.50

4 Kidskin 13.88 Kangaroo 19.50

3 Kidskin 13.88

2 Kidskin 13.88

1 Kidskin 13.88

Live a soft life in these leathers

Kangaroo, 17% stronger than any other dress leather; resists scuffs, scrapes, keeps its rich, handsome appearance after months of steady wear. Soft, pliant, comfortable—lightweight too.

Kidskin. Extra supple, porous, flexible—conforms to the natural contour of your foot. Gives you comfortable wear and feel.

- Strong, springy steel shanks offer extra support.
- Crushproof Perma-counters help support shoe backs.
- Goodyear welt construction . . . no nails underfoot.
- Perma pure vamp linings resist foot germs.
- Long-wearing leather soles and rubber heels.

Advertisement for an extension shoe. *Munsey's Magazine,* c. 1902.

Catalog example of a home shoe repair kit. Montgomery Ward, c. 1925.

Catalog example of high and low top oxfords still available. Sears, c. 1969.

Catalog example of high and low top oxfords still available. Montgomery Ward, c. 1968.

Catalog example of high and low top oxfords with crepe soles. Montgomery Ward, c. 1925.

Catalog example of high and low top oxfords. Montgomery Ward, c. 1925.

Catalog example of popular white leather shoes. Montgomery Ward, c. 1934.

Catalog example of woven leather shoes for summer wear. Montgomery Ward, c. 1939.

Catalog example of casual shoes for casual clothing. Montgomery Ward, c. 1939.

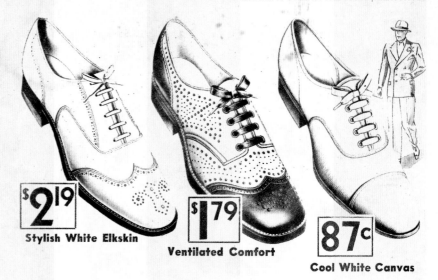

$2¹⁹
Stylish White Elkskin

$1⁷⁹
Ventilated Comfort

87ᶜ
Cool White Canvas

To Determine Correct Size See "How to Measure" on Page 59

Cool Air Conditioned Lightweights ↑   Latest Huarache Style...Cool, Smart ↑

White leather shoes in a variety of styles became a summer staple in the early 1930s and remained until WWII.

Open perforations in basic style shoes and woven leather huaraches offered air flow and cool comfort in summer. These shoes were worn for dress and casual.

As clothing became more casual, footwear followed.

How to Order Shoes under Rationing

Complete safety for your Ration Stamps

when you order your Shoes by mail from Sears

Airplane Stamps No. 1 and 2 are now in effect for Shoes

Most shoes in this catalog are Rationed and a Ration Stamp (either Airplane Stamp No. 1 or No. 2 from Ration Book No. 3) is required for each pair purchased. If you forget to attach ration stamp, we cannot send the shoes.

The government will announce new shoe ration stamps and expiration dates for others from time to time . . . keep in touch with these changes by newspaper.

You can detach stamps from Ration Book only when buying by Mail

Buying shoes from Sears is easy, because OPA permits you to detach shoe stamps from ration book when buying by mail (not when buying at retail). Send just the stamp, not the entire Ration Book.

If we cannot send the shoes you order, or if you return unworn rationed shoes to us for refund, we will send you a special shoe stamp that is good anywhere.

Be sure that stamp is attached carefully to your order blank

Do not hesitate about sending your ration stamp to Sears, because we guarantee the safety of each stamp just as we do your money. We ask only that you use special care in attaching the stamp to your order or letter. Do not send stamp loose in envelope . . . it is very small and might get lost. The best way is to fasten stamp securely in space provided for that purpose on each Sears order blank.

Other Important Facts about Shoe Rationing

Shoe stamps are interchangeable among members of a family. For example, if a husband does not need his stamp, his wife may use it; or both may use their stamps to buy shoes for the children.

Many may qualify for extra ration stamps by applying to local rationing board. Application can be made by the following:

1. Those who do not have at least two pairs of wearable or repairable shoes.
2. Essential workers such as farmers, mailmen, nurses, factory employees who need extra shoes for their work.
3. Those working in an essential industry who require steel toe safety shoes.
4. Children frequently need extra shoes and may obtain them in cases where all ration stamps in family have been used.

Rubber Work Footwear (boots, hi-cuts and work shoes made of rubber) is Rationed but may be bought only with a special certificate from your ration board. Do not send regular ration stamp.

Not all Footwear is Rationed Many types require no stamp

Shoes and slippers made of non-critical materials are Not Rationed and require no ration stamp. Non-Rationed Footwear is available at Sears as follows:

All Women's and Children's Slippers
All Men's and Boys' Slippers
All Infants' Shoes up to size 4
Certain types of Women's Style and Play Shoes
Certain types of Women's and Girls' Oxfords
Certain types of Rubber and Play Footwear]
Catalog Number 15 K 3430, Nurses' Oxford

LASDAM   PAGE 278A . . SHOE RATIONING

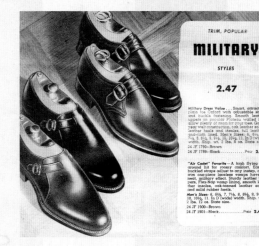

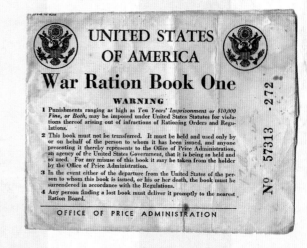

Because many items, like leather and silk, were needed for the war effort, certain clothing items were rationed during WWII.

Summer shoes of Nylon mesh and leather provided cool comfort and a dressier alternative to sandals in the 1950s.

Catalog example of rationed shoes in WWII. Montgomery Ward, c. 1942.

Catalog example of how to order rationed shoes in WWII. Sears, c. 1944.

Example of a War Ration Book, c. 1943. *Courtesy of Todd Nightingale.*

Catalog example of snappy Nylon mesh shoes. Aldens, c. 1952.

BREEZE COOL

Nylon Mesh

Your feet "breathe" in "air-conditioned", wonderfully cool nylon mesh—lasting, handsome, easy to clean! Five of today's smartest two-toners, trimmed in rich mellow leathers. All are Goodyear welt built for longer wear, easy resoling.

6.98 PR. UP

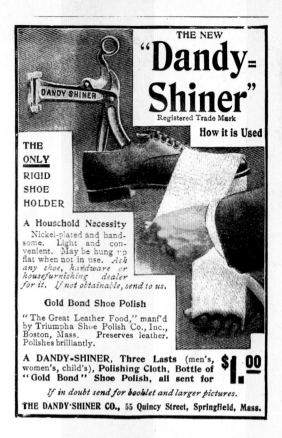

Advertisement for a home shoe shine kit. *McClure's Magazine*, c. 1900.

Catalog example of extreme pointed toe shoes. Sears, c. 1962.

Catalog example of early canvas shoes #1. Sears, c. 1902.

Men's Tennis or Outing Oxfords, $0.40

Weight averages 20 ounces.

No. 15R680 This Oxford is made from a good quality of covert cloth, corrugated rubber sole. Sizes, 6 to 11; no half sizes. Price, per pair..................$0.40

Men's Tennis or Outing Shoes.

No.15R690 This shoe is made from a very good quality of covert cloth, brown kid, lace stays and trimmings; corrugated rubber sole sewed on with waxed thread.
Pair........$0.50

No. 15R691 Boys' sizes, 1 to 5. Per pair, $0.50

Sizes, 6 to 11; no half sizes. Weight averages 28 ounces.

[1] $8.97 [2] $9.77 [3] $9.77 [4] $9.77

Pointed toward style PLUS comfort

Toe shape changed to a very pointed style in the early 1960s, adding to the Beatnik look that had started in the late 1950s and continuing through the British Invasion of the Beatles and other rock bands of the era.

Remember to take good care of your shoes and they will take care of you.

{ Athletic Shoes }

Men desiring fresh air and exercise through vigorous activities at the turn of the twentieth century spent their time golfing, skiing, automobile touring, hunting, hiking, and riding—which all needed specialized clothing: knickers with matching golf coat, swim trunks, wind breakers, hockey jerseys and sweaters, waterproof yellow rain slickers, boxing shorts, and the correct shoes.

Today, men continue their love affair with sports like baseball, football, golf, and basketball. The clothing hasn't changed much in style, but shoes have improved through the decades.

Canvas Shoes

Canvas shoes have been around since the late 1800s, so here's a quick look at their evolution.

For All Uses of Play, Sport or Work Ideal for Children

State Size Wanted

$1.39 For Boys

Men's and Boys' Crepe Rubber Sole Shoe
Cushioned Arch Supports

They're Great For Tennis and Sports

Built-in Arch Cushion reduces foot fatigue. Air Tread cushion insoles. Drill cloth lined Army Duck uppers. Crepe rubber soles. Sturdy outside sole foxing. Inside rubber toe cap. Order half size smaller than shoe.
Men's Sizes: 5, 5½, 6, 6½, 7, 7½, 8, 8½, 9, 9½, 10, 10½, 11, 12. **Please state size.** Ship. wt. pr. 2 lbs. 2 oz.
26 YA 4970—White
26 YA 4971—Navy..Pr.. **89¢**

SIZES for ALL THE FAMILY

There's THRIFT in every step!

LL 3.49 TO 3.79

Rubber suction sole Styles 10 and 11

MM 4.29 TO 4.75

Catalog example of canvas shoe evolution #2. Montgomery Ward, c. 1925.

Catalog example of canvas shoe evolution #3. Montgomery Ward, c. 1933.

Catalog example of canvas shoe evolution #4. Montgomery Ward, c. 1937.

Catalog example of canvas shoe evolution #5. Montgomery Ward, c. 1955.

Catalog example of canvas shoe evolution #6. Montgomery Ward, c. 1968.

Bill Bowerman and Phil Knight changed the face of athletic shoes when they founded Blue Ribbon Sports, a retail outlet, in 1964. Their main product would become known as "Nike®" with worldwide distribution. Major track athlete Steve Prefontaine wore them in competition in 1973, and the rest, as they say, is history.

One of the main dating details is that Nike's stamped the size and year made in their shoes until 1987. The "swoosh" logo was started in 1971, with a "fat swoosh" starting in the late 1970s or early 1980s.

In 1977, Nike began manufacturing their shoes in Taiwan and Korea. In 1981, the firm added Nike Japan and Nike England as their first foreign distributors. And, the shoes were produced in Hong Kong, Ireland, and England in the 1980s. The reissued styles have a tag sewn in at the side rather than on the tongue.

There are many easily available Nike sites across the web to aid with your dating and style names.

Catalog example of early canvas baseball shoes #1. Sears, c. 1902.

Catalog example of early leather baseball shoes #2. Sears, c. 1902.

Catalog example of evolution of baseball shoes #3. Montgomery Ward, c. 1925.

Catalog example of evolution of baseball shoes #4. Montgomery Ward, c. 1934.

Catalog example of evolution of baseball shoes #5. Montgomery Ward, c. 1939.

Men's and Boys' Canvas Baseball Shoes, $1.00 and $0.90.

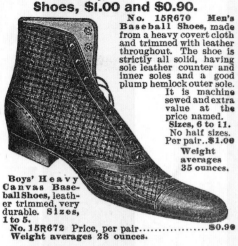

No. 15R670 Men's Baseball Shoes, made from a heavy covert cloth and trimmed with leather throughout. The shoe is strictly all solid, having sole leather counter and inner soles and a good plump hemlock outer sole. It is machine sewed and extra value at the price named. Sizes, 6 to 11. No half sizes. Per pair..$1.00 Weight averages 35 ounces.

Boys' Heavy Canvas Baseball Shoes, leather trimmed, very durable. Sizes, 1 to 5.
No. 15R672 Price, per pair..................$0.90
Weight averages 28 ounces.

Men's Baseball Shoes, $2.20.

No. 15R696 Those baseball players who have had occasion to buy these shoes know that the lowest possible price that has ever been offered on such a shoe is $3.00 per pair and that the best price possible last season was $3.50 per pair. Retail dealers who have bought shoes of a similar grade from leading wholesale houses know that the very best price ever quoted on such a shoe is from $2.35 to $2.65 per pair.

For postage rate see page 4.

Special Sale Price $2⁹⁵

Sprint Shank Model

Bought months ago to make this low Sale Price possible! First quality calf uppers—soft, yet tough and durable. Extra strong stitching. Oak leather tap soles and heels, with flexible sprint shank for speed and comfort. Lined heel. Steel plates between soles protect foot from steel spikes. Black color. Half Sizes: 5 to 11. State size. Ship. wt. 3 lbs.
60 Y 4936—Pair.......Sale Price $2.95

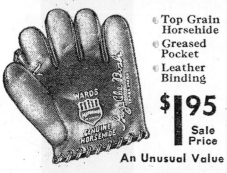

● Top Grain Horsehide
● Greased Pocket
● Leather Binding

$1⁹⁵
Sale Price

An Unusual Value

Men's and Boys' Baseball Oxfords

Strong Flexible Sole

Men's and boys' league model Baseball Oxfords. Strong black chrome side leather. Good wearing leather soles with regulation steel spikes. Unlined. Lace up tightly. State size wanted.
24 B 3405—For Men. SIZES: 6 to 12. Per pair.......$2.98
9 or more pairs. Per pair.......2.79
24 B 3409—For Boys. SIZES: 1 to 5½.
Per pair.......$2.79
9 or more pairs. Per pair.......2.59
Postage, per pair, 12c extra; 9 pairs, 40c extra

High Grade Baseball Oxford
This Baseball Oxford is made with a flexible leather sole which adds speed to your get away when going after a ball or when running the bases. Strong, soft black leather uppers lace up snugly. Smooth insole. Regulation steel spikes.
SIZES: 6 to 11. State size wanted.
24 B 3410—Per pair.......$4.79
9 or more pairs, per pair.......4.59
Postage, 12c extra.

Baseball

The game of baseball dates back to the 1700s in England, with American baseball starting after the Revolutionary War. The game had become an American staple by the 1850s, and continued in popularity after professional baseball started in the 1870s. Here's a look at baseball shoes through the decades.

Anniversary Special—Sprint Shank Baseball Shoes $1⁹⁴
● A $4 Value Elsewhere
● Professional Speed Spikes

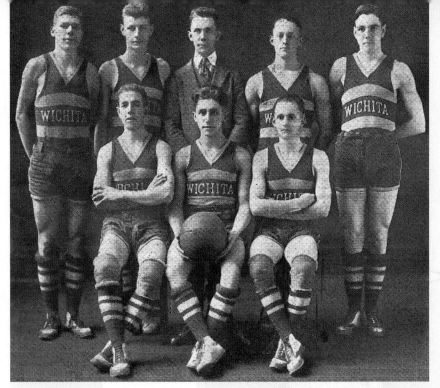

Basketball

Basketball started as a gym class activity in the 1890s, caught on quickly, and moved across America to become a popular indoor game for young men and women. The National Basketball League was established in 1898. Converse introduced Hi-top athletic shoes in 1917 just for playing basketball. Here's a look at how basketball shoes changed by decade.

Photo of early basketball team.
The Wichitan, c. 1918.

Catalog example of basketball shoes #1.
Montgomery Ward, c. 1925.

Catalog example of basketball shoe evolution #2.
Montgomery Ward, c. 1930.

Catalog example of basketball shoe evolution #3.
Montgomery Ward, c. 1939.

Catalog example of basketball shoe evolution #4.
Montgomery Ward, c. 1955.

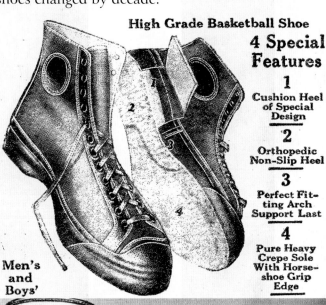

High Grade Basketball Shoe

4 Special Features

1 Cushion Heel of Special Design

2 Orthopedic Non-Slip Heel

3 Perfect Fitting Arch Support Last

4 Pure Heavy Crepe Sole With Horseshoe Grip Edge

Men's and Boys'

Basketball Clothes at Sale Prices
Tufhide Jackets

EVERY price a CUT PRICE! Bright colored, double faced suede cloth. Inside and outside same texture. Cut full with All Wool worsted collar, cuffs and bottom. Pants and shirts listed below match in color.
EVEN SIZES: 32 to 42-inch chest. State size. We Pay Postage.
60 U 5380—Scarlet with white trim.
60 U 5381—Royal blue, white trim.
60 U 5383—Purple with old gold trim. Each..........$3.58

Athletic Shirts

All wool worsted. Chest stripes with one wide stripe in center and one narrow stripe above and below. Round neck style. Cut low under arms. Long body fits well down into pants. Closely knit. Postpaid.
EVEN SIZES: All shirts 28 to 42-inch chest. State size wanted.
60 U 5819—Royal Blue with white stripes. $1.79
60 U 5820—Scarlet with white stripes..... 1.79
60 U 5829—Purple with old gold stripes.... 1.79

Tufhide Pants

Fine double faced suede cloth. About ⅜-inch fiber silk stripe down sides. Loose hanging hip pads. Fly front. Postpaid.
EVEN SIZES: 26 to 38-inch waist. State size.
60 U 5363—Scarlet with white side stripes.
60 U 5364—Royal blue with white side stripes.
60 U 5366—Purple with old gold side stripes.
Per pair..............$1.69

Orders Filled and Shipped Fast!

Special for This Sale Only!

Built special—for this Sale only—by a well known maker of high quality Basketball Shoes. Our prices are the closest we could come to actual manufacturing cost—they assure BIG cash Savings! Built for fast play and long service—uppers of heavy gray duck, gray rubber trimmed with double saddle strap reinforcements. Heavy gray molded sole assures positive grip on the smoothest playing floors. Gray pebble toe cap and double gray foxing assure long wear. Quick shipments. We Pay Postage. State size.
MEN'S SIZES: 6½ to 12.
60 U 4948—Pair.....$1.89
BOYS' SIZES: 2½ to 6.
60 U 4989—Pair.....$1.78

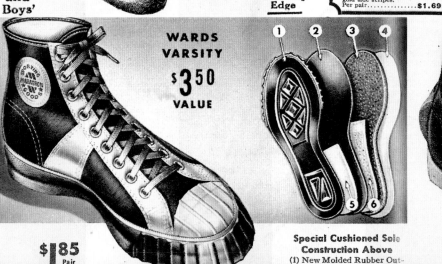

WARDS VARSITY $3 50 **VALUE**

$1 85 Pair

1 2 3 4

Special Cushioned Sole Construction Above
(1) New Molded Rubber Out-

Ⓐ 6.95

Sears Bowling Shoes

Men's

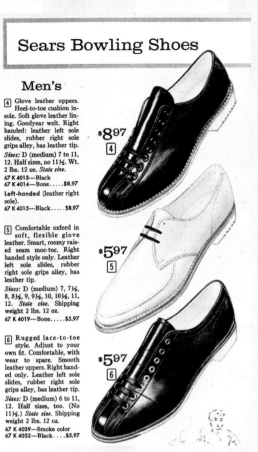

[4] Glove leather uppers. Heel-to-toe cushion insole. Soft glove leather lining. Goodyear welt. Right handed: leather left sole slides, rubber right sole grips alley, has leather tip.
Sizes: D (medium) 7 to 11, 12. Half sizes, no 11½. Wt. 2 lbs. 12 oz. *State size.*
67 K 4013—Black
67 K 4014—Bone.....$8.97
Left-handed (leather right sole).
67 K 4015—Black.....$8.97

$8.97 **[4]**

[5] Comfortable oxford in soft, flexible glove leather. Smart, roomy raised seam moc-toc. Right handed style only. Leather left sole slides, rubber right sole grips alley, has leather tip.
Sizes: D (medium) 7, 7½, 8, 8½, 9, 9½, 10, 10½, 11, 12. *State size.* Shipping weight 2 lbs. 12 oz.
67 K 4019—Bone.....$5.97

$5.97 **[5]**

[6] Rugged lace-to-toe style. Adjust to your own fit. Comfortable, with wear to spare. Smooth leather uppers. Right handed only. Leather left sole slides, rubber right sole grips alley, has leather tip.
Sizes: D (medium) 6 to 11, 12. Half sizes, too. (No 11½.) *State size.* Shipping weight 2 lbs. 12 oz.
67 K 4039—Smoke color
67 K 4032—Black....$5.97

$5.97 **[6]**

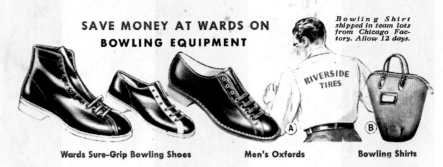

SAVE MONEY AT WARDS ON BOWLING EQUIPMENT

Bowling Shirt shipped in team lots from Chicago Factory. Allow 12 days.

RIVERSIDE TIRES

Wards Sure-Grip Bowling Shoes   Men's Oxfords (A)   Bowling Shirts (B)

Bowling

Bowling has been around with standardized rules since 1895, but didn't gain in popularity until the Depression era. Bowling shoes haven't changed much, but new styles have been added.

Football

Based on the game of rugby, football played in the United Kingdom in the mid-1800s, American football has been played since the late 1800s. The first professional football league was formed in 1903. The National Football League (NFL) was founded in 1922 after using a different name for two years. Football shoes still look pretty much the same as they did a century ago.

Catalog example of bowling shoes #1. Montgomery Ward, c. 1939.

Catalog example of bowling shoes evolution #2. Sears, c. 1962.

Catalog example of football shoes #1. Sears, c. 1902.

Photo of early football team. *The Wichitan*, c. 1918.

Catalog example of the evolution of football shoes #2. Montgomery Ward, c. 1939.

Catalog example of the evolution of football shoes #3. Montgomery Ward, c. 1956.

Men's College Football Shoes, $2.65.
No. 15R667 Those of our patrons who play football and have had occasion in the past to buy first-class football shoes, undoubtedly know that the average price for such a shoe as we are here offering you is from $3.50 to $5.00 per pair.

Wards "Varsity" Football Shoes   **Sole Construction Above**
$5 VALUE

[E] 13.45

[F] 9.75

Men's Popular Crepe Rubber Sole Golf or Sport Oxford

Fine Quality Rugged Golf Shoes at Big Savings!

Golf

The game of golf has been around for centuries, but didn't really become popular in America until an influx of European immigrants in the last few decades of the 1800s brought the game with them. The simple game uses clubs to hit a small ball over a distance and try to put it in a designated hole. There were over 100 golf courses for playing this game in the United States by 1900. Special shoes are worn to improve traction for hitting the ball, and golf clothing is designed for comfort of movement and defeating the elements.

Track

With roots dating back to ancient Greece or before, men have always had running events and track competitions. Races, as rival competitions between members of schools or sports clubs, were heavily promoted in America as early as the 1870s.

The Summer Olympic Games for amateurs, based on the Greek Olympiads, started in 1896. They are currently held every four years. Considered a male dominant sport in the early years, women's sports movements in the early 1920s caused female competitions to be added to the Olympics in 1928.

Catalog example of early golf shoes #1. Montgomery Ward, c. 1925.

Catalog example of evolution of golf shoes #2. Montgomery Ward, c. 1938.

Catalog example of early track shoes #1. Sears, c. 1902.

Photo of early track team. *The Wichitan*, c. 1918.

Men's Professional Running Shoes, $1.95.

Note: Adolph Dassler (Adidas®) has been credited with inventing a track and field shoe with hand forged spikes in 1920, or at least introducing them to runners. But, we know that there were spiked shoes for track guys before then as Spaulding sold spiked shoes for running in the mid-1890s. I wonder exactly what the difference in existing spikes and Dassler's spikes were?

Steel Spikes

Men's Track Shoe

Catalog example of evolution of track shoes #2. Montgomery Ward, c. 1925.

Catalog example of evolution of track shoes #3. Sears, c. 1969.

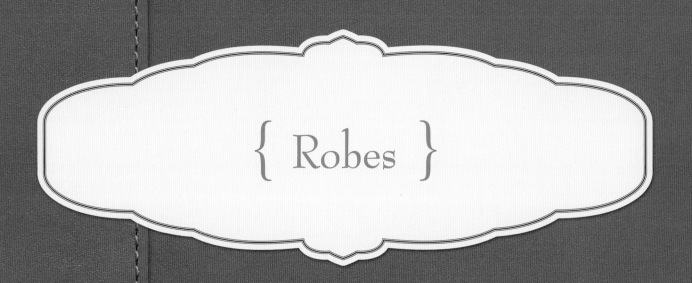

{ Robes }

Catalog example of a warm winter robe. Sears, c. 1916.

Turkish Towels—ds.
Inches.
...is big in size and ...dable for service. A ...priced for this sale, ...res. A rare opportu... ...e in Turkish Towels ...natural cream color. Sold ... about 1½ lbs. ...ly, per pair.... ...**39c**

Superior Quality Ble...
Hemm...
Size, Abou...
No. 96X8554 For ...in towels. The opportu... ...ary 28, 1917, of supplyin... ...for yourself a saving m... ...ter than ordinary in qu... best of service. Woven of cot... tastefully bordered. Extra we... Shipping weight, per pair, abo... Price, during January and ...

Big Bargain Unbleached Turkish Towels— Fringed Ends.
Size, About 13x29 In.
No. **96X8511**
Big value for little money. We have on hand a large quantity of these regular 5-cent Turkish Towels, bought advantageously to sell during this sale. Cream color. Fringed ends. Sold in dozens only. Shipping weight, per dozen, about 1½ lbs. Price, per dozen....... **47c**

Big Value Bleached Turkish Towels— Fringed Ends.
Size, About 13x33 In.
No. **96X8532**
A big value towel at a very low price. One of the best towel bargains we have ever offered. Take advantage of this offering early and lay in a supply. Woven of cotton and bleached all pure white. Sold in half dozens only. Shipping weight of six, about 1 pound. Price, 6 for........**42c**

Large Size Unbleached Turkish Towels—Hemmed Ends.
Size, About 22x38 In.
No. **96X8513**
Get acquainted with this splendid large size towel. It is of good weight and woven of strong absorbent cotton yarn. We purchased them on a low cotton market and can offer you a real bargain. Unbleached or natural cream color. Sold in half dozens only. Shipping wt., of six, about 2 lbs. Price, 6 for........**69c**

Good Quality Bleached Turkish Towels— Hemmed Ends.
Size, Abt. 20x42 In.
No. **96X8534**
Good quality bleached cotton Turkish Towel at a special price. One of our greatest values. Bleached all pure white. Sold in half dozens only. Shipping weight of six, about 2 lbs. Price, 6 for..... **96c**

Specially Priced Double Looped Turkish Towels— Hemmed Ends.
Size, Abt. 21x43 In.
No. **96X8528**
One of our most popular numbers of bleached hemmed end cotton Turkish Towels. A 25 cents each value. Has the necessary weight for daily usage. Sold in pairs only. Shipping weight, per pair, about 15 oz. Price, per pair..... **39c**

Corduroy Weave Bleached Turkish Towels— Hemmed Ends.
Size, Abt. 20x41 In.
No. **96X8529**
Heavy weight and extra value. Woven of very soft absorbent cotton yarn in the new corduroy weave. All white. In great demand for use in hotels and public buildings. Sold in pairs only. Shipping wt., per pair, about 1 lb. Price, per pair.... **43c**

It seems that guys have always had a fascination with robes. At the turn of the twentieth century, a gentleman put on a cotton Cheviot cloth beach robe when he came out of the water after a swim. He wore a heavy terry cloth bath robe after his bath. He donned a dressing gown or room suit to groom and fix his hair before dressing for the day. He adorned himself in a breakfast jacket or house coat to eat his morning meal. And, he snuggled in a blanket robe on a cold winter's night to keep warm in his poorly heated house.

33N1938 — Navy blue and black two-tone.
33N1939—Blue and wine two-tone.
33N1943—Black and old gold two-tone.
Sizes, 34 to 48 inches chest measure. **State size.** Shpg. wt., 2 lbs.
After the day's work is done slip into one of these beautiful All Rayon Brocaded Lounging Robes. Very carefully tailored with the pockets, trimming, collar, cuffs and all underfacings made of genuine Skinner's satin. Attractive Rayon cord girdle. One of the most appropriate gifts for men

$10.98

There were men's robes long before the twentieth century because the Wrapper, Kimono, House Dress, and Bath Robe Makers Union was established in 1901.

Some early robes were as short as a suit jacket, while others were long enough to almost reach the wearer's ankles. And, there were also knee and mid-calf length robes. The majority of robes were made of cotton, wool or Rayon and had a shawl collar, which because of its popularity would later be used as a lapel style for sweaters. Many had up to three patch pockets, they always overlapped in the front, were held in place with a button, and then tied with the sash of matching fabric or silk cording.

Artificial silk (Rayon) jackets and robes even became acceptable cocktail wear during WWI.

Two tone robes of Rayon Brocade with Satin Rayon collar, cuffs, and trim were a well established style by the late 1920s and have remained popular for almost a century. Beacon blankets and wool fabrics made warm, attractive robes to be worn in poorly heated homes.

Catalog example of Beacon blanket robes. Sears, c. 1929.

Catalog example of blanket cloth robe. Montgomery Ward, c. 1925.

Men's Blanket Cloth Robe

The late '20s into the '30s also brought about a Japanese influence with kimono styling, Mandarin collars, and the addition of embroidery.

Smoking jackets, in the styling of actual jackets, appeared as cocktail wear and evening wear in the early 1930s. They were always worn with a tuxedo shirt and tie, with velvet as the most popular fabric for them.

By the late 1930s, buttons were removed, and robes became totally wrap and tie style.

Smoking jackets and breakfast robes had pretty well disappeared and robes were wool for warmth, cotton blanket for comfort, or the tried and true fabric Rayon for a dressier version. Nylon would not come into favorable use for robes until about the end of the '40s and robes remained popular for leisure activities.

Rich Brocade Robe $4.98
Skinner's Satin Trim

Full Silk Lining $7.98
Luxury Jacquard Brocade

WHITTENTON ROBE   DELUXE...WHITTENTON   WARMEST...BEACON CLOTH   FOULARD PULLMAN ROBE   RAYON JACQUARD BROCADE   RAYON LINED BROCADE

Following the WPB regulations for fabric reduction in garments, the sleeve cuffs only appeared in the front for show, but this style remained popular until the early 1960s when there was a return to full turn up cuffs at the sleeves. The WPB regulations also caused the disappearance of tassels on the ends of the sashes, which returned after the war.

Label that is in the Asian robe, c. 1930s.

Example of a hand sewn Asian robe with spiderweb design, c. 1930s. $150-200.

Catalog example showing that whether warm or fancy, robes remained to the knee or below in length. Montgomery Ward, c. 1941.

Catalog example showing satin robes were for dressy occasions. Montgomery Ward, c. 1939.

Catalog example of robes showing sashes replaced braided ties. Montgomery Ward, c. 1945.

Catalog example of fancy satin robes remaining longer length. Montgomery Ward, c. 1949.

The introduction of what we now think of as a TV jacket or Hefner jacket (made popular by Hugh Hefner of *Playboy Magazine* fame) appeared after WWII. It is actually a hip length version of a bath robe and properly referred to as a Lounging Jacket. They were always worn with a shirt, tie or ascot, and slacks for a dressy look in case guests dropped by for a leisurely evening. Since they were worn as a jacket, it was not uncommon for a Lounging Jacket to have shoulder pads just like a suit jacket.

Many robes of the 1940s also had what was called in the catalogs as a "novel button feature", meaning that a button was placed on each side to not allow the sash to slip out of its loops.

Also notable is that the collars on robes followed the width of collars on suits. Wide from the late '30s into the early '50s, changing to skinny in the mid-'50s.

As people got central heating in their homes in the 1950s, robe fabrics became light weight. By the late 1950s, sizing had moved to the back neck either as a separate tag by or attached to the makers label.

From the 1920s on, maker / company labels were sewn into the back neck. And, most robes would have a loop at the back neck for hanging it up on a hook.

Tags from the 1920s through the 1960s were usually paper and sewn to the underside of the left collar.

The late 1950s and early '60s brought about lightweight cotton wrap robes in a kimono style, which were collarless and hit mid-thigh.

■ Example of paper label in robe sewn on underside of left collar, c. 1960s.

□ Catalog example of shorter "Hef" style robe. Sears, c. 1968.

SECTION

3

EVERYTHING ELSE YOU NEED TO KNOW

{ Innovations }

Some of the most amazing and innovative changes and inventions in men's clothing and accessories came during or just after WWI and continued through WWII. These changes, some of which are considered garment basics today, will provide the building blocks needed for dating, with many being covered in the specific garment areas later in this book.

Here's a quick timeline to get you started and give an idea of when the things we take for granted in today's garments came into being:

Year	Innovation
pre-1900s	Intro of pajamas
	Intro of sheepskin lined jackets
	Introduction of canvas shoes
1900	Cuffs added to trousers
	Button down collars introduced by Brooks Brothers for a casual look
1913	First successful slide fastener (zipper)
1914	Introduction of the double breasted suit
	Intro of the button yoke on underwear
	Intro of side tie undershorts issued for WWI soldiers
	Intro of the wristwatch—essentially a pocket watch affixed to a leather strap
1919	Front creases added to trousers

1920s	Labels became commonplace in garments
	Intro of machine knitted clothing: twin sweaters, berets, bathing suits
	Intro of yellow slickers (rubberized cotton) as rain wear
	Intro of Raccoon overcoats
	Belt loops added to men's dress trousers as belts became popular— (braces still worn)
	Intro of pinned or tabbed collars
	Intro of button (barrel) cuffs on dress shirts
	Intro of boxer shorts which were adapted from shorts worn by prizefighters
	Intro of B.V.D.'s—a one piece undershirt and shorts combination
	Intro of pull over sports shirts—which were worn with collar open
	Intro of monogrammed shirts (on the chest towards the waist)
	Intro of elastic waistbands
	Extra seam added to shirt sleeve making it two pieces for better wear
	Intro of the short sleeved shirt
Late 1920s	Intro of swim trunks (sans top)
	Intro of non-prescription sunglasses for the masses
1930s	Intro of the natural linen Palm Beach suit by Sanford Goodall
	Slide fasteners (zippers) sewn into men's trousers
	Intro of formal shirts which buttoned down the front rather than the back
	Intro of the white dinner jacket
	Intro of thigh length coat for playing polo
	Intro of the A shirt (Athletic shirt, wife beater, undershirt) adapted from a tank swimsuit
	Snap fasteners replaced buttons on underwear
	Intro of polo style shirts of knit with short sleeves
	Zippers added to work clothes, sport shirts, and jackets
1932	The Daks Slacks, the first self-supporting beltless trouser, was invented for golfers
1933	Rene LaCoste introduced the crocodile logo embroidered shirt in France
1934	Intro of Jockey shorts (made of jersey knit fabric)
1935	Intro of the T-shirt, tee shirt
1936	Intro of the convertible (loop & button) neck closure on shirts
	Intro of Jockey briefs
	Intro of the Spencer (waist length) jacket
	Intro of Guayabera shirts copied from sugar planters in Cuba
1938	Intro of Beach slacks with a 4" waistband and self straps and buckles for fit
Late 1930s	Popularity of California designed sportswear, Hawaiian prints
	Intro of western wear popularity with novel three button snap cuffs on shirts
	Wool shirts always had pressed creases in the back
	Intro of casual shirts with Boat neck styling
	Intro of the straight bottomed sport shirt made to be worn outside the trousers
	Intro of Hollywood trousers with a high rise, no sewn waistband and lowered belt loops
1940s	Intro of the Bermuda Suit, which was matching jacket and shorts
	Hagger coined the word slacks for casual pants to be worn in the "slack" time between work and sports
1942	Intro of "His 'n Hers" matching shirts
Post WWII	Intro of smoking jackets and short robes
1952	Wash & Wear first marketed for cotton garments

A Real Man's Wrist Watch

Here is the Aviator's model. This New Burlington was built for aviators and is adjusted to keep time to the second anywhere. Fully jeweled—finest nickel movement. Square design. Clear, distinct, military dial. Extra heavy bands. Buckles with sturdy pig skin strap that cannot slip. Send today for beautifully illustrated catalog.

RADIUM DIAL! We furnish this watch with radium when desired using only the highest grade radium. The same as used on the very best scientific instruments. We know positively that this quality of radium will not lose its luminosity for many years; in fact, we believe it will last a lifetime—although we can't claim this definitely as radium has been discovered only a short time.

Only $2.50 a Month!

The superb 21-Jewel Burlington watch, with all these exceptional features, sold direct to you at the rate of only $2.50 per month. Positively the exact price the wholesale dealer would have to pay us. Think of it: Only $2.50 per month for this high-grade, guaranteed watch direct at a remarkable price.

👉 **Send for FREE Watch Book!**

Write today for new Burlington Watch Book. It is absolutely free and prepaid. You will know a lot more about watch buying after you read it. You will know why a man accustomed to a wrist watch will never go without one. Send for this book today and also our special offer. Don't delay — ACT RIGHT NOW!

BURLINGTON WATCH CO., 19th St. and Marshall Blvd., Dept. A277 CHICAGO, ILL.

Write Today for FREE Watch Book

If you could have invested $600 in a Patek Philippe wristwatch with an 18k gold case and handmade in Switzerland in 1950, it could be worth from $2,000 to $20,000 today—depending on style and condition. Wristwatches have come a long way since 1914.

Advertisement for wristwatch to show improvements to styling. *The Red Cross Magazine*, c. 1918.

One of the first wristwatches, which was no more than a pocket watch affixed to a leather strap, c. 1914. Photo taken from TV screen during a broadcast.

Catalog advertisement for Patek Philippe wristwatch, c. 1950. Montgomery Ward, c. 1950.

{ Taking Measurements }

1. Have your measurements taken

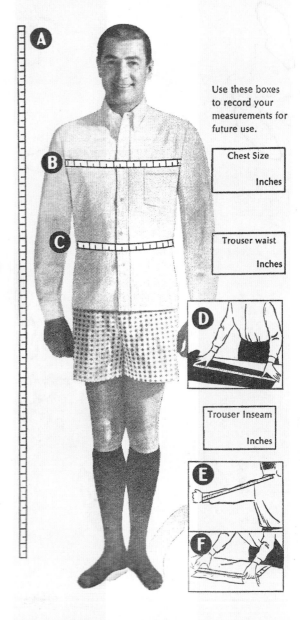

Use these boxes to record your measurements for future use.

Chest Size
Inches

Trouser waist
Inches

Trouser Inseam
Inches

Measurements are more accurate (and clothes fit better) if somebody else takes them for you.

A HEIGHT: measure without shoes.

B CHEST: measure over shirt with tape well up under arms and over shoulder blades.

C WAIST: measure over shirt (without trousers) at position you normally wear slacks. Hold tape firm but not snug.

D TROUSER INSEAM: take well-fitting trousers, lay flat. Measure from crotch seam down leg inseam to trouser bottom.

E SHIRT SLEEVE: wear well fitting shirt, keep arm outstretched. Measure from center collar at back down sleeve to end of cuff.

F NECK: take well-fitting shirt, lay collar flat. Measure from center of collar button to far end of buttonhole.

IT'S EASY TO ORDER CLOTHING . . . JUST MARK IN YOUR EXACT MEASUREMENTS BELOW

Measure from seam at bottom of collar down middle of back to the exact length desired.

Measure from seam in middle of back to seam where the sleeve joins coat at seam in the sleeve.

Take coat sleeves that fit properly and measure the under seam from arm hole to sleeve end.

Place tape over vest around chest, close up underarms and over shoulder blades in back.

Measure around the smallest part of waist over your vest. Hold the tape snug but not tight.

Measure from center seam at back of neck to bottom point of vest for correct length.

Measure from top of waist band down outer seam of trousers to the length wanted.

Measure from snug up in crotch down inseam of trousers to actual length wanted.

Measure around waist over pants. Hold tape snug but not tight. Take with belt off.

Measure around fullest part of seat, snug but not tight. Feet close. Empty pockets.

Encircle Figure Below Nearest Yours, Also Shoulders

Regular Figure | Extra Erect | Flat Chest | Round Shoulders | Stout Figure | Sloping Shoulders | Regular Shoulders | Square Shoulders

IMPORTANT: Read for Ordering Topcoats and Overcoats

Take topcoat and overcoat measures exactly the same as you would for a regular coat. Take chest and waist measures OVER THE VEST. Be accurate. We make all allowances necessary to assure correct fit. Also give the waist and seat measures of pants and be sure to state your height, weight and age.

NOTE—*Do Not Order a Larger Size Than Your Suit Coat.*

FILL THIS IN COMPLETELY BE ACCURATE...DON'T GUESS YOUR HEIGHT AND WEIGHT

	Height	Weight	Age
NECK	Long, Medium or Short?		
SHOULDERS	Regular, Narrow or Wide?		
ARMS	Regular or Large?		
CHEST	Full, Flat or Regular?		
BACK	Regular, Flat, Wide or Prominent Blades?		
FORM	Slender, Regular, or Stout?		
SEAT	Flat, Regular or Prominent?		
SIZE OF COLLAR WORN?			
DO YOU WANT COAT	Snug, Easy or Loose?		
OCCUPATION?			

State Any Difficulty You Ordinarily Have in Getting a Satisfactory Fit

---

Measuring chart for men's clothing. Montgomery Ward, c. 1938.

If you love to buy vintage clothing when you find it and can't always try it on for proper fit, knowing how to measure a garment is the best way to get a good fit for your body.

According to the National Institute of Standards and Technology, the need for mass produced uniforms during the Civil War necessitated the development of standardized sizing. When commercial sizing scales were done after the war, many manufacturers didn't use them, but were known to create their own sizing measurements.

After the turn of the twentieth century and post WWI, menswear sizing had pretty well standardized and has remained so to this day. Since menswear is based on actual measurements, like neck, arm length, waist, and leg length, variations are unusual other than for shrinkage. There are some slight differences in shirts, sweaters, or jackets with S, M, L, XL sizing, and consideration must be given as to whether the garment was to fit close to the body or hang loosely according to the style at the time.

Here are a few tips from catalogs through the years, then I'll follow up with some of my own.

The charts can be a big help, but starting with a garment of your own that fits you well is also necessary. This will help you compare the measurements of your garment with the one you are interested in. Take measurements with a flexible sewing tape measure (not a steel tape) and try to be as accurate as possible.

For a suit or casual jacket: Button or zip the garment and lay it stretched out front side up on a flat surface like a bed, table, or a clean area of the floor. Measure across the chest at the underarms from armpit to armpit; double this figure and you will have the chest measurement. If you measure 22 inches, then double that and you get 44 inches.

As a rule of thumb, subtract 3"-4" for lining, clothing, and movement to get a size. A 47" chest measurement is comparable to today's size 44. The suit pants waist will usually be 6" smaller than the jacket size for a suit.

CHECK SIZE CHARTS BEFORE ORDERING SUITS:

Your size must fall within chart for us to fill your order. Please order only sizes listed.

Men's Suit Chart No. 1

CHESTS:	35	36	37	38	39	40	42	44
WAISTS:	27-29	28-30	29-31	30-32	31-33	31-34	34-37	36-39

Men's Suit Chart No. 2

CHESTS:	36	37	38	39	40	42	44	46
WAISTS:	29-31	30-32	31-33	32-34	33-35	36-38	38-40	40-42

Order SHORT if you're 5'3" to 5'7".

Order REGULARS if you're 5'7½" to 5'11".

Order LONG if you're 5'11½" to 6'3".

The chest measurement should be at least 4"-6" larger than your own chest measures to allow for clothing and movement.

Measure from the top of the shoulder at the seam about half way between the neck and where the sleeve attaches going straight down to the hemline. This is an overall length measurement.

Now, flip the garment over and measure from sleeve seam to sleeve seam across the back shoulders. This is a shoulder measurement and is very important for fit and movement.

Measuring chart for men's clothing. Montgomery Ward, c. 1925.

Men's suit sizing chart. Montgomery Ward, c. 1968.

How To Measure Men's Dress Shirts

How To Measure Neck Size

Take a shirt that fits correctly and lay the collar out flat. Measure from the center of the collar button to the far end of the collar buttonhole. The number of inches is your correct size and the one to give when ordering. Do Not Allow For Shrinkage.

How To Measure Sleeve Lengths

Take a shirt that fits correctly and with a sleeve straight out measure from center of collar band to the far end of the cuff. The number of inches is your correct sleeve length and the one to give when ordering.

You Can Get These Sleeve Lengths				
Neck Sizes:	14	14½	15	15½
You can get these sleeve lengths in neck sizes shown at top of columns.	32 33 34 ..	32 33 34 ..	32 33 34 35	32 33 34 35
Neck Sizes:	16	16½		17
You can get these sleeve lengths in neck sizes shown at top of columns.	33 34 35	33 34 35		33 34 35

Measure from the center back seam at the shoulders across to the sleeve and down the arm with it slightly bent like the previous examples for measuring. This is the sleeve length.

For trousers: fasten all closures, lay the pants down flat, and measure across the inside of the waistband. Double this figure and you will have the waist measurement.

Measure from where the seams cross in the crotch area forward along the closure up to the top of the waistband. This is a front rise measurement.

Flip the pants over and measure from where the seams cross in the crotch area up the back to the top of the waistband. This is a back rise measurement.

Note that the average front rise is 13" and the average back rise is 18". Measurements longer than this will tell you that the pants have a high waist fit and are meant to be worn above the natural waistline.

Measure from where the seams cross in the crotch area down the seam of the inside leg to the hemline. This is the inseam measurement.

And, finally, measure from the top of the waistband down the outer leg to the hemline. This is the outseam measurement.

I also like to check cuff / hemline measurements by laying a leg flat with the creases and measuring across at the very bottom. Double this figure for a measurement to assure a skinny leg fit from the 1920s or late 1950s, early 1960s of about 14"-16", a regular leg fit of about 18"-20", or wide leg fit of 22" or more.

For shirts: Check the sizing on a dress shirt that fits you well. Dress shirts are usually marked as a neck and sleeve length for sizing, i.e. 15 x 33. 15 is the neck size and 33 is the sleeve length. In vintage shirts, the size was sometimes stamped on the tail of a shirt and many launderings will fade or completely take away the ink.

In this case, to get your actual neck size you can either measure around your own neck where a shirt collar lies, or measure the inside of an actual shirt collar that has been buttoned.

Then measure from your center back neck across your shoulder and down your partially bent arm to your wrist or where you like your shirt sleeves to end as shown on the measuring chart. The partial bend allows a little extra length for bending or extending your arm without your shirt sleeve riding up to mid-arm.

Using a shirt that is not marked for size, measure from the center back neck across the shoulder and down the sleeve to the bottom of the cuff. Both methods will give you a sleeve length measurement.

Photo of how to measure the rise on men's trousers.

Measuring chart for men's dress shirts. Montgomery Ward, c. 1938.

Casual and work shirts have been marked as S, M, L, XL since the 1940s. In general, a size Small should fit a 34"-36" chest with room for movement and a 32"-33" sleeve length; a size Medium should fit a 38"-40" chest with room for movement and a 33"-34" sleeve length; a size Large should fit a 42"-44" chest with room for movement and a 34"-35" sleeve length; and, a size XL should fit a 46"-48" chest with room for movement and a 35"-36" sleeve.

Many times a vintage shirt will have no label or a missing one, so no written size is available, or a vintage garment has been improperly laundered or dry cleaned and possibly shrank. In these cases, check the actual chest and sleeve measurements against your own for a proper fit. If a shirt actually measures 38" across the chest, it will more than likely fit like a small as you must remember to include room for movement.

Measuring is hard work!
Is it time to take a breather and cool off?

Bargain Price
Just When You Need a Fan

$5.15

It is always cooler when the breezes blow. Make yourself comfortable with this handy Electric Fan. Take it with you from room to room; use it anywhere you wish. Costs very little to run and our bargain price means a great saving to you on an electric fan of this fine construction.

Keep Cool This Summer

Dependable Quality

The high speed steel fan is 8 inches in diameter and has four blades protected by strong wire guard. Fan is 11½ inches high and has a 5⅜-inch base fitted with three rubber cushions so it will not mar furniture. The fan is adjustable up or down and is held by a convenient thumb nut at the top of the base. The sturdy motor is the universal type and runs on any 105 to 120-volt alternating or direct current. With 6-foot attaching cord and plug.

463 V 395 . . . . $5.15

Postage, 32¢ extra

Montgomery Ward & Co.
[Satisfaction Guaranteed or Your Money Back]
Kansas City Missouri

K-165

Catalog flyer to boost fan sales.
Montgomery Ward billing insert, c. 1925.

{ Fasteners }

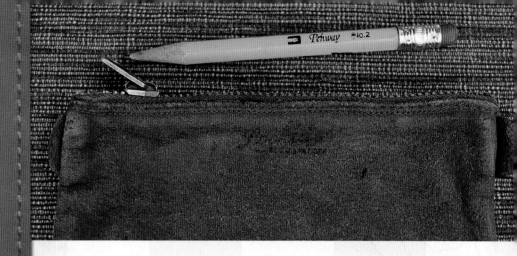

Tobacco bag with Hookless slide fastener,
c. late 1910s. Unknown value.
Photo courtesy of Dale Vest.

{ Talon Zippers }

It's amazing to see how such a simple idea as the slide fastener, later renamed the zipper, has changed the face of clothing and the way we dress. It was an idea whose time had come in 1913 after more than twenty years of trial and failure by many "inventors". The Hookless Fastener Co.'s Hookless #2 was the first successful slide fastener and the basic design has had little modification since that time.

WWI provided opportunities with the Army and Navy Cooperative Co. for military equipment such as spats, leggings, and riding breeches to have slide fastener installed. Then came contracts for fasteners to be used in corsets, health belts, and gloves.

A sturdier Hookless #4 was developed for sleeping bags. The possibilities of its use were endless: purses and handbags, musical instrument bags, vacuum cleaner bags, hat carriers, uniforms, raincoats, pockets of golf bags, and boots.

The word "zipper" was coined in 1922 to dramatize how quickly a fastener worked. The new word was quickly accepted, which increased the acceptance of the device. Within a few years, the slide fastener, which was only sold to manufacturers, had over 100 customers and its uses had been expanded to diaries, ledgers, school bags, pencil cases, hunting boots, and tobacco pouches.

Hookless slide fastener in tobacco bag,
c. late 1910s. Unknown value.
Photo courtesy of Dale Vest.

Zippers were added to work garments in 1926 when H. D. Lee Mercantile Co. bought a million fasteners to put in their union-alls, overalls, and firemen outfits.

The Hookless Fastener Company officially adopted the name of Talon Slide Fastener for its product in 1928.

The creation of the separating fastener in the late 1920s made it possible to put zippers in mackinaw jackets, golf jackets, and sport shirts for outdoor wear. According to James Gray in his book "Talon, Inc.", one manufacturer was looking for new uses for the zipper when he cut an 11" fastener from a pair of galoshes and pinned it into a shirt opening. The "Whizzer Flannel Shirt for men and youths" was born.

During this same time, Hookless decided to sell its fasteners "over the counter" in department stores and for use in home sewing projects. Plako fasteners had been peddled door to door for a few years, so Hookless thought that the need was there. Dritz-Traum, a company already supplying notions and kits to stores, bought the fasteners directly from the factory and packaged them with instructions for sale. Talon slide fasteners were available in nickel silver and NuGild (gold tone) finishes.

■▦ Hookless slide fastener stating name and "Reg. U.S. Pat. Off", c. early 1920s. Unknown value. *Photo courtesy of Dale Vest.*

▦▦ Hookless slide fastener front view, c. 1925-1928. Unknown value. *Photo courtesy of Dale Vest.*

▦▦ Hookless slide fastener back view showing patent imprints, c. 1925-1928. Unknown value. *Photo courtesy of Dale Vest.*

▦▦ Talon Hookless slide fastener front view, c. 1928 to early 1930s. Unknown value. *Photo courtesy of Dale Vest.*

▦▦ Talon Hookless slide fastener back view showing patent dates, c. 1924 to early 1930s. Unknown value. *Photo courtesy of Dale Vest.*

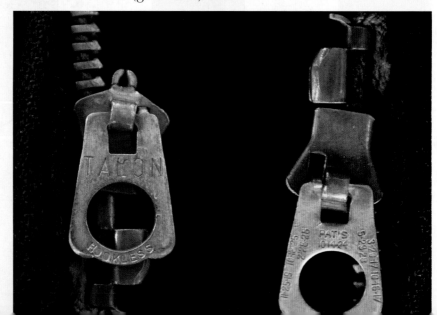

Montgomery Ward introduced shirts with slide fasteners in 1932. To help launch a campaign in 1933 to put the slide fastener in everyday clothing for men and women, Hookless devised an enameling color process to make the zipper match what it was being sewn into.

Hookless had already won a market for slide fasteners in children's clothing and men's work clothes, so they decided to focus on men's casual and dress clothing.

Hart, Schaffner and Marx® and B. Kuppenheimer cautiously placed small orders in 1934 for slide fasteners that would be installed in their suit trousers. The clothing unions completely opposed this new idea. A button fly cost a couple of pennies to install while a slide fastener would cost almost a dollar because of the time and difficulty. This made trousers with zip flies much more expensive.

New equipment had to be engineered to make the fastener application easy and accurate in each type of garment. And, even a new method of constructing trousers to make them better suited for a fastener had to be implemented. Not only was this accomplished, few designers were given the chance for input and to give trousers some style.

Talon package showing zipper pull for heavy jackets, c. 1940.

Talon package showing zipper pull for jackets, sweaters, etc., c. 1940.

Talon jacket zipper pull, c. 1940s. Unknown value. *Photo courtesy of Dale Vest.*

Talon zipper pull from WWII military jodphurs at the bottom of the legs c. early 1940s. Sold in 2009 for $60.

Talon pocket fastener zipper and Talon package illustration, c. 1938. Unknown value.

Catalog example of Talon pocket fastener zipper. Montgomery Ward, c. 1939.

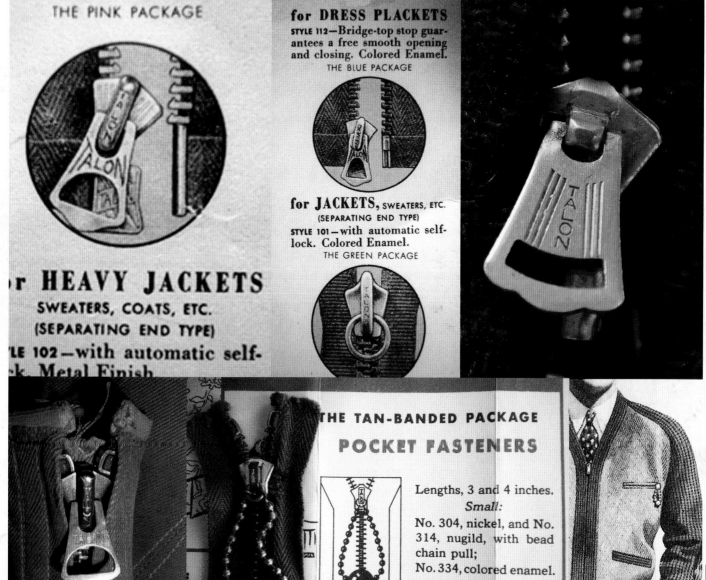

Streamlined Clothes Use Talon Zips

Give clothes fastenings streamlined perfection . . . use **Talons!** Rustproof metal on cotton tape. Wash without harm. Sewing instructions. **State tape color, length.** Shpg. wt., ea., 3 oz.

14ᶜ
Ea.
5-in. Length

Catalog example of Talon zippers for home sewing, c. late 1930s. Sears, c. 1939.

Early Talon separating zipper with unique bottom stop, c. early 1940s. This item sold in 2009 for $165.

Installed early Talon separating zipper with unique bottom stop, c. early 1940s. Unknown value. *Photo courtesy of Dale Vest.*

Improved stop on Talon separating zipper, c. 1940s. $1-5 because of color.

Separating jacket zipper with oversized pull, c. 1940s. $1-5 because of color.

A huge advertising campaign in 1937, coupled with the Duke of Windsor sporting slide fasteners in his trousers, was a boon for the industries involved. According to Gray, in the 1936-37 season over twelve million slide fastener units were sold just for trousers. That same year the board of Hookless Fastener Company voted to adopt its trademark name of Talon.

Zippers were available for home sewing through the catalog by the late 1930s. Separating jacket zippers got improvements, like an easier to install mechanism and their bottom stops. Note that this zipper is grommeted to the fabric at the bottom.

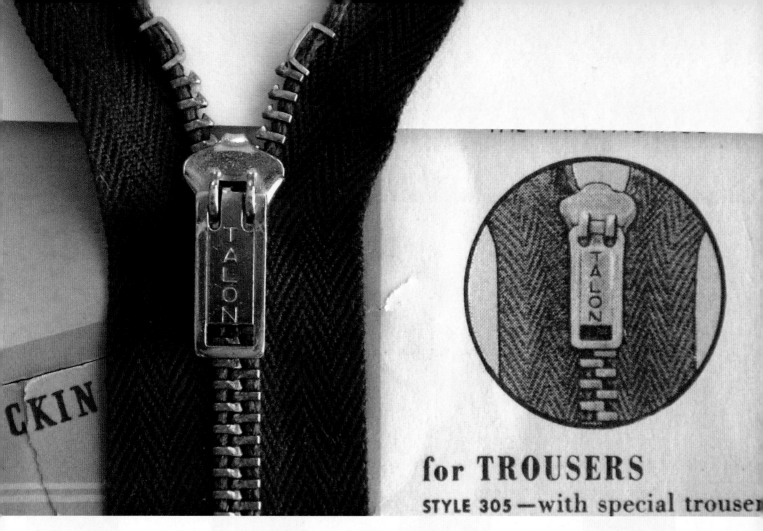

for **TROUSERS**

STYLE 305 — with special trouser

Zippers were not essential to the war effort, but many of Talon's competitor plants closed to manufacture other items or simply went out of business. Talon supplied zippers to the armed services, but because of supply shortages of metals for fasteners they also added the manufacture of gauges, tools, and fixtures for munitions manufacture to their plants.

During the war, zippers were color packaged for the garment for which they were to be used by home sewers. However, a single zipper style was used interchangeably, showing up in men's trousers and women's skirts on manufactured clothing. Plastic zippers, which had been around for almost a decade, were used to ease the shortage of metal ones.

Skirt zipper shown beside Talon package. Package shows trousers zipper to note that many zippers were used for more than one purpose, c. 1938. Less than $1.

Plastic Talon zipper to ease metal shortages, c. 1942. $5-10.

Plastic Talon zipper package bottom, c. 1942. $5-10.

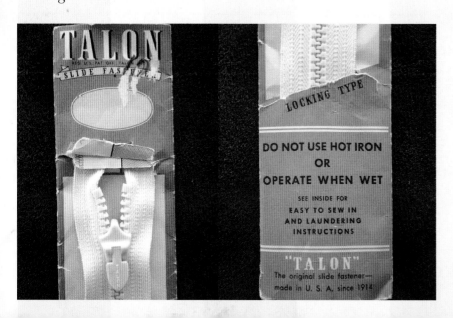

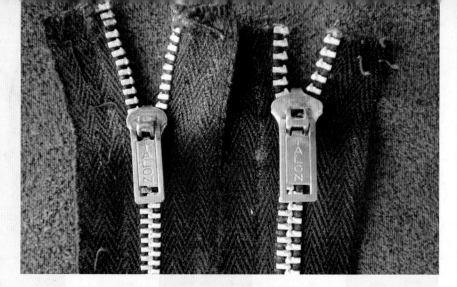

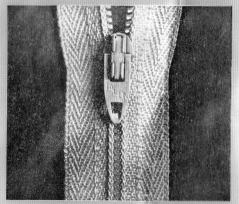

Talon ZEPHYR NYLON ZIPPER

The most remarkable trouser zipper ever!

Made of two continuous nylon coils...the Talon Zephyr is so new and revolutionary in design it makes all other zippers a thing of the past. It's truly the new elegant mark of men's fine tailoring!

First self-locking slider in trousers! Exclusive "Memory-Lock", remembers to lock even if the wearer forgets. Always use the pull tab to open zipper. Never rip fly open.

After the end of the Depression and war, the American public wanted new clothing, and Talon was glad to oblige the clothing manufacturers with plenty of zippers. If you look closely, you can notice subtle changes in the teeth size and zipper pulls.

The company continued to add new products to its line: Big-Zip for men's and boy's jackets, and Little-Zip, a slimmer, lighter zipper for men's trousers, were introduced in the late 1950s.

The year 1960 brought the Zephyr fastener, made of Nylon filament and based on a spiral coil rather than teeth. But best of all, this entire fastener could be dyed the color of the fabric it was to be sewn into and the color could not chip. It was smaller and more flexible than the standard metal zip as well.

By the end of the 1960s, Nylon zippers had pretty well replaced metal zippers in the manufacture of new clothing and for home sewers.

Metal zippers made a comeback in the 1980s, especially for heavier weight fabrics in slacks and jackets, so remember to look at the label for dating.

{ Other Brands of Zippers }

Although Hookless / Talon is one of the most recognizable names for slide fasteners / zippers, they were not the only brand that has been available or used through the decades.

The U.S. clothing manufacturers mainly used zippers made in America and European manufacturers used fasteners made close to home.

▢ Late '40s trouser zipper pull (left) shown beside early '50s trouser zipper pull to illustrate change in zipper teeth size, c. 1940s and 1950s. Less than $1.

▢ Nylon zipper advertisement flyer found in back pocket of NOS trousers, c. 1960. No value.

▢ Catalog example of slide fasteners other than Talon. Montgomery Ward, c. 1935.

▢ Catalog example of slide fasteners other than Talon to compare pulls. Montgomery Ward, c. 1937.

5-INCH LENGTH 8¢

Bargain Sale SLIDE FASTENERS

Wards Slide Fasteners

SEPARATING STYLE

Fine quality Slide Fastener especially constructed to open at bottom. Pre-shrunk cotton. Rust-proof metal. For jackets, cardigans, children's leggings, sports-wear of all sorts.

Colors: Black, gray, navy blue or tan. State color, length.

20 U 4850 — Ship. wt. each, 3 oz.

Length	Price
10-inch Each	27¢
18-inch Each	37¢
20-inch Each	43¢
22-inch Each	45¢
24-inch Each	47¢

NON-SEPARATING

A Slide Fastener you can depend on — securely attached to specially woven cotton tape, pre-shrunk to prevent puckering, made of rust-proof metal.

Colors: Black, white, tan, gray. State color, length.

Ship. wt. 3 oz.

20 U 4848—

Length	
5-inch, Each	17¢
7-inch Each	17¢
8-inch Each	19¢
10-inch Each	21¢
12-inch Each	23¢
24-inch Each	39¢

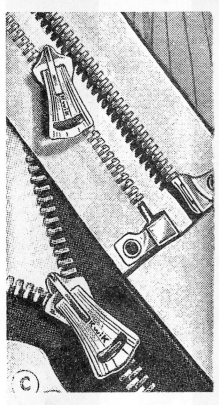

(B) 16 PC 203—Misses' Dres
Even sizes 12 to 20. See Pg. 2
for details. *Postpaid.* Ea...1

(C) 16 PC 220—Child's Dres
Age-sizes 2 to 12. See also P
286. *Postpaid* Ea..........1

(D) 16 PC 214—Misses' Spor
Dress. Sizes: 12, 14, 16, 18, 2
State size. *Postpaid.* Ea....1

"KWIK" SLIDE FASTENERS

- Rust-proof Metal
- Pre-shrunk Cotton Tape
- Locks at Any point

14c
5 to 9-Inch
Closed End

Smooth operating; no rou
edges; cannot open accident
Sew on visibly or invisibl
Instructions included. Lengt
given are for metal parts.

By 1938, there were over forty-five firms in Germany, Great Britain, Italy, Belgium, and Switzerland that were making zippers. Additionally, there were many more zipper factories in at least nineteen other countries throughout Europe.

Invisible zippers with cloth over the teeth were first patented and introduced in the late 1930s. Many companies produced these, but Talon waited to venture into invisible zippers with hidden plastic teeth until the 1960s.

Catalog example of slide fasteners other than Talon to compare pulls and separating bottom. Montgomery Ward, c. 1938.

Catalog example of "invisible" zipper with covered teeth. Montgomery Ward, c. 1938.

Waldes "invisible" zipper with covered teeth in original package, c. 1946. $1-5.

KOH-I-NOOR "KOVER-ZIPS"

A grand type of Slide Fastener that is easier to apply and completely invisible! All metal is hidden by pre-shrunk Cotton Tape. Rust-proof metal; locks in any position. Sewing instructions included. Lengths given are for metal parts.

24c
5 to 9-Inch
Closed End

Colors: White (may be dyed) Black, Navy or Brown. **State color, length.** Ship. wt. 4 oz.

16 C 2505—Closed End Style for dresses, blouses, skirts.

Length	Each	Length	Each
5-inch	24c	12-inch	33c
6-inch	24c	15-inch	39c
7-inch	24c	18-inch	44c
8-inch	24c	20-inch	48c
9-inch	24c	24-inch	55c
10-inch	29c	State length.	

16 C 2516—Open End Style. For all "coat-like" garments.

Lengths	Each	Lengths	Each
10-inch	37c	20-inch	57c
12-inch	39c	22-inch	59c
15-inch	48c	24-inch	63c
18-inch	54c	State length.	

Below is a list of slide fastener / zipper companies and the date they starting selling their fasteners. Note that many companies were in business selling snap fasteners, straight pins, safety pins, staples, paper clips, hook & eye fasteners, buttons, and many other items well before they started producing and selling zippers.

Date	Company
1905 - 1908	C-curity Fasteners
1910	Plako Fasteners
1912	Hookless #1
1913	Hookless #2 or the Hookless Hooker
Early 1920s	Coats & Clark®
1924	E Claire (France)
1924	Kynoch (England) aka Ready Fasteners
1924	Lightning (Canada)
1924	Lion
1924	Zipp or Zipp-Werk (Germany)
1920s	Prentice E-Z Lok
1930	YKK® (Japan)
1931	Waldes® (started selling snap buttons in 1906)
1934	Koh-i-Noor® Kover Zip - hidden zipper (Czech)
1934	Conmar®
1936	Ideal
1930s	Lightning (England)
1930s	Crown by Coats & Clark
1930s	YKK (Japan)
1940s or earlier	Tefas
1940s	DOT (England)
1940s	Kwik (Germany)
1940s	Ri-Ri (Swiss)
1940s	Ritsch (Germany)
1940s	Ruhr (Germany)
1940s	Rapid (Germany)
1940s	Elite (Germany)
1940s	Rheinadel (Germany)
1940s	Serval (owned by Ideal)
1940s	Aero
1940s*	Prym (Germany)
1948	Gripper Zipper by Scovill®
1950s	Harro
Unknown	Falcon
Unknown	Gusum
Unknown	Ready

A garment cannot be older than the zipper that it was originally sewn into. For example, we know from the above information that Waldes started making zippers in 1931, but a quick check of the trademark website tells us that they didn't start producing "separable slide fasteners" (separating zippers) until 1948. So, if your garment has a Waldes separating zipper, then it can't be older than 1948.

NOTE: To maintain your old metal zippers and to keep them sliding easily, rub some wax or soap on the teeth. Please do not use anything spray on (like WD-40®), greasy (like 3-in-One® Oil), or any agent which might wet the area as it can damage, discolor or cause the fabric holding the teeth to weaken.

Finally, a few words of wisdom from a Talon package:

{ Other Fasteners }

Buttons are known to have been used in ancient times (before Christ). Buttonhole machines came into the manufacturing world in 1880.

Original package of Mother of Pearl buttons, approximately .5" in diameter, c. 1930s. $1-5.

Mollusk shell showing how buttons are laid out before they are cut, and an actual 1.25" button after cutting, c. 1940s. Unknown value. *Courtesy of Cathy Mong.*

Variety of bone, wood, and celluloid buttons from men's suits, approximately .5" in diameter, c. 1930s. $5-10.

Card of pearl sport shirt buttons, approximately .5" in diameter, c. 1940s. Less than $1.

Card of washable buttons, approximately .75" in diameter, to take advantage of the wash and wear fad, c. 1950s. Less than $1.

Removable 1" WWII military buttons for ease of cleaning and pins to hold them in place, c. 1940s. Less than $1.

Victorian or Edwardian shoe buttons, approximately .38" in diameter, c. 1900 - 1910. $10-15.

GUARANTEED!

Talon Slide Fasteners are guaranteed. If one should fail under ordinary, everyday wear, return it to us, and we will give you another, free of charge.

TO LAUNDER!

Close the fastener before putting the garment in the water, and keep closed until thoroughly dry. If you put the garment through the wringer, be sure the fastener is flat as it goes through.

Laundering instructions for Talon zipper from original package, c. 1938.

Package of Clinton hook and eye fasteners, c. 1930s. $1-5.

Advertisement for Clinton Safety Pins. Unknown magazine, c. 1900s.

Advertisement for Capsheaf Safety Pins. *Home Needlework Magazine,* c. 1905.

Package of Pinettes safety pins to hold shank and removable buttons in place, c. 1950s. Less than $1.

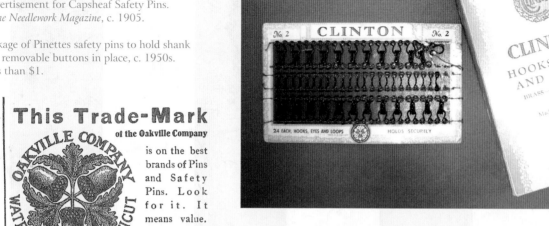

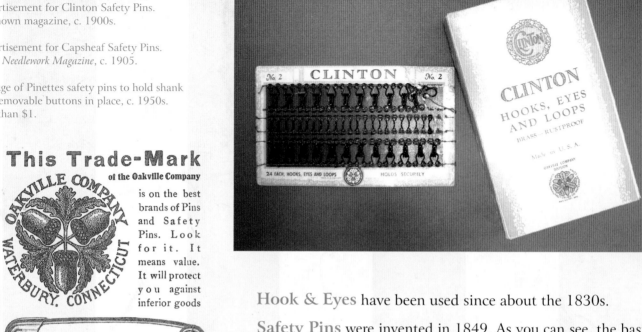

Hook & Eyes have been used since about the 1830s.

Safety Pins were invented in 1849. As you can see, the basic safety pin hasn't changed in the past one hundred and fifty years.

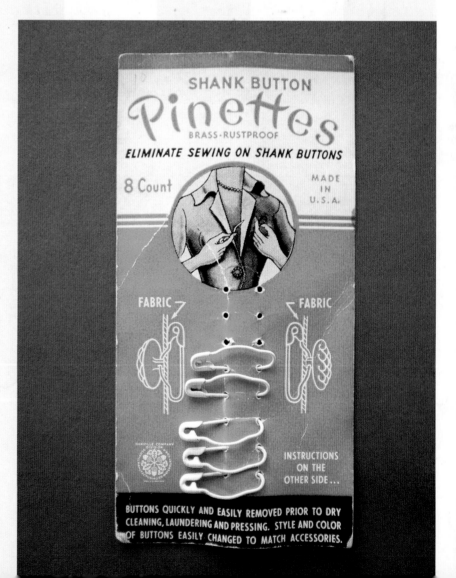

Snaps were first patented in Germany in 1885 to fasten men's trousers and the idea quickly spread around the world. The Ball & Socket Fastener Company is one of the oldest recorded companies for snaps in the US.

In 1921, an article in the *Pittsburgh Press* suggested that men's trouser cuffs be held up with snaps and then could easily be unsnapped, turned down, and the dirt brushed out of them.

In the mid-1930s, someone came up with larger snaps for menswear and they were quickly engaged for that use. Scoville Manufacturing introduced snap fasteners on men's underwear about 1936.

Rockmount® (founded in 1946) claims to be the first company to put snaps on western shirts. However, a snap that looked like a button was shown in 1936 on a work shirt and on cowboy style shirts in Gene Autry western movies as early as 1938.

We also know that some snaps can be dated to their oldest possible use. For example, Scovill Co. started selling Puritan brand snap fasteners in 1892, Dot Snappers® in 1938, Klikit® snap fasteners in 1940, Whipper Snap® in 1967, and Mighty Snap® in 1974. So, if you have a garment with a Whipper Snap, it can't be older than 1967.

Velcro® was patented in 1951; its many uses didn't catch on until it was used on space suits by NASA in the 1960s. The patent expired in 1978, prompting imitations from around the world—mostly known as loop and hook fasteners.

Sometimes when the labels are missing, there are subtle clues in the fastenings. Many times the brand will be etched or embossed in the buttons, or the buckle. We know that these belong to a older item because they are copper, while later buttons or buckles will be brass.

Package of Koh-i-noor snaps, c. 1920s. $1-5.

Catalog example of shirt with snap closures. Montgomery Ward, c. 1936.

Example of Pay Day and Powr House embossed overall fastenings, c. 1940s. Less than $1.

Work Shirts with Plenty of Style .. cut from 79c to

- Main Seams Triple Stitched
- Deep Pleated Back with Smart Half Belt
- Two Pockets, Interlined Collar, Long Tails
- Double Shoulder Yokes

67c EACH

{ Fibers, Fabrics, and More }

{ Manmade Fibers }

If a garment has a tag with a certain stated fabric, that particular garment cannot be older than when the fabric was first put into use, patented or trademarked as the case may be. For example, if you have a garment that says Lastex on a label, then it cannot be older than 1934 when the fabric was invented.

Basic natural fabrics known to have been used since BC:

Silk	Wool	Linen
Cotton	Ramie	Hemp

Fibers used since Colonial Days:

Shantung (Silk)	Angora	Tussah
Doupion	Alpaca	

Manmade fibers and/or treatments	When they came on the market	Manmade fibers and/or treatments	When they came on the market
Acetate	1923/24	Neoprene	1931—synthetic rubber
Acrylic	1944	Nylon	1935/ not used in clothing until 1938/ rationed during WWII
Arami	1961—high temperature resistant	Olefin fiber	1949
Ban-lon	1953	Orlon (Acrylic)	1941—polyacrylic
Bemberg Rayon	1926—name registered in 1964	Perlon	1955—petrochemical based fibers
Cassimere	pre-1920s	Polyester (Terylene)	1941
Celadon	1921	Polyolefin	1961
Celanese	1922	Polypropylene	1961
Cordura Rayon	1929—quit making in 1963	PVC	1926
Crylor	1950s—polyacrylic fibers	Rayon	1910—called Artificial Silk until 1924
Dacron (Polyester)	1953	Rhovyl	1948—polyvinyl chloride fibers
Dralon	1963—polyacrylic fibers	Rilsan	1950s—petrochemical based fibers
Dupont		Rubber	1930
Antron III	1970	Rubberized Cotton	late 1930s?
Dupont Antron	1959-60	Sanforizing	1930—for shrinkage control
Dynel	1950s—polyacrylic fibers	Saran	1941
Fortrel (Polyester)	Early 1970s	Serge	pre-1920s
Fresco	1906—worsted fabric	Spandex	1958-59
Glass Cloth	1936	Sportex	1921
Gore-Tex	1989	Tencel (Lyocell)	1993
Gossamer	1950s—lightest weight fabric of the time	Triacetate	1953-54
Kevlor	1966	Tricotine	1920s
Kodel (Polyester)	1958	Tricot (Nylon)	late 1940s
Lastex	1934	Ultrasuede	1971—not registered until 1974
Lurex	1945	Velon Plastic	1946—plastic film for raincoats
Lycra	1962	Vinyon	1939—polyvinyl fibers
Mercerized cotton	1889	Viyella	1907—cotton and wool blend
Metallic fibers	1946	Washable Wool	1954
Microfibers	1989	Wool Velour	1920s
Modacrylic fiber	1949	Worsted Wool	1870s
Movil	1950s—polyvinyl fibers	Zelan	1938—treatment to repel water

Many of the manmade fibers listed above are patented and may also be trademarked.

By looking at the list, you can see that research during WWII brought about a flurry of new fabrics to ease the shortages caused by the war effort. Newer versions of cellulose-based fabrics, like Viscose and Rayon, improved and proved to be substantially cheaper to produce than the originals.

The real innovations came in the 1950s with synthetic, petrochemical-based fibers to ease the housewives' drudgery of ironing. When these fibers were blended in about equal parts with wool, they became miracle fabrics that absorbed little water, discouraged moths, held their shape, were more lightweight than just wool, and didn't wrinkle as much.

Full synthetic fabrics like Orlon couldn't be ironed. Nylon shirts were passable when hung to dry, but they did not hold their shape well and were hot to wear. Thus, the increased popularity of ventilated and open weave fabrics in the 1950s.

By the mid-'50s, synthetic fabrics were found in many styles of clothing for men including shirts, socks, trousers, and business attire. Some things remained sacred, like 100% cotton for undershirts, Jockey and boxer shorts, and work socks. At least for the first part of the decade.

Nylon t-shirts, athletic shirts, and briefs became available in the mid-'50s, as well as Dacron & cotton blends.

NOS Nylon shirt with fabric stated on hang tag, c. 1950s. $40-60.

{ Common Fabrics Used in Men's Clothing }

Brocade:
A woven fabric with raised design most often used for robes, smoking jackets, and formal wear.

Camelhair:
Fine camel hair woven into a soft cloth, usually tan in color, and used for sport coats and overcoats.

Cashmere:
Fibers from the cashmere goat are often blended with other fibers to produce a soft fabric often used for sweaters, sport coats, and overcoats.

Chambray:
Lightweight cotton fabric usually seen as light blue and used for work shirts.

Corduroy:
Cotton or Rayon fabric with a cut pile and wide or narrow cords used for slacks, jackets, shirts, and sports coats.

Gabardine:
Cotton, Rayon, or wool fabric with a tight weave and fine ribbed effect. Mostly seen in 1940s through 1960s clothing, but still in limited use today.

Linen:
Flax plant fibers woven into a fine or heavy fabric used for shirts, slacks, suits, and sports coats.

Madras or Madras Plaid:
A woven plaid of Indian cotton that became popular in the 1960s for its "bleeding" qualities, which made it fade with each laundering.

Palm Beach Cloth:
A blend of mohair and cotton fabric designed to be worn in warm weather. Not used by, nor to be confused with Sanford-Goodall's Palm Beach brand.

Seersucker:
Crinkled cotton fabric with permanently woven stripes, mostly seen as blue and white, and used for suits, casual shirts, sports coats, slacks, and shorts.

Tweed:
A textured fabric woven of many colors of wool and mostly used for suits, trousers, sports coats, jackets, overcoats, and hats.

Velour:
A velvet-like fabric that can be woven of natural or synthetic fibers and is usually identified with jogging suits of the 1980s and 1990s.

Worsted Wool:
Wool fabric woven after the fibers have been smoothed and made smaller in diameter. It is softer, smoother, and lighter weight than regular wool and can be used in any garment to replace wool.

NO MORE WASHEE WASHEE - MELICAN MAN WEAR CELLULOID COLLAR AND CUFF.

Make your shirt money buy full value

You choose a shirt for its attractiveness, but you want it to wear. Signal Shirts combine style, comfort and service, and save you shirt money.

It will surely satisfy you, as Signal Shirts have satisfied thousands of others. You never had a shirt to stand up so well under hard service.

Signal Tubtest Coat Style Shirts
UNION MADE

Signal Shirts are made of **Tubtest** fabric, of fast and durable color. "You can't fade a Signal Shirt." They please railroad men because they are comfortable, yet fit perfectly; the neckband does not bind; buttonholes are strong, and the buttons are fastened on TO STAY. They satisfy because they are excellent work shirts, while still dressy enough for every day wear.

◻ Victorian trade card stating, "No more washee washee—melican man wear celluloid collar and cuff.", c. 1880s. $10-15.

◻ Advertisement showing Signal Tubtest Union Made shirts. *The Railroad Trainman*, c. 1917.

{ Fabric Processes }

Fabric shrinkage in garments has always been a problem. Early efforts at laundering usually led to a smaller, tighter fitting shirt, and was still a problem by the late 1800s. Shrinkage was controlled by wetting the fabric, then letting it dry while tension was applied.

Sweet Orr used their Ace of Spades process as early as 1908 to control denim shrinkage.

Cluett & Peabody, owner of Arrow shirts, figured out how to control shrinkage of their detachable collars with a process called "Clupeco" in the early 1900s. When soft collars were added to dress shirts in the 1920s, the collars were good, but the shirts shrank.

Hilker-Wiechers made their Signal shirts and overalls with Tubtest fabrics "that will not fade and means the least amount of shrinkage and guarantees long wear", according to an April 1917 ad in *The Railroad Trainman*.

"Rely-on-sized", a process used by the maker of Big Yank clothing, is thought to have been patented sometime in the late 1920s to reduce shrinkage. It would be in direct competition with Sanforized.

The Sanforizing process was invented by Sanford Cluett and patented in 1930 by Cluett & Peabody as a way to decrease shrinkage of cotton fabric to 1% before it was cut into garments, and afterwards with the laundering process.

Thus, cotton made a comeback over silk as a favorite for dress shirts in the 1930s because cotton shirts would no longer shrink and become too small to wear. Many other garments, like casual shirts, work shirts, trousers, and other garments made of cotton quickly appeared advertising Sanforized.

Other less known processes were introduced to reduce shrinkage, but never gained the popularity and exposure of Sanforized.

New Water-Finish Process

SANFORIZED

Cluett, Peabody & Co., Inc. permits use of its trade-mark "Sanforized," adopted in 1930, only on fabrics which meet this company's rigid shrinkage requirements. Fabrics bearing the trade-mark "Sanforized" will not shrink more than 1% by the Government's standard test.

NOTE THE WORDING: From the first advertising in the 1930s until about 1949, the wording for Sanforized was "shrinkage less than 1%". Sometime between 1950 and 1954 the wording changed to "shrinkage no more than 1%". If the wording accompanies Sanforized on a label, this little bit of information makes it easier to date.

Sanford Cluett continued his quest to control shrinkage in other fabrics and in 1940 patented Sanforset® to control the shrinkage and stretch in Rayon to 2%. In 1948, he patented Sanforlan® to control shrinkage in wool, which was trademarked in 1950. Sanforized plus® followed in 1955 for wash & wear smoothness without ironing, and then Sanford plus 2®, a version of durable press. Sanfor-knit™ was the process for cotton and cotton blend knits, and Sanfor-set™ was to control shrinkage and give easy care.

Catalog example of the new "water finish process" for shrinkage control. Montgomery Ward, c. 1931.

Catalog example of "Yukon Permana Shrunk" shirts. Montgomery Ward, c. 1932.

Catalog example of "Sanforized" for never shrink shirts. Montgomery Ward, c. 1932.

Catalog example of "mill shrunk" cotton fabric for denim, which had been around since the early 1900s. Montgomery Ward, c. 1934.

Advertisement showing how the wording changed for Sanforized fabric from "shrinkage less than 1%" to "shrinkage no more than 1%". *Ladies Home Journal*, c. 1954.

Label showing Sanforset, a fabric process patented in 1940. This label dates to after 1976 because of the cotton seal.

Catalog example of Buck Skein fabrics treated with Du Pont processes. Sears, c. 1935-36.

After the death of Sanford Cluett in 1968, the Sanforized process was licensed for use in other countries, and by the late 2000s more than 100 countries held licensing agreements for its use.

The basic thing to remember about a Sanforizing notation on a label is that is does not necessarily date a shirt to the 1930s. It was introduced in 1930, but was used until the early 1970s in the United States for clothing.

In 1941, Sears introduced its "cravenette" treatment for coats to make them shed water, repel wind, and compete with Buck Skein, which already did those things. Within a few years, rubberized cotton gabardine or Zelan treated gabardine were used to shed water and keep the wearer dry.

Buck Skein was known as a leader in fabrics sold on the open market, and also the men's coats they made from their fabrics. The company teamed with Dupont on some fabric processes to be able to promote clothing that was windproof, rainproof, waterproof, and stormproof, and to guarantee against fading, shrinking, or losing its texture.

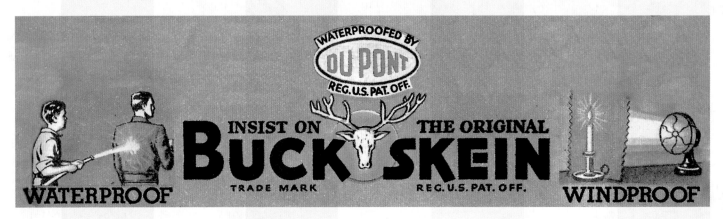

Since many synthetic fabric garments were thought to be hot and uncomfortable in the 1940s, the first "wash-and-wear" cotton shirts came about in the mid-1950s that required only pressing, not full ironing.

This was a boon because of frequent laundering. Cotton blends of 35% cotton and 65% polyester appeared in the early 1960s along with "perma press" fabrics to hold pleats and creases intact without any ironing. Many companies had their own versions of the permanent press process. In 1973, perma-press moved forward to "durable press" in which the fabric was chemically treated to be wrinkle resistant.

In the 2000s, permthrin fabric treatment was developed to repel insects, a process was developed to add UV protection to fabrics or clothing, and you can waterproof about anything with a simple spray from a can.

{ Caring for Wool Garments }

Whether you love to wear wool shirts, trousers, hats or caps, jackets, or suits, care must be taken to keep a vintage garment in optimum condition.

1. Don't wear the garment on a daily basis. Let it rest at least a day between wearings.

2. If the garment gets wet, hang it up in an out of the way place and let it dry naturally.

3. Brush the garment occasionally to help rid dust, soot, or smog build-up. It's absolutely amazing what blows in the wind.

4. Have the garment cleaned occasionally even though it is not noticeably dirty or stained. This will remove dust, after shave aromas, and body oils. Yes, unbeknownst to you, even the oil from your hands can transfer to what you are wearing.

5. Certain unlined garments like sweaters can be hand washed. Its the lining in garments that will cause problems with shrinkage. Never use hot water, and never wring a wool garment as it can render the garment out of shape. Instead, squeeze the sweater gently to get rid of some of the rinse water and then roll in absorbent bath towels to remove the excess water. Never dry a wool garment in the dryer as you are surely risking shrinkage. Block (shape) a sweater and let it dry naturally.

6. Try to remove any accidental stains immediately by dabbing with a clean damp cloth. If an over-the-counter spot remover for dry cleanable fabric used according to the directions doesn't work and the stain remains, then take to a dry cleaner as soon as possible. Be sure to point out the stain and tell them what caused it to make the stain removal easier.

7. If you live in a part of the country that has moths that damage wool items, it is best to have your item dry cleaned before storing it away for the summer. Hanging in a closed bag with cedar blocks, or a light mist with diluted lavender oil will help keep the bugs away.

{ Speaking of Wool Garments ... Moths }

Moths have been a problem in many parts of the United States for decades, with cedar being used in various fashions such as blocks, chests, and closets, to deter them. Mothballs and dry cleaners also helped to fight the nuisances.

If you are shopping and find a wool garment you are considering, be sure to hold it up to the light of a sunny window or powerful ceiling light to assess if there are any holes from moth damage.

If you bring home a wool garment and are unsure if it has been recently dry cleaned, or you see slight moth damage, it is a good idea to put it in the freezer for a couple of days, remove, and let it thaw a day or two, and then return the item to the freezer for a few more days. The extreme temperatures of the freeze and thaw cycle will kill any moth larvae and prevent its spread throughout the garment and any other wool garments it might have contact with. Then have the garment dry cleaned for sanitary reasons and to reveal any moth damage that was hidden so it can be repaired.

A separate tag or label notation about a garment being "Moth Proof" generally only appeared in the 1950s and '60s.

{ Getting Rid of Funky Smells }

Sometimes you will buy a shirt, jacket, coat or sweater that has a funky underarm smell and even laundering and / or dry cleaning doesn't help. Or, you think a garment is clean and odor free, yet when you wear it, your body heat triggers an unpleasant aroma.

Remember that deodorants or antiperspirants were not always available many decades ago, and they didn't always work well when they were used. The resulting smell in clothing is caused by bacteria. To combat the lingering bacteria, just spray the offensive underarm area inside and out with Lysol®. I have also heard that a spray of vodka works to eliminate bacteria, but have never tried it.

Advertisement showing mothproof bags for wool garments. *The Dry Cleaner*, c. 1935.

Label showing that garment is mothproof, c. 1960s.

Label showing that garment is mothproof, c. 1960s.

Sometimes you will buy a garment online and when it comes in the mail and you open the package, the smell is almost overwhelming. Even though a garment might be clean when it is packaged, the act of enclosing it in a Ziploc® or other sealed bag to mail will get some odors activated —especially in the heat of summer. If you hang the garment outside in the shade for a couple of hours, hopefully with a slight breeze, a lot of times the smell will disappear.

If a garment smells like cigarette smoke and airing it out doesn't seem to help, again Lysol comes to the rescue. I have also sprayed my garments with Febreze® after wearing them to a place that allowed smoking, which seemed to work well for me, but many people are allergic to the product or just don't like its smell.

It seems that the catch phrase today in online selling is "comes from a smoke free home". Well, their home might be smoke free, but with the high percentage of smokers from decades past, it is probably a safe bet that the garment didn't spend its entire existence in a smoke free environment.

Vintage clothing that has been stored with moth balls can also pose an aroma problem. Sometimes a good spray with Lysol and hanging outside in the shade with a breeze for a few days can minimize or eliminate the smell.

For a garment you really love and just can't seem to get rid of the smells, you can take it to your dry cleaners and have it "ozoned". It is a relatively inexpensive treatment, somewhat higher than dry cleaning, and could be well worth the extra cost. Ask your local dry cleaner about this process.

Remember that smell is subjective. I have a highly sensitive sense of smell and am bothered by aromas that don't seem to bother others. If you are a smoker, or live with one, you may be desensitized to the smell of smoke on clothing.

Most vintage items have had a previous life. We don't always know how much an item was worn, how it was taken care of, or where it came from. But, we can look over the item and see its condition:

* Has it had improper storage resulting in moth damage or mildew?

* Is the seat of the trousers thinning or threadbare?

* Are there rips & tears, and have they been repaired well, repaired poorly, or are they untouched?

* Are there stains?

* Does it look like new?

Of course, all damage is subjective to the eyes of the seller and the perspective of the buyer.

This is a basic chart of how online sellers should rate vintage garments as to condition as suggested by the

eBay Vintage Clothing & Accessories Board.

MINT: The article has never been worn or used.
Note that some sellers also use the term NOS (new old stock) synonymously with mint. The item should have 1. original hang tags still on it; 2. affixed pricing; 3. original folds; and / or 4. sometimes be in the original sealed package or box as proof of unused / unworn condition.

NEAR MINT: The item is possibly worn, but with little or no signs of wear.
Note that some sellers use the term NWOT (new without tag), but if the original tags are missing, the big question is why? Many times the vintage item / garment may look like new, but without its tag has more than likely been worn.

EXCELLENT: Worn with NO flaws. That should mean not even the tiniest holes, small stains, or replaced stitching. If the seller has made a repair, they should disclose that fact.

VERY GOOD: Worn with minor flaws, such as a missing button or repaired seam, which should be noted in the listing.

GOOD: Minor flaws as noted, wearable, or minor repairs required.

FAIR: Numerous flaws noted, possibly wearable after care or repair.

POOR or TRASHED: Damage can not be repaired. These pieces can be worn, but are usually sold to theater production companies, for crafts, or as study pieces to use as a pattern.

If you are purchasing online and cannot examine the garment for yourself, please ask specific questions as to its condition if it is not stated in the listing. I consider two or three tiny moth holes or a couple of well done repairs the maximum damage I will tolerate in a garment for collecting or selling, unless it is an extremely rare item, like a 1920s jacket to wear by the fire after a fox hunt. These flaws might not bother you in the least, or you might consider the same amount of damage makes the item unwearable. It is personal perspective, but you need to have the facts.

{ One of the Most Collectible Current Designers }

Although not designing during the years this book covers, Ralph Lauren deserves a special mention for his vintage-inspired pieces and collectability of certain garments.

We all love to slip into a comfy Polo shirt and jeans for any occasion from church to mowing the lawn. Unfortunately, these Polo shirts are in abundant supply and overflow the racks at the local thrifts. This is not the Ralph Lauren that needs mentioning.

Its the unusual Ralph Lauren sweaters and jackets from the 1980s and early 1990s, and his vintage inspired clothing, that people are looking for and willing to pay for: the RL bear, the P wing, the extreme and unique designs, or even the extremely hard to find items like a long bill cap. These are the new collectibles and vintage style pieces that are rivaling Big E Levi's, turn of the twentieth century chinstrap shirts, and overalls in terms of collectability.

Ralph Lauren started selling Polo® (brand) neckties in 1967 and expanded to menswear almost immediately. The company garments were made in the United States until its first plant in Hong Kong opened in 1983. Note that this was the same year that Hong Kong was reclassified from a British Crown Colony to a dependent territory (but, still under Britain). In 1997, Hong Kong's sovereignty was transferred to China, but their governments remain independent and they operate as independent countries.

By the opening of the 1990s, Ralph Lauren also had overseas plants in Thailand, Singapore, China and Indonesia with Uruguay being added by 2000. By the late 2000s, the company also has manufacturing plants in Sri Lanka and Honduras.

Ralph Lauren ski sweater, c. 1980s. Sold on ebay in 2009 for $480.

Ralph Lauren Indian blanket jacket, c. 1970s. Sold on ebay in 2009 for $525.

Start Date	Brands of Ralph Lauren
1967	Polo Ralph Lauren® (blue label)
1977	The Polo Club®
1978	Polo Western Wear® (in a joint venture with Gap)
1980	Double RL® or RRL (vintage style sportswear)
1981	Polo University by Ralph Lauren® (suits) (expired 2004)
1983	Ralph Lauren 1983® (expired 2008)
1984	Polo Country Store®
1985	Polo RL Est. MCMLXVII®
1986	Est. MCMLXVII RL Polo®
1987	Polo Golf®
1988	Polo PRLC®
1988	Polo Ralph Lauren Sportsman®
1988	USA Polo Club®—t-shirts (expired 2001)
1988	Polo USA®—sweatshirts (expired 2009)
1989	RRL®
1989	Chaps Ralph Lauren CRL® (expired 1997)
1990	Polo Chino Authentic Dry Goods Est. 1967 Ralph Lauren® (expired in 2004)
1991	Polo Bear by Ralph Lauren®
1991	Stadium®
1991	Polo L 91 Athl Dept® (polo bear)
1993	RRL Ralph Lauren®
1993	RRL Ralph Lauren Est 1993®
1993	Polo Sport®—ended in 2005
1995	Polo Sport Ralph Lauren®
1995	RL Jeans® (expired in 2005)
1995	CRL® (expired in 2008)
1996	Lauren Ralph Lauren®
1996	RL® (logo shown as stars in our flag)
1996	RL by Ralph Lauren® (TM pulled in 1997)
1996	Polo Jeans Co.® (expired in 2006)
1997	Polo Sport Technical® (TM pulled in 1998)
1998	RLX—Ralph Lauren Extreme® (outdoor sports apparel)
1999	Ralph Lauren Sport®
2004	Rugby Ralph Lauren® (college apparel)
2007	Polo Denim®

Date	Noteworthy dating clues:
1971	Ralph Lauren introduces the polo player on horseback as his logo
1972	Introduction of "Polo" knit mesh short sleeve shirt
1981	introduced the American Collection
1989	began selling through Robert Redford's Sundance Catalog
1994	Purple Label (highest end line of suits and sports coats)
2005	Black Label (high end suits and sport coats)

Chaps, established in 1978, and Chaps RL, established in 1988, are labels licensed to / owned by Warnaco, Inc. under their WPL #125.

There are great vintage clothing bargains and collectible pieces to be found across the internet if you just take a little time. Explore the fashions of the past to decide what you like best or will look best on you.

The number one thing to remember is that you are purchasing a vintage garment that has had a previous life. It has been worn, sat on, stored, used, wadded up in the back seat of a car, had Coke spilled on it, and who knows what else.

That is, unless it is a NOS (new old stock) item that is definitely vintage with its original price tags and has not been laundered or cleaned. Get to know grading terms or the vintage condition chart and its abbreviations.

The bust, on the other hand, can be that a NOS shirt may have been stored improperly for sixty or seventy years and has stains that are not removable. Or, that NOS wool garment might be full of moth holes and only usable as a pattern. I feel it fair to warn you that sometimes moth damage in a wool garment will not show up until a garment is dry cleaned. Some online sellers do not clean their items before selling, so read the listing carefully or ask.

If you are searching an online auction site like eBay®, Specialist Auctions, Bonanzle®, or a specialized website by a certain seller, remember that what you see is what you get. And, sometimes you don't see very much, so ask questions before you spend your money. Honest and conscientious sellers photograph, describe, grade, and provide measurements.

Unfortunately, many do not know how to date a garment, or even care, and everything they sell ends up as "vintage '40s" (the hottest decade right now), "antique" or just "vintage" without a decade. This is where using this book and doing your own research will pay off, as you will know if a garment is genuine, from the decade stated, and worth the money being asked. Or, whether the seller is way off base in his or her pricing.

You are the buyer. You have the power.

If you have any questions about a garment, ask them. If you want to see more or different pictures, ask for them. Be sure to check the stated measurements against the ones you have previously taken of your own clothing and body and noted for future use. This will assure a better fit and prevent returns.

Check the seller's feedback rating and read the remarks. eBay feedback ratings are transferable to other sites rather than the person having to build a reputation on the new site.

Be sure to find out about a return policy. On eBay, for example, you pay for the item and its shipping. If you are not pleased with your purchase, you can send it back for a refund—but, you have to pay to have it return shipped at your own expense. So, in essence, that's money you spent that you have nothing to show for.

If you are new to online buying, there are books available to guide you. Check them out and avoid potentially costly mistakes.

{ Bibliography }

1920s Fashions from B. Altman & Company. NY: Dover Publications, 1999.

Aldens Catalog, Spring and Summer 1952. Chicago, IL.

Amesen, Eric. *Encyclopedia of United States Labor Working Class History, Vol 1 A-F*. NY: Taylor & Francis Group, 2007.

Art in Knitting Vol. 16. Chicago: Novelty Art Studios, 1917.

Artise, Bridgett, and Jen Karetnick. *Born Again Vintage*. NY: Random House, 2008.

Berendt, John & The Editors of Esquire Magazine. *Esquire Fashions for Men*.

Berendt, John & The Editors of Esquire Magazine. *Esquire's Encyclopedia of 20th Century Men's Fashions*.

Borsodi, William, Ed. *Men's Wear Advertising*. NY: The Advertisers' Cyclopedia Co., 1910.

Blum, Stella. *Everyday Fashions of the Twenties*. NY: Dover Publishers, 1981.

Boilermakers' and Iron Ship Builders Journal, c. 1920.

Broadway Magazine, September 1907.

Bridges, John and Bryan Curtis. *A Gentleman Gets Dressed Up*. TN: Rutledge Hill Press, 2003.

Brotherhood of Locomotive Firemen and Engineers Magazine. Vol. 12 Jan-June 1888.

Brotherhood of Locomotive Firemen and Engineers Magazine. Vol. 34 Jan-June 1903.

Brotherhood of Locomotive Firemen and Engineers Magazine. Vol. 39 July-Dec. 1905.

Brotherhood of Locomotive Firemen and Engineers Magazine. Vol. 45 July-Dec. 1908.

Brotherhood of Locomotive Firemen and Engineers Magazine. Vol. 52 Jan-June 1912.

Brotherhood of Locomotive Firemen and Engineers Magazine. Vol. 54 Jan-June 1914. *Brotherhood of Locomotive Firemen and Engineers Magazine*. Vol. 59 July-Dec. 1915.

Brotherhood of Locomotive Firemen and Engineers Magazine. Vol. 62 Jan-June 1917.

Brown, Patty. *Ready-To-Wear Apparel Analysis*. NY: Macmillan Publishing, 1992.

Chicago Mail Order Catalog, 1933.

Chicago Woolen Mills Catalog, 1937.

Consumers Union Reports Buying Guide Issue, December 1940.

Country Gentleman Magazine, February 1949.

Fairchild's National Directory and Digest, Vol. 17 - 1920. NY: Fairchild Publishing Co., 1920.

Fashions of the Early Twenties: 1921 Philipsborn's Catalog. NY: Dover Publications, 1996.

Field & Stream, December 1951.

Friedel, Robert. *Zipper: An Exploration in Novelty*. NY: W. W. Norton & Co., 1996.

Gene Autry's Sensational Collection of Famous Original Cowboy Songs and Mountain Ballads. Chicago: M.M. Cole Publishing Co., 1932.

Good Housekeeping, January 1937.

Good Housekeeping, August 1953.

Good Housekeeping, September 1953.

Gray, James. *Talon, Inc. A Romance of Achievement*. Meadville, PA: Talon, Inc., 1963.

Home Needlework Magazine, January 1905.

Hopkins, James Love. *The Law of Trademarks, Tradenames and Unfair Competetion, 3rd Ed*. Cincinnati: W. H. Anderson Co., 1917.

How American Shoes Are Made, Third Ed. MA: United Shoe Machinery, 1966.

Hunter-Trader-Trapper Magazine. January 1924.

Ladies Home Journal, February 1954.

Ladies Home Journal, December 1954.

Ley, Sandra. *Fashion for Everyone*. NY: Charles Scribner's Sons., 1975.

Lindroth, Linda & Deborah Newell Tornello. *Virtual Vintage*. NY: Random House, 2002.

Machinist's Monthly Journal, c.1912.

Marsh, Graham and Paul Trynka. *Denim*. Great Britain: Indigo Productions, 2005.

McCall's Magazine, December 1910.

McCall's Magazine, June 1967.

McClure's Magazine. c. 1900.

"Milestones in ARS Research". Agricultural Research Magazine, November 1983. <ars.usda.gov>

Mirken, Alan, editor. *1927 Edition of The Sears, Roebuck Catalogue*. Crown Publishers, 1970.

Montgomery Ward Catalog. c. 1910.

Montgomery Ward Catalog. Spring and Summer 1925.

Montgomery Ward Sale Catalog. August 1928.

Montgomery Ward Sale Catalog. Baltimore, Maryland, Book No. 3, 1928.

Montgomery Ward Sale Catalog. Albany, N.Y., c. late 1920s.

Montgomery Ward Sale Catalog. Baltimore, Maryland, c. late 1920s.

Montgomery Ward Sale Catalog. Baltimore, Maryland, c. late 1920s.

Montgomery Ward Sale Catalog. Baltimore, Maryland, Book No. 1, 1929.

Montgomery Ward Sale Catalog. February 1930.

Montgomery Ward Sale Catalog. Book No. 6, Fall 1930.

Montgomery Ward Sale Catalog. c. early 1930s.

Montgomery Ward Sale Catalog. c. early 1930s.

Montgomery Ward Sale Catalog. Book No. 3, 1931.

Montgomery Ward Sale Catalog. Book No. 2A, 1932.

Montgomery Ward Sale Catalog. Mid Winter 1932.

Montgomery Ward Sale Catalog. Spring 1933.

Montgomery Ward Sale Catalog. February 1933.

Montgomery Ward Sale Catalog. Albany, N.Y. July 1933.

Montgomery Ward Sale Catalog. December 1933.

Montgomery Ward Sale Flyer. Albany, N.Y., c. 1934.

Montgomery Ward Sale Catalog. April 1934.

Montgomery Ward Sale Catalog. June 1934.

Montgomery Ward Sale Catalog. July 1934.

Montgomery Ward Sale Catalog. August 1934.

Montgomery Ward Sale Catalog. Book No. 5, Summer 1934.

Montgomery Ward Sale Catalog. January 1935.

Montgomery Ward Sale Catalog. March 1935.

Montgomery Ward Sale Catalog Supplement. March 1935.

Montgomery Ward Sale Catalog. April 1935.

Montgomery Ward Sale Catalog. July 1935.

Montgomery Ward Sale Catalog. August 1935.

Montgomery Ward Sale Catalog. Albany, N.Y., c. December 1935.

Montgomery Ward Sale Catalog. November 1936.

Montgomery Ward Sale Catalog. August 1937.

Montgomery Ward Sale Catalog. Mid Winter 1937.

Montgomery Ward Sale Catalog. February 1938.

Montgomery Ward Catalog. Spring and Summer 1938.

Montgomery Ward Sale Catalog. October 1938.

Montgomery Ward Sale Catalog. February 1939.

Montgomery Ward Sale Catalog. August 1939.

Montgomery Ward Catalog. Fall and Winter 1939-40.

Montgomery Ward Sale Catalog. February 1940.

Montgomery Ward Sale Catalog. November 1940.

Montgomery Ward Sale Catalog. February 1941.

Montgomery Ward Catalog. Fall and Winter 1941-42.

Montgomery Ward Sale Catalog. February 1942.

Montgomery Ward Catalog. Spring and Summer 1945.

Montgomery Ward Catalog. Fall and Winter 1950.

Montgomery Ward Catalog. Fall and Winter 1956.

Munsey's Magazine. Vol XXIX, No. 3, June 1903.

National Car & Locomotive Builders Magazine. c. 1888. (books. google.com)

National Cloak & Suit Company Catalog. 1915.

National Geographic Magazine. December 1926.

National Shoe Manufacturers Association. *shoediction.* New York: no date.

O'Hare, Kate Richards. "Prison Labor for Private Profit; a report submitted to the Joint Committee of Prison Labor 1925." *NYC Daily News Record* 06-29-1925. <womhist. alexanderstreet.com>

Outdoor Life - A Magazine of the West, September 1923.

Peacock, John. *Men's Fashion - The Complete Sourcebook.* NY: Thames & Hudson, 1996.

Pope, Jesse Eliphalet. *The Clothing Industry in New York.* University of Missouri, 1905.

Railroad Trainmen's Journal. Jan-June 1899.

Reynolds, Charles B. *Washington Standard Guide.* NY: Foster & Reynolds Company, 1922.

Schoeffler, O. E. *Esquire's Encyclopedia of 20th Century Men's Fashions.* NY: McGraw-Hill, 1973.

Scott, Clarice L. and Hagood, Anne F. *Mending Men's Suits.* Washington D.C. Agricultural Research Administration, January 1943 rev 1946.

Sears, Roebuck and Co. Consumers Guide Fall 1900. IL: DBI books, 1970.

Sears, Roebuck and Co. 1902 Edition reprint, U.S.A.: Bounty Books, 1969.

Sears, Roebuck and Co. Catalog. 1916-17.

Sears, Roebuck and Co. Catalog. Fall and Winter 1929-30.

Sears, Roebuck and Co. Sale Catalog. August 1936.

Sears, Roebuck and Co. Catalog. Fall and Winter 1935-36.

Sears, Roebuck and Co. Catalog. Spring and Summer 1940.

Sears, Roebuck and Co. Catalog. Fall and Winter 1944-45.

Sears, Roebuck and Co. Catalog. Fall and Winter 1948.

Sears, Roebuck and Co. Catalog. Spring and Summer 1949.

Sears, Roebuck and Co. Catalog. Fall and Winter 1956.

Sears, Roebuck and Co. Catalog. Spring and Summer 1956.

Sears, Roebuck and Co. Catalog. Spring and Summer 1962.

Sears, Roebuck and Co. Catalog. Fall and Winter 1962.

Sears, Roebuck and Co. Catalog. Fall and Winter 1968.

Sears, Roebuck and Co. Catalog. Spring and Summer 1969.

Shaw, Albert, editor. *"The American Monthly Review of Reviews - An International Magazine."* Vol XVI - July - December 1897: 228.

Shih, Joy. *Fashionable Clothing From the Sears Catalog - Mid 1960s.* PA: Schiffer Publishing, 1997.

Skinner, Tina. *Early 40s Fashionable Clothing From the Sears Catalogs.* PA: Schiffer Publishing, 2002.

Smith, Joyce A. *Fabric Care Symbols.* Ohio State University. <http: ohioline.osu.edu>.

Spedden, Ernest R. "The Trade Union Label; A Dissertation." Johns Hopkins University, 1909.

"Standardization of Women's Clothing". National Institute of Standards & Technology, 2003. <museum.nist.gov>

Sterns, David M. "New Textile Research Brings You Better Clothes." *Popular Science* May 1941: 105.

Stowell, Charles Jacob. "The Journeymen Tailors' Union of America; Thesis." University of Illinois, 1917.

Sullivan, James. *Jeans: A Cultural History of An American Icon.* NY: Gotham Books / Penguin Group, 2006.

Tabbler's Temptations. "The History of Trademark Law" <tabblerone.com>.

Thadeus. "Davids Co. V. Davids Mgf. Co." <supreme.justia.com>.

The American Dry Cleaner (magazine), April 1935.

The Frisco Employees Magazine, October 1927. St. Louis, Missouri.

The Frisco Employees Magazine, April 1928. St. Louis, Missouri.

The Jewish Communal Register of New York City 1917-1918, 2nd Ed. New York City: Kehi Ilah NYC / Lipswitz Press, 1918.

The Journal of the American Medical Association, August 12, 1933.

The Locomotive Engineer, a Monthly Journal. c. 1888.

The Red Cross Magazine, June 1918. Chicago, Illinois.

The Red Cross Magazine, July 1918. Chicago, Illinois

The Texas Rancher Supply Company Catalog, Spring and Summer 1937. Fort Worth, Texas.

The Staff of the National Bureau of Economic Research. *Income in the United States, Vol. II.* NY: National Bureau of Economic Research, 1922.

The Wichitan 1918. Wichita High School Yearbook. Wichita, Kansas.

The Wichita Beacon Newspaper. April 23,1943. Wichita, Kansas.

True Romances Magazine. November 1923.

United Shoe Machinery Corporation. *How American Shoes Are Made, Third Edition.* U.S.A. 1966.

Van Horn, Carl E., and Herbert A. Schoffner. *Work in America,* Vol. One. <abc-clio.com>

MISCELLANEOUS WEBSITES USED:

answers.com

answers.yahoo.com

archiviavintage.blogspot.com

artlevedev.com

athleticscholarships.net/history

books.google.com

census.gov

docs.google.com

docsouth.unc

doityourself.com

ebay.com

encyclopedia.com

fabriclink.com

fda.gov

freepublic.com

german.about.com

kipnotes.com

learningseed.com

legal-dictionary.thefreedictionary.com

levisguide.com

museum.nist.gov

pds.lib.harvard.edu

phrontistery.info

privateline.com

redcloud.co.jp

rn.ftc.gov

scripophily.com

snopes.com

specialistauctions.com

sportsartifacts.com

supreme.justia.com

textileaffairs.com

textilecare.com

thefedoralounge.com

uspto.gov/patents

uspto.gov/trademarks

vintageadbrowser.com

vintagecityclothing.com

vintageties.blogspot.com

wikipedia.com

WishbookWeb.com

{ Index }